KNOWING RIGHT FROM WRONG

To Dagmar,

In gratitude for
your support and
your prayers.

Thomas Williams LC

23 - Sept - 2008

KNOWING RIGHT FROM WRONG

A CHRISTIAN GUIDE TO CONSCIENCE

THOMAS D. WILLIAMS, LC, ThD

NEW YORK   BOSTON   NASHVILLE

Unless otherwise noted, Scriptures are taken from the NEW REVISED STANDARD VERSION of the Bible. Copyright © 1989 by the Division of Christian Education of the National Council of The Churches of Christ in the U.S.A. All rights reserved.

Scriptures noted RSV are taken from the REVISED STANDARD VERSION of the Bible. Copyright © 1949, 1952, 1971, 1973 by the Division of Christian Education of the National Council of the Churches of Christ in the U.S.A. Used by permission.

Scriptures noted NEB are taken from THE NEW ENGLISH BIBLE WITH APOCRYPHA, copyright © 1961, 1970, 1989 by Oxford University Press, Inc. and Cambridge University Press, Inc. Used by permission of Oxford University Press, Inc.

Scriptures noted NIV are taken from the HOLY BIBLE: NEW INTERNATIONAL VERSION®. Copyright © 1973, 1978, 1984 by International Bible Society. Used by permission of Zondervan Publishing House. All rights reserved.

Scriptures noted NKJV are taken from the NEW KING JAMES VERSION. Copyright © 1979, 1980, 1982, Thomas Nelson, Inc., Publishers.

Scriptures noted NJB are taken from The New Jerusalem Bible, © 1985 by Darton, Longman, and Todd, Ltd. and Doubleday.

FaithWords
Hachette Book Group USA
237 Park Avenue
New York, NY 10017

Visit our Web site at www.faithwords.com.

Printed in the United States of America

First Edition: September 2008
10 9 8 7 6 5 4 3 2 1

FaithWords is a division of Hachette Book Group USA, Inc.

The FaithWords name and logo are trademarks of Hachette Book Group USA, Inc.

Library of Congress Cataloging-in-Publication Data

Williams, Thomas D., LC, ThD
Knowing right from wrong : a Christian guide to conscience / Thomas D. Williams.—1st ed.
p.   cm.
ISBN-13: 978-0-446-58201-8
ISBN-10: 0-446-58201-8
1. Conscience—Religious aspects—Christianity.   I. Title.
BJ1278.C66W55   2008
241—dc22   2008000767

CONTENTS

INTRODUCTION

"Conscience vs. duty in Guantánamo." I scratched my head, but there it was again, emblazoned across the front page of the *International Herald Tribune* on October 20, 2007. Wherever I turned, conscience was popping up as the most important moral buzzword of the day. It seemed to me that everything from news stories to my own work as a theologian and spiritual director was being framed in terms of "conscience."

The daily news is replete with talk of conscience. A Florida judge recently tossed out the plea bargain in the case of a teacher who had sex with a teenage student, saying the lack of jail time "shocks the conscience of this court." In Virginia, the mother of a twenty-three-year-old murder victim, a former Marine, appealed to someone "with a conscience" to come forward so she can know what happened to her son. And the wife of a victim of the 9/11 attacks celebrated the conviction of Zacarias Moussaoui, calling him a man of "no conscience, no soul." Conscience is truly everywhere.

In my personal life as a spiritual guide, people often ask for help resolving doubts of conscience. They want to know how to form their conscience, whether to obey it, and what to do when their conscience conflicts with outside authority or popular opinion. How does conscience come into play in the life of a Christian?

Yet the more I realized that conscience was being invoked in every possible context, the more I saw that people meant very different things by conscience. As in the Guantánamo case, for some it seemed that conscience was a justification for disobeying authority. For others, conscience was a synonym of moral sensibility, as in "a person of conscience." For others, conscience was the final arbiter of right and wrong, superior to all other moral guides. For still others, conscience was a severe task-master, from which human beings desperately need to be liberated so they can lead happy and productive lives. Could any sense be made of this cacophony?

As a professional ethicist, I was used to dealing with conscience in a more theoretical sense, drawn from centuries of moral analysis. Precise definitions made conscience intelligible, almost tame. In the safety of the college classroom, conscience can be treated antiseptically, far from the front lines of moral decision-making. By contrast the real world often seems like the ethical Wild West, where anything goes and the prize goes to the one who draws fastest and shoots hardest. As good people wrestle with decisions that affect not only their own lives, but the lives of their loved ones and sometimes even legal policy, conscience is a wild card that can be played at any time. "Acting in conscience" trumps any other sort of moral reasoning, and in comparison the *content* of our ethical choices seems to fade in importance.

The contemporary world with its rapidly changing moral landscape presents complex ethical dilemmas that our grandparents never dreamed of. The spiraling technical progress that characterizes our age—everything from Internet and iPod to cloning and the human genome project—challenges us with ever new and uncharted moral dilemmas. No longer are nearly all of our moral choices cut and dried, with textbook answers and ready formulae to apply. Advances in end-of-life care, to take just one salient example, offer new possibilities in caring for the elderly and dying that carry with them a series of moral considerations that eschew a quick and easy verdict. Should life be prolonged at any cost? Where do we draw the line between "ordinary" and "extraordinary" care? Is it ever right to pull the plug? In the face of these dilemmas, what kind of light and certainty can conscience really give?

This was the daunting task that faced me as I sat down to write this book. Given this scenario, how are Christians to think about conscience? How can we separate the wheat from the chaff, embracing notions of conscience consistent with our faith while discarding views that conflict with our basic understanding of the human person and his illustrious vo-cation in Christ? On a practical level, what of the countless ethical ques-tions that are never mentioned in the Bible? Should Christians seek a common moral voice on hotly debated moral issues, or simply accept a diversity of opinions on vexed ethical questions?

The growing confusion surrounding conscience cries out for literature that will help today's Christian sift through the many opposing voices. Answers must be given to urgent questions regarding the nature and role of conscience, its biblical foundations and moral reliability. This book seeks to provide Christians with a fresh set of categories by which to think about conscience and its function in their lives. It will explore the relationship among conscience, freedom, faith, truth, and happiness. Without oversimplifying complex problems, this text will address in straightforward, accessible language the major issues swirling around conscience and its capacity to guide us through today's moral jungle. Above all, I hope that the following pages will give you the necessary tools for *knowing right from wrong*.

KNOWING RIGHT FROM WRONG

I

THAT STILL, SMALL VOICE

The Idea of Christian Conscience

Like so many morality tales, *The Adventures of Pinocchio* talks about growing up. Growing up, in this context, doesn't just mean getting older—it means getting better. Master storyteller Carlo Collodi paints a portrait of a wooden marionette who longs to be a real boy, but to do so he must first become *good*. Pinocchio keeps straying from the right path, betrayed by false friends and his own weakness of character. By his constant wanderings and thoughtlessness he causes great suffering to others, especially his poor father, the woodcarver Geppetto.

Fortunately, early in his adventures Pinocchio meets an important figure who will accompany him with wise counsel. In the 1883 Italian original, Collodi calls this wise voice the *grillo parlante* ("talking cricket"), rechristened "Jiminy Cricket" by Walt Disney in his 1940 animated film. In the movie version, the figure of Jiminy Cricket becomes explicitly identified with Pinocchio's conscience. Look how Disney introduces Pinocchio to the idea:

> *Blue Fairy:* Prove yourself brave, truthful and unselfish, and someday you will be a real boy.
> *Pinocchio:* A real boy!
> *Jiminy Cricket:* That won't be easy.
> *Blue Fairy:* You must learn to choose between right and wrong.

Pinocchio: Right and wrong? But how will I know?

Jiminy Cricket: How'll he know!

Blue Fairy: Your conscience will tell you.

Pinocchio: What are a conscience?

Jiminy Cricket: What are a conscience! I'll tell ya! A conscience is that still, small voice people won't listen to. That's just the trouble with the world today.

Shortly afterward, Jiminy Cricket formally gets enlisted as Pinocchio's conscience. The Blue Fairy has Jiminy Cricket kneel before her, as she pronounces these words: "I dub you Pinocchio's Conscience, Lord High Keeper of the Knowledge of Right and Wrong, Counselor in moments of temptation and Guide along the straight and narrow path. Arise, Sir Jiminy Cricket."

Despite Pinocchio's initial enthusiasm about having his very own conscience, he soon gets distracted with offers of theater and Pleasure Island, which seem far more attractive than school and homework. The cricket—his conscience—seems little more than a bothersome nuisance, keeping him from more agreeable pursuits. Pinocchio even takes ridicule for listening to his conscience. Here's how Disney describes the meeting between Pinocchio's irresponsible friend Lampwick and Jiminy Cricket:

Lampwick: [picks up Jiminy] Hey, who's the beetle?

Jiminy Cricket: Put me down!

Pinocchio: He's my conscience. He tells me what's right and wrong.

Lampwick: What? You mean to tell me you take orders from a grasshopper?

Though simplistically portrayed, Pinocchio's struggles are something all of us can identify with. We all have heard the voice of conscience, urging us to do the right thing. Sometimes we listen, sometimes we don't. We resent its nagging, but we recognize that it is right. Sometimes we wish we could simply turn it off or at least adjust it to fit our whims and appetites. And we, too, may wonder, *Why should I take orders from a grasshopper?*

My own epiphany of conscience happened in the fifth grade. My homeroom teacher was a man named Mr. Cruse—one of the few male teachers in my Catholic grade school. Despite his notorious temper I liked him a lot and learned much from him. He was, however, someone to be reckoned with. He took no guff from the students and commanded respect.

One day during gym period, two other boys and I clambered up on top of a row of freestanding metal lockers in the boys' locker room to gain access to the windows. Down below, on the red brick patio, a few students were engaged in conversation. We called out to them and proceeded to remove our navy blue uniform neckties and toss them down to our accomplices below.

Somewhere in the midst of this childish game of toss-the-ties, Mr. Cruse appeared out of nowhere, like a specter conjured up from the netherworld. He reached up and grabbed me by the collar, hauling me down from the lockers as if I were a bag of nacho chips and swinging me solidly into the opposite row of lockers with a sharp bang. He glared at me and barked: "Were you spitting and throwing things out the window?"

"No, I wasn't," I whimpered.

He then moved on to the other two and the whole scene quickly dissipated. For some reason, however, more than self-justification or the embarrassment of getting caught in our actions, I felt profound remorse for having lied to Mr. Cruse. It is true that I hadn't *spat* out the window, but I had most certainly thrown something.

For the next few days, the feeling of having done wrong gnawed at me, until finally I got up the nerve to approach Mr. Cruse at school to apologize. "I just wanted to tell you that I am very sorry because I lied to you the other day in the locker room," I said. "I *did* throw my tie out the window."

Mr. Cruse responded, "That's okay. . . . And I'm sorry I got so mad at you." And that was the end of that particular crisis of conscience.

Not nearly all my bouts of conscience have ended so favorably. Often my responses to the urgings of conscience have simply been to put off the good I know I should do or to ignore them completely. Yet fortunately, conscience is still there, like a glowing ember that refuses to go out, reminding me and calling me to be my best self (and to write books about it). The moral life is a continual struggle to be true to what we are called to be. In this ongoing battle, where would we be without conscience?

A GUIDE TO GOODNESS

Conscience is indeed, as Jiminy Cricket proclaimed, a guide, and a very insistent one at that. But where does it lead us? Not just to efficiency or productivity, but to *goodness*. Conscience provides more than a pragmatic calculus of costs and benefits, pointing to the most successful outcome. In fact, it often impels us to do things that apparently promise only woe. It judges not the *efficiency* of our actions, but their *moral quality*, their "goodness" or "badness." When our consciences admonish us for telling a lie, they don't fault us for the outcome of the lie (getting away with it or getting caught, the shame we avoid by lying, etc.). They judge the *act of lying* itself and reprimand us for engaging in a wrong action.

This moral judgment is more important than we may think. It affects not only our productivity or outward success, but our very quality as human beings. Being good means succeeding in humanity. A morally bad person is like a blind chauffeur, or a fingerless piano player, or a tone-deaf singer. Just as eyesight is essential to a chauffeur's trade, moral goodness is the key to our "trade" as human beings. A lack of goodness is not just some random defect or privation, but the absence of the most essential element of what we are. Like Pinocchio, who became a real boy only when he learned to be *good*, we cannot flourish as human persons unless we, too, become good. That's where conscience steps in.

But what does it mean for a person to be good? "Good" is more than what appeals to me, what I find to be pleasant or useful. Something is *good* when it is fully what it was *meant* to be. By extension, something is "good for me" when it helps me to be what *I* am meant to be. In philosophical terms, goodness is the perfection of nature. A good watch does what a watch should do; it keeps time accurately. A good watch may or may not have diamond studs, or a fine leather band, or bear the name of Patek Philippe. No matter how well adorned or finely crafted, a watch that does not keep time is not a good watch.

So what can be said about a good person? What quality makes or breaks a person as good or bad? It is not intelligence, good looks, social graces, or economic status. If we are told that "Laura is a good person," what do we really know about her? We cannot infer that she is a world-class figure skater, an accomplished opera singer, stunningly attractive, or an expert cryptographer. What we *do* know is that she is unselfish, honest, loyal, generous, and kind. In other words, we know that she is *morally* good. If we fail at moral goodness, we have failed at humanity. Nothing else can make up for it. Lots of money, a brilliant career, recognized accomplishments—none of these means anything if we are not good. Goodness is not an accessory to who we are; it *determines* who we are as persons.

Regardless of the abundance (or dearth) of other qualities and talents, moral goodness always tips the balance, qualifying someone as good or bad *as a person*. Let's take an extreme example to illustrate this. What if, for instance, we were to draw up a "human values report card" for Adolf Hitler? It might look something like this:

Hitler, Adolf	
Bravery	B
Leadership	A
Intelligence	B+
Willpower	A+
Oratory	A+
Grooming	C-
Moral goodness★	F
Value as a person	F

Despite Hitler's high marks in other areas, his final grade as a person reflects his *moral* life. Moral goodness stands head and shoulders above all the other values we may possess. It is more important to be good than to be smart. It is more important to be good than to be beautiful. Moral goodness is even more important than health, wealth, and popularity. When we do good, we are behaving in accordance with the truth of our being. We are what we were meant to be. Wrongdoing, on the other hand, is the *denial* of this truth of being; it is moral falsehood. Conscience reminds us of truth—not abstract truth but the truth of who we should be and what we need to do to get there.

Recognizing the importance of goodness helps us appreciate the value of conscience. Conscience directs our actions to the pursuit of good—a good that attracts what is most noble in us. Certain choices make me a better person; others detract from my goodness. All of us have experienced that natural tendency that urges us with the force of a mandate to *do good and avoid evil.* This compelling interior inclination was not taught to us by anyone (though much of its *content* is learned—for example, that we should be humble, generous, and poor in spirit). At the same time we are free to accept it or ignore it. What is this elusive concept we call conscience? Where does it come from?

MORAL SENSE AND PRACTICAL JUDGMENT

According to some, conscience is the awareness that there is a moral dimension to one's conduct, together with the urge to prefer right over wrong. Others would say that conscience is conformity to one's own sense of right conduct. Still others speak of a practical judgment regarding the moral quality of our actions or the voice of God in the soul. When we stop to examine the nature of conscience, several qualities emerge.

1. CONSCIENCE IS MORE THAN A FEELING

We usually feel good after doing what is right and feel bad after doing what is wrong, but conscience itself is not the feeling. Many activities produce feelings, but the activities themselves are not feelings. We may feel good playing the saxophone or attending a birthday party, but music and parties are not feelings. We don't feel too good sitting in the dentist's chair, but a dentist's chair is not a feeling either. A feeling is the result of something else—an effect. In the moral sphere, when we know we have done wrong we often feel guilty, but guilt and conscience are two separate things. Conscience may make us aware of our guilt, which in turn can make us *feel guilty*, but conscience is not guilt.

Conscience is an act of reason rather than a feeling. In fact, it is a part of reason itself, not a distinct faculty. Conscience is the mind thinking morally, evaluating the goodness or badness of our actions. The judgments of conscience are not isolated moral intuitions, but *reasoned conclusions*, even when they happen instantaneously. Sometimes these judgments emerge so spontaneously that they seem more like instincts or feelings than rational judgments. But if we look more closely, we realize such judgments are the result of habits of reason. Remember what Agatha Christie's wonderful sleuth, Hercule Poirot, says about such intuition:

But what is often called an intuition is really *an impression based on logical deduction or experience.* When an expert feels that there is something wrong about a picture or a piece of furniture or the signature on a cheque he is really basing that feeling on a host of small signs and details. He has no need to go into them minutely—his experience obviates that—the net result is *the definite impression that something is wrong.* But it is not a *guess*, it is an impression based on *experience.* (*The ABC Murders*, italics added)

When you feel bad after criticizing a good friend behind her back, your conscience is judging your action in the light of moral principles. It tells you that you have done wrong: *You should be true to your friends. It is wrong to betray them.* In reality this process is often immediate and moral judgments become second nature, but they continue to be *rational* judgments. You don't just *feel* as if you've done wrong—you *know* it.

This important distinction between reason and feelings can save us from some common errors. Sometimes we could think that since we don't feel bad about certain actions they must not be wrong, even though we know they violate basic principles of right behavior. We may even experience a feeling of power or accomplishment, for instance, after taking revenge on our enemy. Other times we can feel terrible, even guilty, even when we know we have behaved properly. A young lady who breaks off a relationship with a man as soon as she is certain he is not right for her may feel like a heel, while in reality she is doing the right thing by saving him from a tougher heartbreak later.

2. CONSCIENCE INVOLVES MORAL JUDGMENT
As we can see from the example about backbiting, conscience takes a general norm or principle (*It is wrong to betray one's friends*) and applies it to a concrete action (*I just betrayed my friend behind her back*) to conclude with a moral judgment (*I have done wrong*). The principles applied are *moral* principles, that is, they refer to right and wrong. They may be as simple as the Golden Rule, which urges us to treat others as we would like to be treated, or as specific as a principle, such as "Christians should always go to church on Sundays."

Since everyone has a conscience, everyone—Christians and non-Christians alike—have moral principles they refer to, perhaps without realizing it. Everyone evaluates his conduct by some standard, some ideal. Perhaps for some the universal moral code may culminate in "Do no harm" or even "It is evil to smoke" or "Always recycle," yet even here they make their moral judgments based on these general norms. The only way we can judge the moral quality of our actions is through their conformity or nonconformity to some more general principle.

Conscience's moral judgment itself, however, no longer occurs at the level of a principle, but at the level of a personal choice. In other words, conscience doesn't stop at acknowledging general moral norms but applies them to specific actions. It is my *free* and *deliberate* choices that form the matter of conscience's judgments. Conscience itself is not a choice, but the evaluation of a choice as morally good or bad. Where there is no personal freedom, there is no responsibility. Where there is no responsibility, there can be no praise or blame. It is my *free* choices—the good ones and the bad—that conscience addresses.

3. Christian Conscience Is Interpersonal

For Christians, the awareness that we have done wrong affects not only our moral character, but our relationship with God. We know that when conscience tugs us in a certain direction or judges our actions after the fact, God has not been foreign to this process. Our choices do not occur in an isolation chamber. The Holy Spirit enlightens our consciences and calls to mind what he expects from us, while also giving us strength to do the right thing. God accompanies us throughout and urges us to greater love and virtue. Thus our obedience or disobedience to conscience is a response we make to God himself and directly affects our relationship with him.

Conscience evaluates our decisions not only in terms of abstract right and wrong, or by their conformity to "right reason," but far more specifically and importantly in relation to what the Lord wants from us. "God's will" becomes an overriding criterion for determining what we should do and for judging whether or not we have done it. When conscience urges us forward, it does so by insisting: *This is what God wants from you!*

Awareness of this relationship enhances our effort to follow conscience. Legend has it that when it came time for Saint Peter to suffer martyrdom in Rome, he became frightened and left town. Jesus appeared to him, approaching on the road in the opposite direction. Peter asked, "Where are you going, Lord?" (in Latin, *"Quo vadis, Domine?"*). Jesus replied, "I am going up to Rome to be crucified again." Peter was overcome and turned right back to Rome to face the fate awaiting him. To this day the church of *Quo Vadis* stands along the Appian Way at the location of the alleged meeting.

Sometimes only love can conquer fear.

To say that a Christian's conscience is interpersonal does not mean that this interpersonal dimension is lacking for non-Christians, but it may not be explicit or recognized. What non-Christians may interpret as the "voice of reason" or simple human integrity, Christians understand to include the quiet involvement of the Holy Spirit, who is active in the lives of all persons, urging them to goodness and drawing them to himself. Even without knowing it, a person who strives to be true to conscience inevitably comes closer to God.

ETHICAL EYESIGHT

Conscience is to the soul what the eyes are to the body. It lets in light and allows us to see things as they really are. Our eyes reveal the physical properties of things, while conscience unveils the moral quality of our actions. Conscience, like eyesight, is personal and intimate, but objective. It is personal in the same way that seeing is personal. We all see the same thing, but we see it in our own way.

Ten persons with healthy eyes will recognize that the American flag is red, white, and blue and adorned with stars and stripes. If a fellow comes along saying it is green, yellow, and chartreuse and features giraffes and triangles, we would immediately conclude that our friend was suffering from impaired vision (if not worse). Conscience, too, looks at moral reality and communicates what it sees. If conscience is sound, it will communicate moral truth.

If a person's cornea is deformed, he may see things as taller and thinner than they actually are. Without an operation or corrective lenses, he will never be able to judge distance, depth, or form correctly. Some art historians suggest, for example, that the elongated figures of El Greco's paintings are due to a visual dysfunction rather than a revolutionary artistic technique. The same can happen with our consciences. If they get bent out of shape, we will judge our actions in a distorted way—things that are wrong will seem right, while things that are right may appear wrong.

Today conscience is often glorified as an unerring guide of conduct, the single undisputable reference point for good and evil: "This is a personal matter between me and my conscience." "You follow your conscience, I will follow mine." "As long as it is okay according to your conscience, it is all right." But there is a problem with this way of thinking. Just as our eyes don't impose form on what we see, but simply recognize the form that is there, so, too, conscience doesn't *determine* right and wrong, it merely *acknowledges* it.

Though conscience judges, it doesn't *create* good and bad, any more than my eyes create the reality they are seeing. I cannot make a bad action good by simply declaring it to be so. My conscience is not the ultimate foundation of moral value. It gauges my actions according to an objective order of right and wrong that transcends it. Otherwise, conscience would possess no moral authority in our lives, since, as the great Christian apologist C. S. Lewis notes, "Those who create conscience cannot be subject to conscience themselves."

In the case of human inventions, *we* write rules for the game. But in the case of *right* and *wrong,* there are fixed standards. The willful killing of an innocent person—to take an obvious example—is always morally wrong, and it is up to us to conform ourselves to this standard instead of conforming the standard to our opinions or preferences.

In the depths of our consciences we recognize the existence of a law we did not write, but which we feel we must obey. We have the power to *choose* right or wrong—but we do not have the power to *declare* what is right and wrong and have it be so. We can decide we do not need oxygen, but after a minute or so our bodies will remind us that they were not consulted in the decision. We could decree that rat poison is healthy, but if we eat it we are buying a one-way ticket to the county morgue. Certain things are the way they are despite our opinions or personal wishes, and this is true in our moral lives as well.

There is, of course, plenty of grey in the moral landscape. Sometimes there may be more than one right road. Moreover, many issues we feel strongly about may not even be "moral" questions at all. A teenager who wears his hair too long or sports a tattoo may appall his mother and father, but at the heart of it, there is nothing intrinsically right or wrong about hair length or body adornments (the obedience of a child to his parents, of course, is another matter). Here, too, conscience helps us to distinguish between moral imperatives and simple social mores or questions of etiquette. Not every practical question is a moral matter, and many times our deliberations may revolve more around clarifying our own tastes and priorities than the application of ethical principles.

Many true moral quandaries themselves do not admit of an easy, black-and-white answer. Take the area of bioethics. Especially today, with the dizzying advances of the medical sciences, the sheer number of variables makes many moral problems so complex that a slight shift in circumstances may substantially change the moral conclusion. Furthermore, the radical differences of opinion found even among ethical "experts" may make us legitimately wonder whether a right or wrong answer even *exists*, let alone whether we can find it.

Yet even in the midst of all the grey, conscience continues to prod us toward conscientious moral decisions. It won't allow us to abdicate our ethical responsibility just because the answers do not immediately emerge with pristine clarity. We are called to be good, both in the simple decisions of every day and in the anguished choices that decisively shape our lives.

THE GIFT OF CONSCIENCE

Regardless of their simplicity or complexity, right and wrong are not arbitrary but *reasonable*. The moral law is not the invention of some whimsical lawgiver. Fairness, for example, is good—really good. God did not sit down one day to invent the Ten Commandments in order to make our lives difficult, but in order to show us the path to goodness and happiness. God does not command honesty, justice, temperance, and religion because he feels like it, but because they are truly good for us. He loves us, and the moral law we discover within us is his gift to us. What is *morally* good is also really good for us. Our ability to distinguish right from wrong—conscience—is the precious tool that we have to choose well and to build a good life.

Our consciences guide us in much the same way a compass helps a ship stay on course. A compass indicates north, south, east, and west. If the compass is true, all the helmsman need do is follow the arrow north and he will be sure of sailing north. If the compass is faulty, it may read north for what is actually southeast. Instead of going to Nova Scotia, he may wind up in Havana. That is, he will be *subjectively* correct but *objectively* in error. For the sailor who really wants to reach his destination, a well-tuned compass is essential. For a person who truly wants to be good, a well-tuned conscience is indispensable.

Even though conscience often seems more like a ball and chain than wings, if we really think about it, conscience—especially for a Christian—is one of the most precious gifts we have received. Conscience provides a sure guide for the use of our freedom. It allows us to become the persons we were meant to be. And when we stray from the right path, conscience calls us back and shows us the path. It opens the door to conversion and repentance.

Having examined in broad strokes what conscience *is*, we now turn to what conscience *does*. How and when does it act? What are its scope and limitations? Can conscience err, and if so, how does this come about? We will examine these questions more closely in the next chapter.

Questions for Study and Discussion

1. In what sense does conscience guide us to success? It what sense does it guide us to failure?
2. What is the defining mark of humanity? What does it mean to have succeeded in being a person?
3. Is it more important to be smart or to be good? Why?
4. How is wrongdoing like falsehood? In what way is every sin a "lie"?
5. Conscience often seems like a feeling—we feel good when we do the right thing and bad when we don't. In what sense is conscience more than just a feeling?
6. What does it mean to say that conscience is essentially "interpersonal"?
7. Is there always a morally right thing to do in every situation?

Questions for Personal Reflection

1. What is the first time you can vividly recall your conscience reproaching you for doing wrong or urging you to do right? How old were you? What were the circumstances?
2. Do you consider conscience to be a gift? Are you grateful for it? Or does it seem more trouble than it's worth?
3. Is being a morally good person the most important thing to you, or is some other ideal more important?

2

THE ROLE OF CONSCIENCE

What Conscience Does . . . and Doesn't Do

As marvelous as conscience is, it cannot do everything. Some would like to assign a nearly omnipotent role to conscience, as if it were responsible for all our decisions and choices, and even the moral law itself, but this is far from the case. The role of conscience is modest, but extremely important.

The acts of conscience are properly called *judgments*, not *decisions*. In reality our consciences *decide* nothing. When I think about telling a lie as a way out of an embarrassing situation, my conscience *judges* my proposed action in the light of moral truths, but it doesn't "decide" what the right thing is. As much as I would like to write my own moral law sometimes, that would be beyond the competence of conscience. In fact, even if I *tried* to create my own moral law, my conscience would judge that attempt itself as something morally reprehensible.

Decisions, on the other hand, are different from judgments. When conscience provides moral guidance and promptings, I must then *decide* whether to heed it or not. In other words, conscience counsels, guides, and urges, but in the end, we must decide whether to listen to it or ignore it. Conscience does not create the law and does not dictate right and wrong but testifies to a moral truth that transcends it.

A simple way to look at this distinction is by comparing it to the division of powers in a government. We have the legislative branch, which sets forth laws, the judicial branch, which judges people's behavior by the law, and the executive branch, which enforces the laws. By this analogy, conscience would represent the judicial branch of government. It doesn't make the laws, since it isn't a legislator. It doesn't enforce them, since it doesn't have this power. It merely *judges* our activity according to a law that it didn't create and urges us to behave well.

We are called to live up to a moral ideal that is given to us. That is why conscience can become so uncomfortable. Unlike our decisions, the judgments of conscience don't directly depend on our free will. Conscience evaluates our actions whether we like it or not. How does this work? What mechanisms are involved in the judgment of conscience?

Before, During, and After

Three technical words are frequently applied to the judgment of conscience. Moral philosophers often distinguish among *antecedent, concomitant,* and *consequent* conscience. These erudite terms refer to the *what* and especially the *when* of conscience.

Antecedent Conscience

Antecedent conscience comes into play *prior* to our actions, evaluating the moral quality of what we propose to do. It assesses our plans and then warns or encourages, commands or forbids. If I find a twenty-dollar bill and consider pocketing it, even though I have a good idea who dropped it, antecedent conscience kicks in and protests that such an action would be unethical. It forbids me to do it and commands me to try to restore the bill to its legitimate owner. The antecedent role of conscience carries special importance since it exercises influence over my actions rather than simply evaluating them once they are performed.

Concomitant Conscience

Concomitant conscience judges my actions *in the moment* I carry them out. *Concomitant* means *simultaneous* and refers to the conscience's moral appraisal of my actions that accompanies the actions themselves. Once again the principal act of conscience is moral *judgment*, and this judgment extends beyond the single action itself to the moral agent, that is, to me— the one performing the action. Not only is the *action* right or wrong, *I* am right or wrong to carry it out. Conscience approves or condemns, testifying to the moral law and to God's will for me.

While I am patiently listening to a friend's problems, for example, concomitant conscience assures me that I am doing a good thing and encourages me forward in my endeavor. This judgment of moral reason is often accompanied by interior pleasure or pain—the satisfaction of knowing that I am doing the right thing, or the uncomfortable feeling of knowing I am doing wrong.

CONSEQUENT CONSCIENCE

Finally, *consequent conscience* judges my actions *after* I have brought them about. Looking back on what I have done, conscience censures me if I have done wrong, and I often feel an accompanying sense of guilt. Conscience bears witness to what I have done or failed to do and calls my actions up before my eyes. If I have done well, conscience lauds my efforts and I often experience an interior peace for having used my freedom well. Again, conscience applies general principles to my specific actions. If I have wasted time out of laziness, neglecting my obligations, consequent conscience chastises me for my dereliction of duty: *You should be more responsible in using your time well. You have acted badly.*

These three categories of conscience can be graphically represented as follows:

	Before (Antecedent)	During (Concomitant)	After (Consequent)
Good action	Commands	Approves	Praises
Bad action	Forbids	Censures	Reproaches

CONSCIENCE AS A HERALD

Conscience has no authority of itself but carries moral weight because it testifies to a higher moral truth. Conscience speaks for Another. Saint Bonaventure wrote that conscience "is like God's herald and messenger; it does not command things on its own authority but commands them as coming from God's authority, like a herald when he proclaims the edict of the king. This is why conscience has binding force." If conscience were just a passing whim or a personal opinion, it might be interesting, but it would not be *authoritative*. We could rightly heed or ignore it. Yet we find that this is not the case. When conscience speaks, it does not offer suggestions; it passes judgments and issues commands. It is the witness of God himself, who knows our inmost being, our deepest thoughts, motivations, and intentions.

Conscience involves both dialogue with oneself and dialogue with God, who is the Author of the moral law. It is he who calls us to fidelity. Because conscience entails dialogue, it also entails listening and opening ourselves up to God's voice. For this reason conscience has also been rightly called an inner "sanctuary" where God speaks to man in the depths of his heart. Since God is the Author of both the moral law and human reason, the two walk hand in hand and confirm one another. Our reason acknowledges the goodness of what the law commands.

That great explorer of human conscience, John Henry Newman, wrote about the authority of conscience with these unforgettable words:

> The rule and measure of duty is not utility, nor expedience, nor the happiness of the greatest number, nor State convenience, nor fitness, order, and the pulchrum. Conscience is not a long-sighted selfishness, nor a desire to be consistent with oneself; but it is a messenger from Him, who, both in nature and in grace, speaks to us behind a veil, and teaches and rules us by His representatives. Conscience is the aboriginal Vicar of Christ, a prophet in its informations, a monarch in its peremptoriness, a priest in its blessings and anathemas, and, even though the eternal priesthood throughout the Church could cease to be, in it the sacerdotal principle would remain and would have a sway. (*The Letter to the Duke of Norfolk*)

Christians benefit from the clear teaching of God's Word, whose authority they acknowledge. But nonbelievers have a conscience as well, and they, too, have access to the moral law. God has written a law on the human heart, a law man discovers but did not create (Rom. 2:14–15).

How Conscience Can Err

If conscience is God's herald, we could logically suppose that it is infallible. After all, if conscience speaks for God, and God never errs, how could conscience err? Appealing to divine authority would lend respectability to a belief in the inerrancy of personal conscience. I think we have already established that this cannot be so, since many people "acting in conscience" do things that are manifestly wrong and often hurt others or themselves. Are they lying when they claim to be following conscience? Perhaps sometimes, but not necessarily.

Let's take a look at the ways and reasons conscience can err.

A Poorly Formed Conscience

As our Creator, God is the Author of human reason; yet human reason is fallible. Just as we can make mistakes in our mathematical calculations so, too, we can in our moral judgments. Since conscience is simply the mind thinking morally, it can err the same way our mind errs in other areas. Sometimes this is because one's conscience is poorly formed. It is possible, for example, for a child to be brought up with a false sense of values regarding some important moral questions, such as forgiveness of one's enemies, honesty, purity, or obedience to legitimate authority. A suicide bomber may actually think he is doing a good thing by destroying his own life and the lives of many innocent people. Like a deformed eye, a poorly formed conscience judges evil to be good and good to be evil.

Faulty Application of Values

Even if a person has a sound set of values, he can make a mistake in *applying* his principles to a particular action. The mind can think well or badly. A person who knows full well that killing an innocent person is wrong may still approve of abortion or euthanasia, either because he mistakenly feels that a person is not really a person until being born, or because "compassionate" killing is somehow exempt from the general norm. Because conscience is a human and imperfect judgment, it needs to be instructed—and sometimes corrected.

Conscience Used Improperly

Moreover, like reason, conscience is an instrument or *tool*. A tool will render good results only when wielded properly. For a tool to yield the results we hope for, two things are needed. First, the tool itself must be working properly. A hammer with a loosely attached head will only cause problems when we try to pound nails into the wall. Similarly, we can exert ourselves mightily with a dull handsaw without ever cutting through wood. As a tool, our consciences must be in good working order, trained in their knowledge of good and evil, if they are to provide good moral judgments.

Second, to be effective a good tool must be *used well*. In baseball, no matter how good your bat, if you have no intention of hitting the ball, it is senseless to step up to the plate. Conscience, as we saw earlier, supposes an underlying intention to be good. If, deep down, we don't want to do the right thing, conscience won't be very effective.

The Obligation of Conscience

How seriously should we take Jiminy Cricket's admonition to "always let your conscience be your guide"? How absolute is "always"? After all, if conscience can sometimes err, it would seem that we needn't obey it in every circumstance. Maybe right now my conscience is judging incorrectly. Must I still obey it?

Conscience is *always* our best guide. Since conscience represents an honest judgment of right and wrong, we must always follow it. Even when it is wrong, we do not *know* it is wrong. True, if we have doubts about the goodness or badness of a certain action, we are obliged to investigate. Forming and informing our consciences is part of moral duty. Yet an erroneous conscience still binds us. Saint Paul very clearly says that even when conscience is wrong—out of scruple or simple error—we would be wrong to disobey it (see Rom. 14:23).

We are often responsible for the errors of conscience, the process by which our consciences became deformed. Maybe we never took the time to learn about the duties of our state in life, or the ethics of our profession, or Christian teaching regarding our relations with other people. Or perhaps through habits of doing wrong our consciences have become dulled to moral goodness and no longer nag us as they should. Even here we must obey conscience. The guilt then would lie not in the present act, or the present judgment of conscience, but in the neglect that has deafened us to the internal promptings of truth. Once we get the sense, however, that conscience might not be judging well, we are obliged to rectify it as best we can.

Often when we think of conscience, we think primarily of its *negative* role. As a sort of inner policeman, it keeps us from overstepping ethical boundaries and blows the whistle when it catches us doing wrong. Yet this is only half the story. Conscience also has an eminently positive role in the moral life. Let us look at it more closely in the next chapter.

Questions for Study and Discussion

1. Why are the acts of conscience more properly called "judgments" than "decisions"?
2. Give three examples of the antecedent conscience in action.
3. What is the role of the consequent conscience?
4. In what sense is conscience said to be a "herald"? What is the role of a herald and how is conscience similar?
5. If conscience is the voice of God in the soul, how can it err?
6. Can you think of any situations in which it is better *not* to follow your conscience?

Questions for Personal Reflection

1. Are you most attentive to your conscience before, during, or after you act? Should it be more active at other times?
2. Is your conscience truly the guide to your decisions and actions, or do other motivations sometimes gain the upper hand? If so, what are they?
3. Do you experience God speaking to you through the voice of your conscience?

3

COACH OR REFEREE?

The Motivating Role of Conscience

Conscience is most often associated with moral restraint. Socrates, for example, spoke of his *daemon* as a restrainer rather than a promoter of action. Some of the most poignant examples from great literature paint conscience in this light. Think, for instance, of Edgar Allan Poe's "Telltale Heart," in which a guilty conscience gnaws so desperately at the killer that, despite his perfectly executed plan, he ends up turning himself in. Think, too, of Nathaniel Hawthorne's *Scarlet Letter*, or Shakespeare's *Macbeth*, or any number of other classic works where conscience is portrayed especially as a persistent and intransigent reminder of moral guilt.

Is conscience, then, only the awareness that we have done wrong? As we saw in the last chapter, judgment of *past actions* forms just a part of the activity of conscience. The most important role is that of antecedent conscience, which urges and compels us to act in a certain way. Prior to our actions it can *command*, *forbid*, or *permit*, depending on whether the action we are contemplating is right, wrong, or morally indifferent. In this antecedent function, conscience is not only on the lookout for evil; more importantly, it encourages us to do good, to seek perfection in all we do. When an opportunity arises to visit an elderly person who is lonely, to assist a struggling coworker new to the job, or to lend an understanding ear to a friend going through hard times, our consciences spur us on to positive action.

Just as the moral life means more than coloring within the lines, so conscience means more than making sure we keep the rules. An ethics limited to the avoidance of evil may be little more than an excuse to live selfishly, expecting nothing from others and offering nothing in return. As C. S. Lewis wisely observed in *Letters to an American Lady*: "Nothing gives one a more spuriously good conscience than keeping rules, even if there has been a total absence of all real charity and faith." We are called to more than rule-observance, and right conscience does more than alert us to evil.

Conscience, then, has an important role of approving, instigating, and inspiring us to positive action. This positive role of conscience is not exhausted in urging us to fulfill our obligations. It pushes us beyond strict obligation toward an *ideal*. True, obligation is a key concept when it comes to morality, but doing the right thing goes much farther. Actions may be bad, acceptable, good, or excellent, with plenty of grey area in between. Conscience urges the good person to generosity beyond the minimum required.

In this sense, too, the subjectivity of conscience becomes evident. We have insisted on the important *objective* dimension of morality. Right and wrong are not human inventions. Yet the *subjective* aspect is deeply important as well. Universal moral norms necessarily describe obligations that are common to all and are generally expressed in prohibitions. *Thou shalt not kill; thou shalt not steal; thou shalt not commit adultery . . .* The range of possibilities for doing good, however, is much vaster than this: *Love one another as I have loved you . . .* Conscience invites us to climb higher, according to the gifts received and our real possibilities of doing good. Here, too, the Holy Spirit's role in conscience is paramount, since it is he who whispers to us in secret and suggests acts of generosity and even of heroism.

COACH OR REFEREE?

To illustrate the positive role of conscience, we can take an example from athletics. In sports, or in any parlor game for that matter, the *rules of the game* and the *object of the game* are two different things.

Pull out the card accompanying your game of Monopoly or Pictionary and you will find two separate headings. First, the card will describe the "object of the game"—what you must do to win and how you go about it. Next, you will find a series of "rules of the game"—a list of norms and prohibitions that all players must abide by (how much time you have to move, what words or symbols you may use, etc.). Now the rules of the game are important, but they form only the *context* in which the game is played. They are not central to the venture. The real meat of the game is its *object*, what you are trying to accomplish.

In the case of athletics—say a game of football—the *object* of the game is to *score points* (touchdowns, field goals, safeties) and keep your opponent from doing the same. Whichever team scores most points at the end wins the game. This is accomplished through a series of complex plays involving all the members of the team. Much creativity and strategy is involved in playing the game well.

The *rules* of the game, on the other hand, involve what can and cannot be done to achieve this end. The "rules" include how many players may be on the field, how long the teams play, and where players may be at different times. They also proscribe a whole series of moves, such as "roughing the kicker," "offside," "illegal motion," "pass interference," or "facemasking."

In our comparison of Christian life with a football game, where does conscience fit in? It all depends on how we understand the game. If we conceive of the Christian moral life essentially as rule-keeping, logically we will associate conscience with the referee. He enforces the *rules*. If we think of the Christian life in terms of the object of the game, our conscience becomes more like a coach. The coach focuses on the object of the game: scoring points. Let's see how this works.

The negative view of conscience would liken the role of conscience to that of a referee or umpire. Decked out in his black-and-white striped shirt, a referee runs up and down the field, looking closely for any sign of foul play. He has no interest in who wins or loses, or even in the quality of the game. His sole concern is keeping the players within the boundaries of the rules. As soon as he spots an infraction, he begins wildly blowing his whistle, simultaneously throwing a flag in the air. This is his hour. This is what he gets paid for.

The relationship between the players and the referee is a strained one. They are obliged to show respect and begrudgingly recognize that he is a "necessary evil" for the sport, but they probably won't be inviting him out for a beer after the game. They generally avoid him and do their best to fly below the radar. During the game, any attention from him will not be a good sign. They endeavor to play the game avoiding run-ins with the ref.

If conscience is nothing but a moral referee, we are in sad shape. How can we get excited about forming a good conscience, when conscience exists only to catch us in wrongdoing? How can we develop a good working partnership with our consciences when conscience is practically our enemy? More to the point, doesn't this purely negative view of conscience say something terrible about our outlook on the moral life itself?

Realistically, how many players think about the football game solely in terms of avoiding penalties? How many, at the end of the game, would be spraying champagne on each other's heads because they succeeded in getting through the game with no penalties (despite the fact that their team got creamed, 56–3)? That is an absurd scenario, but perhaps no more absurd than reducing morality to the mere avoidance of wrongdoing. If we view the Christian life as something much bigger—a mission or adventure—then we will begin to view conscience more as our *coach* and less as a referee.

If we think of conscience as our athletic *coach*, things change considerably. The coach is the players' closest ally. He wants them to win as badly as they want it. He works them hard to get the best out of them but loves them as a father. He keeps their attention on the final goal of the game and only peripherally on the rules. Sure, the rules are to be respected, but they are not the focus of the game. Similarly, the Christian life is not about "not stealing" or "not committing adultery." It is about the high adventure of loving God and neighbor, throwing in our lot with the Jewish carpenter from Nazareth, wherever that may take us. It is about, in Jesus' own words, having life and having it in abundance (see John 10:10)!

As a coach, conscience pushes us forward. It reminds us of our goals and ideals and searches for ways to grow in love and for opportunities to do good. Do you remember the scene in the 1981 film *Chariots of Fire* where one of the British runners, Harold Abrahams, hires a famous personal trainer, Sam Mussabini, to personally coach his running? Mussabini watches tapes of Abrahams to see where he can improve, where he can eke out the reduction of a few milliseconds in his hundred-yard dash. A good conscience is like that, too. It doesn't settle for a bare minimum but urges us on to greater virtue.

THE URGE TO DO GOOD

In the Acts of the Apostles, Peter characterizes Jesus' life with the simple phrase: "He went about doing good" (Acts 10:38 RSV). Jesus didn't conceive of his mission as an endeavor to avoid evil. He had come to earth for a reason: to achieve our salvation. By the same token, he sends his followers out with a mission: to do good, to evangelize, to bear witness to him. "As the Father has sent me, even so I send you" (John 20:21 RSV). A good Christian conscience will help us embrace the mission to which we have been called and carry it out with perfection.

Many of Jesus' parables underscore the positive nature of the Christian life, and by extension, the empowering role of conscience. In Jesus' description of the Last Judgment (Matt. 25), all the nations appear before the judgment seat of God, where Christ separates them as a shepherd separates sheep from goats. Those on his right are rewarded with eternal life, while those on his left are sentenced to eternal fire.

From a moral perspective, the striking feature of this judgment scene is the kind of behavior being evaluated. It seems, in fact, that the reason for this judgment has little to do with the *evil* done or avoided, and more with the *good* achieved or neglected. The damned are not taken to task for their fornications, murders, extortions, and drunkenness, nor are the blessed praised for avoiding such misdeeds. The blessed are received into the kingdom because of their works of charity for their neighbors (giving food and drink, clothing, visiting, consoling), which Jesus takes as done to himself.

Other gospel parables reiterate the same message. The parable of the good Samaritan (Luke 10:29–37), the parable of the rich man and Lazarus (Luke 16:19–31), and the parable of the talents (Matt. 25:14–30) all speak of the Christian obligation to bear fruit and not merely to "follow rules." The parable of the talents is especially illustrative. A man leaving on a journey calls his servants and entrusts his property to them during his absence, to one servant five talents, to another two, and to the third, one. The first two servants trade with the talents received and double them, whereas the third buries the money. On the master's return he demands an account of their stewardship and praises the first two servants for their trustworthiness, giving them further responsibilities and inviting them to "enter into the joy of your master" (vv. 21, 23 RSV). On seeing that the third servant made no return on the money entrusted to him, the master censures him for his laziness and has him cast out into the "outer darkness" (v. 30 RSV).

Once again the contrast in conduct centers on positive fruitfulness versus barrenness, here represented by yielding a profit through industrious trading versus burying one's money and returning it intact but without further yield. The moral message stresses both the fact of stewardship, and the obligation to bear fruit through industry and ingenuity. The parable clarifies that rendering an account for what one has received means more than restoring it safely to its rightful owner; it involves showing an *increase*. Although specific gifts vary both in quantity and kind, responsibility for productivity and multiplication is demanded of all. One is required to yield in proportion to the gifts one has received.

If the Christian mission is essentially proactive, then the role of conscience will center on spurring Christians on to greater self-giving and fruitfulness. The exhortation to "keep the faith" doesn't mean burying it! It means sharing it. If we are called not only to "play by the rules," but to "score goals," then our consciences will more closely resemble an inspiring coach than a meticulous referee.

LEGALISM VERSUS LOVE

A positive view of conscience helps to overcome an ugly moral legalism that sometimes threatens the Christian life. Those who truly love God could never be satisfied with "keeping their consciences clean." When you love someone, you are not content with not offending them, you want to do more.

Think, for example, of a mother caring for her sick child whom she loves. How would you characterize her "morality"? She is not concerned with merely doing her "duty" or fulfilling her parental obligations. She is not thinking, *What am I absolutely required to do for my child in this situation?* No! Motivated by love, she doesn't want to know the minimum she is *obliged* to do, but rather the maximum she *can* do for the good of her child. She looks for the most competent doctor, consults other parents, obtains the most effective medicines, and is even ready to give her own blood if necessary. Why? Because she is motivated by love and not merely by obligation.

For those who want to love God authentically, for those who really want to be the best they can be, conscience is an invaluable guide for choosing the path of greater love and self-giving. It reminds us when we have let up in the pursuit of our ideal and encourages us to tend ever higher. Few writers have expressed the motivational power of love better than Thomas à Kempis in *The Imitation of Christ*:

> Love is a great thing, greatest of all goods, because it alone renders light every burden and bears without distinction every misfortune. Because it carries a burden without feeling it, and renders sweet and pleasing every bitterness.
>
> The lover flies, runs and rejoices; he is free and nothing can restrain him.
>
> Love feels no burden, values no labors, would like to do more than it can do, without excusing itself with impossibility, because it believes that all is lawful and possible for it to do.
>
> In fact, it is ready to do anything, and it performs and effects many things in which he who does not love, faints and succumbs.
>
> When fatigued it does not become tired; when pressed it does not work through constraint; when threatened it is not disturbed; but like a lively flame and a burning torch, it mounts upwards and securely overcomes all opposition.
>
> Whoever loves knows well what this voice says.

In short, for those who live by love rather than by legalism, conscience provides a sure orientation for the right use of freedom. It pushes us not with threats of punishment but with the interior motivation of a loving heart.

We have already caught a glimpse of how a Christian conscience ties faith to moral choices. Now it is time to delve more deeply into the relationship between conscience and Christian belief. Christians may wonder how their faith in Jesus Christ affects their conscience. What does the Bible say about conscience and how can believers forge an authentically "Christian conscience"? To these questions we now turn.

Questions for Study and Discussion

1. Is conscience more properly a restrainer of evil or a promoter of good?
2. Where does a good conscience push us?
3. In what sense is the image of conscience as a referee inadequate?
4. Describe how a good Christian conscience is like an athletic coach.
5. What is the difference between the "object of the game" and the "rules of the game" in the moral life?
6. How do Jesus' parables encourage us to think of conscience in a more positive light? Give some examples.

Questions for Personal Reflection

1. Do you experience the promptings of conscience more in a negative or a positive direction?
2. In your following of Christ, do you find yourself more motivated by love or by fear? How does he want you to act?
3. Do you find the Christian moral life to be an exciting adventure, or more of a necessary burden?

4

THE LAMP OF THE BODY

What the Bible Tells Us About Conscience

Why does a Christian need conscience anyway? With God's Word to guide us, why fall back on a rational calculation of right and wrong? Why bring conscience into the equation? In a word, isn't Scripture enough?

The answer, of course, is yes and no. God's Word is indeed enough, sharper than any two-edged sword, and contains the saving truth we need to know God through his son Jesus Christ. Yet the Scriptures themselves attest to the importance of conscience. They teach us much about discerning right from wrong, and what it is that God expects from us. His Word resounds in our consciences, and conscience, in turn, calls us to be faithful to his Word. Conscience, in sum, is a thoroughly *biblical* concept.

Christianity begins with God's own self-revelation in his Son Jesus and continues with the gift of faith to believe in him and follow him. It cannot be reduced to a moral message or an ethical code. Yet following Jesus does have an important moral dimension, too. It involves free choice and shapes our actions and decisions. Thus while Christianity is broader and deeper than morality, it does include a very specific moral code essential to the Christian life. Being a Christian means subscribing to a specific body of doctrine as well as a singular lifestyle, in imitation of Christ and in obedience to his teaching. Christian conscience, as the mind thinking morally, shares its basic form and structure with the structure of human reasoning. At the same time its points of reference are distinctly Christian, both at the level of *intention* and the level of *content*.

PRINCIPLES OF CHRISTIAN CONDUCT

The question of Christian morality ties in directly to the question of eternal salvation. In his gospel account, Saint Matthew relates how a man approached Jesus and asked, "Teacher, what good deed must I do, to have eternal life?" He specifically wanted a guide for his behavior that would be pleasing to God and thus could serve as a compass for his choices. Jesus responds, "If you wish to enter into life, keep the commandments." Jesus accepts the premise of his interlocutor (the relationship between actions and eternal life) and answers him directly. He offers norms that will guide the man's ethical decisions. The specific content of these norms becomes even clearer when the man questions him further: "Which ones?" Jesus answers, "You shall not murder; You shall not commit adultery; You shall not steal; You shall not bear false witness; Honor your father and mother; also, You shall love your neighbor as yourself" (Matt. 19:16–19).

Christian conscience needs points of reference—principles, prescriptions, norms—in order to bring the general goal of "being holy as God is holy" down to earth. So Jesus reaffirms the commandments given to Moses on Mount Sinai. Yet he doesn't stop there. He will add his own unique contribution to the moral law in the Sermon on the Mount and elsewhere, notably making the commandments extend not only to external actions but also to internal attitudes and intentions. He will also command love not only of neighbor, but even of one's enemies, and will require that his followers be merciful, "as your heavenly Father is merciful" (see Luke 6:36). But while making it more demanding, he does not reject the old Law. Rather he states unequivocally: "Do not think that I have come to abolish the law or the prophets; I have come not to abolish but to fulfill. For truly I tell you, until heaven and earth pass away, not one letter, not one stroke of a letter, will pass from the law until all is accomplished" (Matt. 5:17–18).

Yet even the most precise moral precepts demand the mediation of conscience. We know that we are not to murder, to commit adultery, and that we are to love God above all things and our neighbor as ourselves. In practice, what does this all mean? Discernment is necessary. So is the translation of general norms to my specific case here and now. Sometimes this discernment is ridiculously easy. Since I am not to murder, it would be wrong for me to pick up a pistol and shoot my mother-in-law, though she is really getting on my nerves. I am not to steal that television set I see in the store window. Other times, the discernment is far more complex. Does the termination of a pregnancy constitute murder? How about the creation of several embryos *in vitro* in order to implant one in the womb of a sterile woman?

The issues get trickier still when we talk about the application of the *positive* precepts that enjoin us to do (and not merely avoid) certain things. How am I to "love my neighbor"? What does that mean for me today? How much time should I devote to community service? Do I condone my coworker's immoral activity out of compassion or make known my disapproval? Do I dedicate my entire waking existence to caring for my aged father or do I entrust him to a nursing home? Here conscience has its work cut out for it!

Biblical norms shape our outlook on life and the way we approach God and other people. But the Bible also enjoins us to be discerning, and to seek out God's will. It lays the basis for a truly Christian understanding of conscience. Let's look more closely.

KNOWLEDGE AND MORAL RESPONSIBILITY

Conscience is all about knowing right from wrong. Here, too, the Bible has much to say about the importance of moral knowledge. We can see this by looking at the reality of sin. In the Bible, sin comprises a double dimension, the *objective* dimension of an action or omission in disaccord with God's will, and the *subjective* dimension of intentionality, tied closely to knowledge of what God wants. Let's take the example of the sin of idolatry. Worshiping a false god is simply wrong, whether we know it or not. It becomes especially grave, however, when we *deliberately* do it, knowing that it is wrong.

In several passages of the Old Testament we find the idea of sinning *unintentionally*, through ignorance (Ezek. 45:20; Lev. 4:2, 13–14, 22–23, 27–28, 5:14, 18–19; Num. 15:22–24, 27–28). Though such sins must be atoned for, there is no question that the punishment stipulated for *deliber-*

ate sin, committed with full knowledge, is far weightier. In this sense, the Bible confirms what we know intuitively: some degree of knowledge is necessary for there to be personal responsibility. Knowledge of God's will is considered a grace, and the just Israelite begged God for it. Without light from above conscience is incapable of fully knowing God's will. In fact, one cannot even know the depths of one's own heart. The psalmist, after praising God's law as a source of wisdom, joy, and enlightenment, offers the following prayer to God: "But who can detect their errors? Clear me from hidden faults" (Ps. 19:12). Even for the person who desires to be true to God, moral discernment requires divine assistance.

In his teaching, too, Jesus links moral responsibility with knowledge of right and wrong. On the cross, Jesus prays for those who put him to death with the words "Father, forgive them; for they do not know what they are doing" (Luke 23:34). Why does Jesus add the expression "they do not know what they are doing"? He seems to be offering his Father a possible *motive* for granting forgiveness, meant to attenuate the guilt of his executioners. Just as knowledge confers responsibility, ignorance lessens it.

Nowhere does the relationship between moral responsibility and knowledge come across more clearly than in Jesus' parable of the unfaithful steward (Luke 12:41–48). The master returns at an hour the servants do not expect and it is not a pretty sight. On evaluating the situation, Jesus offers the following verdict:

> That slave *who knew what his master wanted,* but did not prepare himself or do what was wanted, will receive a severe beating. But *the one who did not know and did what deserved a beating* will receive a light beating. From everyone to whom much has been given, much will be required; and from the one to whom much has been entrusted, even more will be demanded. (Luke 12:47–48, emphasis added)

From this moral story we can draw several lessons.

First, it is clear that right and wrong do not depend solely on one's *intention*, because both servants deserve a beating for their conduct, whether they realize it or not. There is an objective standard according to which the servants' behavior can be qualified as good or bad. It is Saint Paul who writes: "Do not be deceived; neither the immoral, nor idolaters, nor adulterers, nor sexual perverts, nor thieves, nor the greedy, nor drunkards, nor revilers, nor robbers will inherit the kingdom of God" (1 Cor. 6:9–10 RSV). Certain behavior is pleasing to God and other actions are displeasing to him. Yet the servants' *knowledge* of what was expected of them affects their personal responsibility. Here there is a difference between *objective* right and wrong, determined by correspondence to what the master wanted (God's will), and *subjective* responsibility and culpability.

Second, ignorance of the master's wishes attenuates guilt but doesn't necessarily remove it. Jesus says that "the one who did not know and did what deserved a beating" for what he has done will receive a light punishment. The one who is privy to his master's wishes is clearly more responsible for his conduct than the one who had only his good moral sense to guide him. But the other bears some responsibility as well. We understand that even those without an explicit knowledge of God's will are still responsible for their conduct and possess at least a rudimentary sense of right and wrong. Even with no precise awareness of his master's wishes, the conduct of the servant (beating his fellow servants, drunkenness) was hardly exemplary, and he knew it.

Some degree of moral knowledge is accessible to all, through the natural law written on the human heart, as I mentioned in chapter 2. In an important passage, which also has relevance to our discussion of conscience, Paul writes:

> When Gentiles, who do not possess the law, do instinctively what the law requires, these, though not having the law, are a law to themselves. They show that what the law requires is written on their hearts, to which their own conscience also bears witness; and their conflicting thoughts will accuse or perhaps excuse them on the day when, according to my gospel, God, through Jesus Christ, will judge the secret thoughts of all. (Romans 2:14–16)

For those who have the benefit of divine revelation, conscience testifies to the moral law as communicated through God's Word. Yet all possess some knowledge of what God expects, and conscience bears witness also to this natural law inscribed on the human heart. Saint Paul does not merely acknowledge that conscience acts as a witness; he also reveals the way in which conscience performs that function. He speaks of "conflicting thoughts" that accuse or excuse the Gentiles with regard to their behavior. The term "conflicting thoughts" clarifies the precise nature of conscience: it is a moral judgment about man and his actions, a judgment of either acquittal or of condemnation, according as human acts are in conformity or not with the law of God written on the heart.

Third, the responsibility attached to *knowing* the master's will is compounded by the added factor of *trust*. "From everyone to whom much has been given, much will be required; and from the one to whom much has been entrusted, even more will be demanded." God does not require the same response from everyone, and the accountability of each depends on what he has been given. At the Last Supper, Jesus would say to his apostles: "I do not call you servants any longer, because *the servant does not know* what the master is doing; but I have called you friends, because *I have made known to you everything that I have heard from my Father*" (John 15:15 NSRV, emphasis added). To his "friends" God gives knowledge of himself and of his will, on trust. From these he expects more. He assigns a mission to each, a "vocation," and he looks for faithful correspondence to his plan. Thus conscience does not look only to a universal list of moral norms, applicable to all, but also to the *specific response* he expects from me alone. This is, incidentally, an important reason not to compare ourselves with others, since only God knows what he has given to each one and what he expects as a response.

In his epistle, Saint James plainly lays out the close connection between knowledge of the moral law and personal responsibility, specifically as regards sin. "Anyone, then, who *knows* the right thing to do and fails to do it, commits sin" (James 4:17, emphasis added). By this definition, sin consists not only in morally reprehensible action or inaction but requires moral knowledge as well. Jesus says something similar in regard to the Jews' rejection of him: "If I had not come and spoken to them, they would not have sin; but now they have no excuse for their sin" (John 15:22).

Yet though moral knowledge is a necessary condition for *sin*, it is also vital in order to lead a life pleasing to God. Knowledge of God's will is a blessing, not a curse. Saint Paul prayed for the Colossians that "through perfect wisdom and spiritual understanding you should reach the fullest knowledge of his will and so be able to lead a life worthy of the Lord, a life acceptable to him in all its aspects" (Col. 1:9–10). Throughout Sacred Scripture knowledge of God's will is never considered a burden, but a great blessing and the key to wisdom and happiness.

MORAL SIGHT AND BLINDNESS

We have already seen that conscience functions like a sort of moral eyesight, and this is confirmed in Jesus' words. "The eye is the lamp of the body," he says. "So, if your eye is healthy, your whole body will be full of light; but if your eye is unhealthy, your whole body will be full of darkness. If then the light in you is darkness, how great is the darkness!" (Matt. 6:22–23). In what way is conscience a lamp? Not that it *produces* light, but that it allows light in. Conscience is a gift, just as eyesight is. Without it, we stumble about in the dark. Light, is, of course, the first gift, without which eyesight would be useless, and Jesus himself is the light. At the same time, our eyes allow us to see the light. Moral blindness is the worst of evils, sometimes worse than sin itself. When we sin, we prefer darkness to the light and repentance is always possible; when one is spiritually blind, he no longer distinguishes between light and darkness.

Light is to the eyes what moral truth is to conscience. Knowledge of this truth is essential for acting rightly. In Saint John's Gospel we read how Christ cures a man born blind. At the end of the narrative Jesus exclaims that he came into this world for judgment so that the blind may see, and those who do see may become blind. On hearing this, some of the Pharisees near him said to him, "Surely we are not blind, are we?" At this Jesus responded, "If you were blind, you would not have sin. But now that you say, 'We see,' your sin remains" (John 9:40–41). Perhaps ignorance of God's will would have been a justification, but their insistence that they see makes them responsible for their lack of acceptance of God's plan.

Conscience, like eyesight, not only discerns light and darkness, right and wrong, but also various shades of *grey*. A good conscience detects the relative importance or weight of the moral principles to be applied. Though moral goodness means a loving devotion to the *whole* of moral truth rather than a pick-and-choose approach to morality, conscience also distinguishes a hierarchy among moral norms. Jesus railed against the Pharisees for their lack of this discernment, denouncing them for "straining out gnats and swallowing camels," a colorful way of saying that they had their priorities backwards (see Matt. 23:24). As an example of this, Jesus says: "Woe to you, scribes and Pharisees, hypocrites! For you tithe mint, dill, and cummin, and have neglected the weightier matters of the law: justice and mercy and faith. It is these you ought to have practiced without neglecting the others" (Matt. 23:23).

Jesus specifically teaches that certain precepts of the law—justice and mercy and faith—are "weightier" than others, in this case, the exact tithing of herbs. A good conscience not only recognizes what is right and what is wrong but discerns which activities take precedence. It arranges our moral priorities according to God's will.

Nowhere does the Bible support the claim that conscience is an infallible guide or the final judge of our moral character. Just as a person may be nearsighted, farsighted, astigmatic, or even totally blind, so, too, with conscience. Blindness to moral truth occurs just as physical blindness does. Jesus says that an hour is coming when people's consciences will be so obscured that "those who kill you will think that by doing so they are offering worship to God" (John 16:2). Paul describes those who in later times will renounce the faith as those "whose consciences are seared with a hot iron" (1 Tim. 4:1–2). Even in his own case, Paul is circumspect about the judgment of his conscience. "My conscience does not reproach me," writes Paul, "but that is not enough to justify me: it is the Lord who is my judge" (1 Cor. 4:4 NJB). It is the Lord, in fact, "who will bring to light the things now hidden in darkness and will disclose the purposes of the heart" (1 Cor. 4:5). Unfortunately, the human person seems especially susceptible to blindness of *his own* moral situation, which is the proper domain of conscience.

Look, for instance, at the well-known case of King David and his double sin of adultery and murder. After committing adultery with and impregnating Bathsheba, the wife of Uriah the Hittite, David tries to get Uriah to sleep with his wife, to cover up his sin. When this attempt fails, David has Uriah sent to the front lines of battle to be killed, so that David's adultery will not be found out. Once Uriah is dead, the last obstacle is removed and David marries the widowed Bathsheba and everything seems resolved. Despite his heinous crime, David goes on with life as if nothing had happened.

To rouse David's lethargic conscience, God sends the prophet Nathan to bring his sin before his eyes. Nathan tells David a story about a rich man with all sorts of sheep who takes a poor neighbor's only little lamb to serve to guests, since he doesn't want to take one from his own flocks. At this, David becomes filled with righteous anger and declares: "As the LORD lives, the man who has done this deserves to die; he shall restore the lamb fourfold, because he did this thing, and because he had no pity." At this, Nathan immediately retorts, "You are the man!" (2 Sam. 12:5–7). David saw so clearly in the abstract, but his conscience was blind to his own reality.

Sometimes those with the greatest interest in changing others have the greatest need of change themselves. Jesus notes the very human tendency to acute perception of others' faults coexisting with near blindness to our own.

> "Why do you see the speck in your neighbor's eye," he asks, "but do not notice the log in your own eye? Or how can you say to your neighbor, 'Let me take the speck out of your eye,' while the log is in your own eye? You hypocrite, first take the log out of your own eye, and then you will see clearly to take the speck out of your neighbor's eye." (Matthew 7:3–5)

A dull conscience regarding our own wrongdoing and need for conversion can coexist with meticulous keenness in observing our neighbor's smallest faults. Jesus reminds us that we must convert ourselves before helping others to convert.

CONSCIENCE AND JUDGMENT

Conscience does indeed judge our actions, not in order to condemn us, but to rectify our conduct. It helps us put our house in order, in preparation for that final judgment where Christ himself will judge our actions. Conscience, then, not only helps us to be good persons here and now, it also aids us in following Christ with its reward of eternal life. Jesus tells us that "the Son of Man is to come with his angels in the glory of his Father, and then he will repay everyone for what has been done" (Matt. 16:27). He will repay us according to our actions, and conscience helps us know what he is looking for.

Scripture tells us that God's judgment is *just*; it is *fair*. "As I hear, I judge; and my judgment is *just*" (John 5:30), says Jesus. What does justice mean here? Obviously it means that people get what they deserve, or that their reward or punishment in some way corresponds to their free actions. That doesn't mean, of course, that anyone deserves the glory of heaven, since "all have sinned and fall short of the glory of God" (Rom. 3:23). Justification is, to be sure, a free gift of God's grace, through the redemption that is in Christ Jesus. Put in another way, no one gets *less* than he deserves, though clearly many will get *more* than they deserve.

My good conduct cannot *earn* my salvation—Jesus won salvation by his obedience and death on the cross—but it is a necessary *condition* for salvation. It manifests my response to the gift Christ holds out to me and shows whether my faith in him is real, or merely lip service. Scripture leaves no doubt that judgment deals specifically with *human conduct* and *free choices*. God will judge "all people impartially according to their deeds" (1 Pet. 1:17). Indeed, God's righteous judgment will be revealed when "he will repay according to each one's deeds" (Rom. 2:6).

The most fundamental of these choices or "deeds" is belief in Jesus Christ and the acceptance of the salvation he offers, yet this belief and acceptance are not merely *intellectual* acts of assent. They imply a correspondence to his grace in our lives. Saint James writes that "faith by itself, if it has no works, is dead" (James 2:17). Good works, in fact, are the substance and expression of our faith. Faith becomes real, "takes flesh," through our personal decisions and moral choices.

Since God's judgment is just, no one is responsible for what he doesn't know or for what he is incapable of performing. Christian tradition holds that *"Ad impossibilia nemo tenetur"* ("No one is obliged to do the impossible"). We will be judged for our conduct, our behavior, our attitudes, our choices—free, deliberate, *mine*. These are not accidents of birth or ill fortune. To do or not to do, to speak or remain silent, to believe or not to believe, to act or refrain from acting, to trust or to doubt, to attend to or neglect . . . all of these are *my* choices, for which I am accountable. Judgment underscores the importance of good conduct, which in turn underscores the importance of conscience, by which we know what good conduct *is*.

GOOD CONSCIENCE

But the Bible tells us still more about conscience. A Christian is called to act in all sincerity, in the knowledge that God knows and sees all things. We are summoned to act uprightly before God, in full transparency. In short, we must truly *want* to be good. This sincerity before God bears the name of a "good conscience" or "pure conscience." Without this basic moral honesty it is futile to worry about the right workings of conscience. It would be like concern for having a very precise compass when you really have no intention of following it.

"Good conscience" includes two vital dimensions. The first is a heart-felt desire to do the right thing. A person of good conscience isn't looking for an excuse to do his own will, searching for a loophole in the moral law that will permit him to get out of his obligations. A person of good conscience truly wants to please God in everything he does. And because he wants to please God, he ardently desires to know what God wants from him, here and now. With this base, the judgments of conscience in particular matters often hit the mark. Purity of conscience leads to exceptional moral clarity, while without it conscience easily errs. As Jesus states, "Anyone who resolves to do the will of God will know whether the teaching is from God or whether I am speaking on my own" (John 7:17). In this case we see that having a good conscience—being resolved to do God's will—leads to interior illumination and discernment.

Second, a good conscience means the awareness of having done one's best. This is a source of immense peace of soul and confidence to stand before God. How beautiful it would be to be able to exclaim, like Saint Paul, "Brothers, up to this day I have lived my life with a clear conscience before God" (Acts 23:1). "Conscience" here refers to the state of one's soul before God. A "good conscience" or a "clear conscience" means that even after a careful self-examination one discovers no deliberate evil. True, if our consciences are functioning well we will always find imperfections and areas where we can be more generous, but a clear conscience means a consistently sincere effort to live well. Paul uses a similar expression when he says, "Therefore I do my best always to have a clear conscience toward God and all people" (Acts 24:16).

Purity of conscience requires a choice, not only of a specific act, but more fundamentally of *whom we will serve.* "No slave can serve two masters," Jesus declares (Luke 16:13). If we wish to serve our unruly passions, the world with its vanities, the demands of our pride and sensuality, *and* Jesus Christ, we will inevitably fail. Moral conscience either reigns supreme or becomes no more than an annoying hindrance to the attainment of our baser aspirations. When the judgment of conscience is downgraded to just one of the factors in making a decision, morality invariably cedes to more pragmatic considerations.

Saint Paul exhorts us not to be conformed to the world, but to be transformed by the renewal of our minds. Only then will we be able to "discern what is the will of God—what is good and acceptable and perfect" (Rom. 12:2). It is the "heart" truly converted to the Lord and to the love of what is good that is really the source of true judgments of conscience. In order to "discern what is the will of God," knowledge of God's law is certainly necessary, but it is not sufficient. What is needed is a sort of connaturality between a person and the true good. Such a connaturality develops through the virtuous attitudes of the person himself. This is the meaning of Jesus' saying that "those who do what is true come to the light, so that it may be clearly seen that their deeds have been done in God" (John 3:21). A pure conscience readily discerns the good, just as the pure heart sees God (see Matt. 5:8).

A bad conscience, on the other hand, is not just a conscience that errs. It reflects the hard-heartedness that closes itself off to moral truth. It is voluntary blindness to God's light and deafness to his voice. More than simply "not knowing," a bad conscience implies that we "do not want to know"—perhaps explicitly, perhaps implicitly through a more subtle negligence in investigating what we ought to know. Let's say, for example, that a person often drinks more than he should. At times he wonders whether such an excess of alcohol could be displeasing to God, but rather than look for guidance, he pushes the thought out of his head for fear that if he finds out he is wrong, he will have to modify his behavior. That way he can keep drinking heavily without "knowing" he is offending God. Bad conscience involves a choice not to allow God and his will to guide our actions.

THREE LEVELS OF CONSCIENCE

From the preceding considerations, we can distinguish three separate levels of conscience. Although they are distinct, they relate closely to one another and influence one another. The first, most fundamental level is that which we have just considered: the level of *good conscience*. This primary level involves the firm decision to love God above all things, to *do good* and *avoid evil*. Accepting Christ as the Lord of our lives carries with it an active desire to please him in all things, which means in turn knowing his will. This fundamental decision sets the tone for our consciences and all our moral choices.

The second level of conscience is the knowledge of moral norms and the principles of right conduct. These include the Ten Commandments, the moral teachings of Jesus such as the Beatitudes, and especially the "great commandments" to love God with our whole hearts and our neighbor as ourselves. Along with these precepts, this second level entails knowledge of the vices and sins that displease God, as well as the virtues and attitudes that please him most, such as faith, humility, trust, temperance, and so forth. It also means knowing Jesus himself as the model of Christian life.

The third level, finally, comprises the application of both our general disposition toward God and our knowledge of his will to our specific situation. This level, the most proper to conscience, asks, *What would Jesus do? What does God want from me personally, concretely, now?* It draws light from its knowledge of moral principle as well as from the Holy Spirit, who aids in discerning the proper and holy thing to do. The third level also includes *self-knowledge*, a clear picture of our actions, motivations, and intentions. We could summarize these three levels graphically as follows:

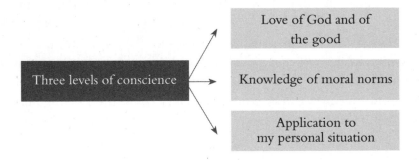

All three levels are absolutely essential to the good workings of moral conscience. A vague decision to "love God" without an active effort to know what pleases and displeases him leads to an ambiguous, sentimental love that doesn't manifest itself in holiness of life. A true love of God, or at least the *effective desire* to love him, leads to an earnest endeavor to discover his will and to get to know Christ's life as a pattern for our own.

Knowledge of moral norms, on the other hand, is worth little without love of God and a firm resolution to pursue goodness. Without this fundamental motivation we will not apply what we know to our own lives. Either we will experience frustration in knowing what we should be doing without the necessary drive to live accordingly (in which case conscience becomes nothing but a nagging reminder of the life we should be living), or we follow the moral precepts legalistically, without love. In the latter case, more often than not our point of reference will be our own perfection rather than God's glory. This serves us little, puffing up our vanity without effecting any real change on our moral character.

Finally, wanting to be good without a sound knowledge of objective ethical principles results in moral subjectivity, where my moral code is anchored only in personal "insight" and "moral feelings," rather than the solid grounding of God's will for me. In other words, in trying to do the right thing, I will have no sure point of reference. What "feels right" to me becomes more important than God's revelation of his will or the proven principles of the natural law.

For a good moral life, the three levels of conscience must be interlocked. They work together as one, informing and perfecting each other. Love impels us to study, to know, and to apply and provides the further impetus to live according to what we have discovered.

CONSCIENCE AND CONVERSION

Conscience helps not only those who earnestly strive to please God in all things, but also those who sometimes lose sight of God. When we have the misfortune of wandering from the Father's house, preferring our will to God's, conscience does not abandon us. Jesus called himself the Good Shepherd, who goes out to search for the lost sheep that has strayed away. He often does this through the promptings of conscience.

We have seen that the great Christian apologist John Henry Newman referred to conscience as "the aboriginal vicar of Christ." This is, perhaps, the most moving role of conscience, so like Christ who came "to seek out and save the lost" (Luke 19:10). It speaks softly but insistently, testifying to Christ's truth and reminding us of the greatness to which we are called and reminding us of the possibility of forgiveness. Thus conscience often provides the initial incitement to conversion.

At the Last Supper, Jesus tells his disciples that when the Spirit of truth comes, he will "convince the world concerning sin" (John 16:8 RSV). Conversion requires convincing of sin; it includes the interior judgment of the conscience. But this interior judgment becomes at the same time a new beginning of the bestowal of grace and love. In this "convincing concerning sin" we discover a double gift: the gift of the truth of conscience and the gift of the certainty of redemption. It convinces us both of our need for forgiveness and the possibility of forgiveness. The Holy Spirit searches the depths of man's heart and leads him to the complete truth about himself and about who he should be.

How necessary God's grace is, not only to purify us of the sins we are aware of, but also to see better, to know right from wrong! Blindness to one's own sin and the silence of conscience is a more dangerous sickness of soul than sin itself. If one sins but conscience remains intact, one has the necessary tools to recognize one's error and turn to the Lord in repentance and sorrow, sure of receiving forgiveness. Yet when one fails to recognize one's own faults, this path of conversion is closed off to him. He is further removed from truth and goodness than the one who fell.

The tremendous evil of blindness to one's own guilt comes across with great force in Jesus' parable of the Pharisee and the publican (Luke 18:9–14). In the end the self-righteous man comes out as the one who is truly lost. The tax collector with all his undisputed sins stands more justified before God than the Pharisee with all his undeniably good works. Jesus does not downplay the weight of sin and evil, or the importance of moral goodness. Rather he underscores the need for all to take stock of their moral guilt and to ask for God's mercy in all humility. The Pharisee, despite the good works he lists off, also has sin for which he needs forgiveness, yet he is blind to this need. He sees only his goodness and no longer recognizes his need for mercy. His "clear conscience" masks a situation of objective wrong to which he is blind. It forms an impenetrable shell that deafens him to the voice of God.

The publican, on the other hand, suffers under the cries of conscience that convict him of sin. But this suffering is blessed and moves him to seek the forgiveness of God. "God, be merciful to me, a sinner!" (Luke 18:13). Through his conscience, the publican is in touch with God's truth, the truth about his own moral evil and neediness. Jesus communicates effectively with sinners, since their acknowledgement of wrongdoing opens them to conversion. The self-righteous, who believe they have no need of conversion, are shielded from grace.

Guilt alone—the knowledge of our sin—does not purify. Good conscience does not redeem man but opens him up to redemption. When I feel bad, rather than trying to eliminate the guilty feelings, I should seek to rectify the *cause* of those feelings—to set things right again. This involves personal effort, but above all it involves God's forgiveness. Grace is already active when conscience recognizes our *failures* to follow God's will, but conscience also points us to the need for grace, for a forgiveness we cannot bestow on ourselves.

Therefore a troubled conscience is not the finish line but the starting gate. It is an invitation to self-examination, to repentance, to conversion, to recourse to God's pardon. Conscience does not merely *recognize* our wrongdoing; it *incites* us to sorrow, remorse, contrition, and compunction. More than mere guilt, or simple regret at the way things are, it moves us to set things straight. In the end, conscience prods us to seek forgiveness from God. The Letter to the Hebrews assures us that if the blood of goats and bulls was able to purify the flesh of the defiled, "how much more will the blood of Christ . . . purify our conscience from dead works to worship the living God!" (Heb. 9:13–14).

Conversion comprises three important moments, or stages, exemplified in the parable of the prodigal son (Luke 15:11–32). Far from the Father's house, the son experiences the inner workings of conscience. First, the son "came to himself." This refers to the awakening of conscience, which leads to reflection and self-examination. "How many of my father's hired hands have bread enough and to spare, but here I am dying of hunger!" (Luke 15:17). London's Tate Gallery displays an oil painting by William Holman Hunt entitled *The Awakening Conscience* (1853), which depicts a young woman experiencing a moral epiphany: she suddenly realizes that what she is doing is wrong. At certain moments of our lives, God gives us the grace to "come to our senses," to wake up and realize what is really important, and to want to change.

Next comes the decision to ask forgiveness and to change, sometimes called a "firm purpose of amendment." The prodigal son says: "I will get up and go to my father." Acknowledgement of sin remains sterile if not accompanied by a real decision to change, with God's grace. To simply realize that we are lying in the mud doesn't help much, unless we decide to grasp the hand that offers to pull us out.

Finally, we have the confession of sin and the pardon God freely gives. "Father, I have sinned against heaven and before you; I am no longer worthy to be called your son" (Luke 15:18). Recognition of sin means more that realizing we have made mistakes; it means realizing that we have offended a Father who loves us, and deserves better. Again, this blessed journey begins with the insistent prodding of conscience that obliges us to confront the moral truth of our lives.

These brief reflections, while not nearly exhausting the biblical teaching on conscience, should at least give us a point of departure and some basic principles to work with. We have seen that there is an objective standard for right and wrong, that knowledge is essential for moral action, that our knowledge is imperfect and needs divine illumination, that moral precepts require the mediation of conscience, that conscience begins with love of God and a sincere pursuit of goodness, and that conversion and repentance begin with the prodding of conscience. A good start for our study!

Alongside these fundamental biblical considerations, however, a further question emerges. If Jesus himself is truly the Christian model, what does his example teach us about conscience and its role in our lives? Did Jesus, in fact, have a conscience? If so, what were its points of reference for his own moral life? On the basis of what norms or guidelines did he use his human freedom and make moral choices? Let us look more closely at these important questions.

Questions for Study and Discussion

1. With God's Word to guide us, why do we need conscience? Isn't Scripture enough?
2. How does conscience help us to imitate Christ?
3. Why does a Christian conscience need concrete principles or norms of behavior? What are some of these?
4. What does the Bible tell us about knowing right and wrong, good and evil? Is knowledge of right and wrong necessary for freedom and moral responsibility?

5. In what way is conscience like a lamp? How do Jesus' words regarding sight and blindness, darkness and light, apply here?
6. What are the three levels of conscience, and how do they work together?

Questions for Personal Reflection

1. What does it mean to you to have a "good conscience"? Would you say that you always act in good conscience? Some of the time? Most of the time?
2. How well do you know what God expects from you in your life? Do you make an effort to find out?
3. Do you see yourself as needing conversion? Where, especially?

5

DID JESUS HAVE A CONSCIENCE?

Putting on "The Mind of Christ"

The Christian life is all about following Jesus. As the perfect human being, Christ is our model and our guide to right conduct. A Christian is called to make Christ his standard and the pattern for his whole existence. Following Christ means imitating him and often asking ourselves: *What would Jesus do?* As Saint John writes, very succinctly, "Whoever says, 'I abide in him,' ought to walk just as he walked" (1 John 2:6).

Yet "walking as Jesus walked" implies a substantial task for our consciences. First, we must study Christ and learn how he walked. Knowing him well is a necessary condition for imitating him. Second, conscience must help us translate the actions of Jesus in first-century Palestine to our own situation in the twenty-first century. Jesus, called to be the Savior of the world, was born in a stable, traveled about by foot, called disciples to himself, preached, healed the sick, and gave his life on the cross. Here you are, perhaps, in urban America, wrestling with a transitional job, invasive friends, a deadbeat husband, and two unruly kids. To "behave like Jesus" requires stretching a moral bridge between two very different situations. In other words, it requires the mediation of conscience. It is conscience that allows us to take a model—Christ—and apply the general principles that we see in his conduct to our own particular circumstances.

When Jesus is presented as a model for our lives, three objections often leap to mind. The first could sound something like this: *Adopting Christ as a moral standard puts the bar way too high. Jesus was God, after all. We admire Christ the way we admire the greatest of moral heroes. But no one is commanded to be heroic. How can Christ, not only as God but as moral hero, be a normative model for Christian ethics? He is the pinnacle of morality, but are Christians bound by this?*

The Christian moral tradition invites believers to heroism but does not require it. No one is ethically bound, for example, to throw himself into a frozen lake to save a drowning child, though we consider the action not only praiseworthy but heroic. This is what we mean by "above and beyond the call of duty." By making Jesus our model, aren't we setting ourselves up for an exercise in frustration?

The second objection stems from Jesus' divine nature. We have a hard time getting our minds around the idea that Jesus is *both* God and man. We cannot help but assume that, being God, Jesus just had to find things easier than they are for us. After all, Jesus walked on water, calmed the tempest, multiplied food, cured lepers, and raised the dead. How much could he have *really* struggled with moral choices? How hard could it really have been to do the right thing? We get the feeling that the gospel's description of Jesus' suffering and even his moral struggles involves a little dramatic flourish, like Mom's pretending to eat a spoonful of spinach to get the baby to do so, too. Why would Jesus need a conscience if he spontaneously wanted only good?

The third objection has to do with the immense difference between Jesus' situation and our own. Not only did Jesus live in a world radically different from ours, but even in context his own life hardly seems fit for imitation. He presents himself to the world as its Savior, the longed-for Messiah. He is the center of his own message, calling himself "the way, and the truth, and the life" (John 14:6) and demands love and unconditional loyalty from his followers. How can this be imitated? Similar behavior from any of us would rightly be construed as megalomania. Jesus' mission was so singular, so unique, that it seems to escape imitation. How much of the content of Christ's moral life is derived from his specific mission as Redeemer? How much is meant to be a normative pattern for the life of Christians? How can we know the difference?

These questions are vital, and in answering them we will unearth some important principles for understanding and forming our own consciences. Jesus invites us to follow him, to learn from him, to imitate him, so there must be a way. His conscience will be the key.

THE ROLE OF CONSCIENCE IN JESUS' LIFE

Jesus was a man. A staple belief of Christians from the very first centuries was that Jesus Christ was "true God and true man." He had human sentiments and emotions, human senses and impulses, and more importantly, a human intelligence and a human will. Like us, Jesus was free, and he had to discern from day to day and moment to moment how he was to use his freedom. When he woke up every morning, he had to decide what he was going to do with his day. When someone treated him badly, he had to decide how he was going to react. When it comes to imitating Christ and doing "what Jesus would do," nothing could be more important than the way he made choices. Jesus is a model for Christians of following one's conscience.

We might imagine that for Jesus, the Son of God, the moral life was a no-brainer. This isn't the picture we get from the New Testament. The author of the Letter to the Hebrews goes to great pains to explain to his readers the extent to which Jesus shared in our humanity. Jesus, he writes,

> had to become like his brothers and sisters *in every respect*, so that he might be a merciful and faithful high priest in the service of God, to make a sacrifice of atonement for the sins of the people. Because he himself was tested by what he suffered, he is able to help those who are being tested. (Hebrews 2:17–18, emphasis added)

We do not, he continues, "have a high priest who is unable to sympathize with our weaknesses, but we have one who in every respect has been tested as we are, yet without sin" (Heb. 4:15). This is a very bold claim. To say that Jesus was tested in every respect as we are means moral struggle. It means conscience.

Two compelling scenes of moral deliberation from the Gospels exemplify this struggle with special vividness: the temptations in the wilderness and the agony in the garden of Gethsemane. Here the interior combat becomes especially fierce. Let's take a closer look at both.

THE TEMPTATIONS IN THE WILDERNESS (LUKE 4:1–13)

The Gospels tells us that right after his baptism, before beginning his public ministry, Jesus went out to the desert and fasted there for forty days and forty nights. This is how Luke described it: "Jesus, full of the Holy Spirit, returned from the Jordan and was led by the Spirit in the wilderness, where for forty days he was tempted by the devil. He ate nothing at all during those days" (Luke 4:1–2). In one of the truly great biblical understatements, Luke tells us that after forty days without food, Jesus "was hungry" (Luke 4:2 RSV)!

Luke goes on to describe three of the devil's temptations. Here it is worthwhile to remember what a temptation *is*. For there to be temptation we must have at least two options—a fork in the road, so to speak. In a Christian context, the temptation must be toward something *contrary* to what we *should* be doing, contrary to God's will for us. The temptation must be appealing, or we would not be "tempted." This was the case for Jesus in the wilderness. The devil appeals to Jesus' noblest sentiments, presenting him with alternative ways to fulfill his mission, suggesting that they are more attractive and immediately successful than the way marked out by God's will. In this scene we learn much about Jesus' conscience and how it worked.

First the devil says to him, "If you are the Son of God, command this stone to become a loaf of bread," to which Jesus replies, "It is written, 'One does not live by bread alone'" (Luke 4:3–4). How easy it would have been to produce a little bread! Later Jesus would turn gallons of water into fine wine, multiply loaves and fishes to feed five thousand people. What could it hurt to procure a little continental breakfast in the wilderness? Yet it was not the time for eating. That was not the way the Father wanted Jesus to use his power. And Jesus has recourse to Scripture: "One does not live by bread alone." Not long after he would tell his apostles: "My food is to do the will of him who sent me" (John 4:34). Here Jesus demonstrates the truth of this claim.

The devil rarely tempts us to do extravagantly bad things, like robbing banks and blowing up bridges. He begins with little things, "inconsequential" things. Our consciences know that "technically" they are wrong, yet they seem so small and unimportant and the benefit so great ... *Maybe just this once it won't matter.* And once we have dialogued this far, our minds begin to invent all sorts of justifications for what *we* want to do, because we are no longer concerned with the one question that matters: what does *God* want us to do?

Next the devil leads Jesus up and shows him in an instant all the kingdoms of the world. And the devil says to him, "To you I will give their glory and all this authority; for it has been given over to me, and I give it to anyone I please. If you, then, will worship me, it will all be yours" (Luke 4:6–7). What a delightful offer! All the kingdoms of the world at his feet! Jesus had come to establish his kingdom, and there it was being offered to him on a silver platter, without the tedious preaching, the rejection, the cross. . . . What a good, noble prospect! Yet, of course, with one string attached: Jesus must kneel before God's enemy and worship him.

And Jesus answers him, "It is written, 'Worship the Lord your God, and serve only him' " (Luke 4:8). Jesus' conscience evaluates not just the noble goal that the devil holds out to him, but the immoral *means* that he must employ to achieve it. Not for any good end will Jesus stoop to an evil means. How often we are tempted to obtain good things with bad methods. Tell a little lie, make a little concession, and how much better things will be!

Take a topical example for today's Christian. God loves life, he wants married couples to have children, but a child isn't coming. How about a surrogate mother? Why not *in vitro*? Why not artificial insemination? How about cloning? Since the intention is so good, surely God wants us to try *every means possible.* . . . If only the end matters, then the means to get there shouldn't be so important. The actual method is swallowed up, subsumed by the overriding "good intention." Yet Jesus' example and his own clear conscience tell us something different. No matter how badly we want something, there are some means that are morally off-limits. And if God really wants something, he never intends to get it through immoral means.

Remember, too, that the enemy of our souls rarely asks us to do "bad things." He asks us to do good things *in a bad way*. He suggests that if God's way seems difficult, there must be a shortcut, an easier way to accomplish the same thing. He twists things, distorts them, turns them on their heads to confuse us. He encourages us to pursue things that *feel good* (though we know they're not), or he shows us how attractive bad things can be, like Eve gazing at the forbidden fruit, finding it "good to eat and pleasing to the eye, and that it was enticing for the wisdom that it could give" (Gen. 3:6 NJB). Jesus teaches us that one thing alone matters: God's will.

Back to our story. Finally, the devil pulled out all the stops. He took Jesus to Jerusalem and placed him on the pinnacle of the temple, saying to him,

> If you are the Son of God, throw yourself down from here, for it is written,
>
> > "He will command his angels concerning you,
> > to protect you,"
>
> and
>
> > "On their hands they will bear you up,
> > so that you will not dash your foot
> > against a stone."
> > (Luke 4:9–11)

How clever Satan is! He seems to say to himself: *So this one is devoted to Scripture. . . . Scripture he shall have.* The devil, too, can cite the Bible, not of course looking for truth, but manipulating it for his own purposes. He looks for our soft spots, chinks in our armor. He doesn't attack where we are strongest, but where we are most vulnerable. If we are pious, the devil will offer pious temptations; if lazy, he will suggest inaction; if rebellious, he will tempt us there.

And thus he proposes something really wonderful to Jesus: *Show your trust in God, and people will believe in you when they see you rescued by the angels.* What could be better than actively exercising his trust in his good and loving Father, which will bring so many people to believe in him . . . ? Later, as Jesus hung on the cross, the Pharisees would tempt him in a similar way: "Come down from the cross and we will believe in you" (see Mark 15:31–32). Again Jesus doesn't enter into a debate with the devil; he simply shuts him down. His answer is short and to the point: "It is said, 'Do not put the Lord your God to the test'" (Luke 4:12).

What the devil proposes as trust, Jesus calls by its true name: *testing God.* What is the difference? Testing God means forcing his hand, obliging him to act. We do things *our way* and then expect God to patch things up. Trust is different. It means doing things *God's way*, with the assurance that he will bring everything to a fruitful finish. The difference may seem subtle. The ability to distinguish between the two is also the work of Jesus' well-honed conscience.

It is no coincidence that Jesus deflected Satan's darts so handily after a long period of prayer and fasting. Later he will recommend to his disciples that they "watch and pray" so as not to fall into temptation (see Matt. 26:41). Jesus' body was weakened, but his spirit was fortified.

GETHSEMANE (MATT. 26:36–46)

In Christ's agony in the Garden of Gethsemane, Jesus' human conscience also shines with particular brilliance. The night before he died, following the Last Supper with his disciples, he went to the Mount of Olives and prayed earnestly to the Father that "if it is possible, let this cup pass me by" (Matt. 26:39 NEB). With a clear understanding of the torments that awaited him, Jesus is mortally afraid. He would prefer to do anything else. How excruciating obedience to the divine will can be sometimes! How hard to do what God is asking us when it is so contrary to our nature!

And though his fear and absolute repugnance to the coming torture make him *sweat blood*, his resolution remains firm not to do his own will but that of the Father—in everything and in spite of everything.

This passage can teach us some especially important lessons regarding conscience. It was, after all, Jesus' conscience that kept him faithful to his mission. Let's look at a few of the salient traits of this interior struggle.

The first outstanding characteristic of Gethsemane is the *intensity of the spiritual battle*. Anyone who thought Christ's obedience was easy need only look here to see how far that is from the truth. On the one hand we have the Father's will—that his only Son give himself over to a terrible, ignominious death for the salvation of the world. On the other hand we have Christ's human nature that recoils in horror before the prospect of what God is asking of him. Think for a moment of the pathos of Christ's words: "My soul is very sorrowful, even to [the point of] death" (Matt. 26:38 RSV). Here the words of the Letter to the Hebrews are not only confirmed, they are surpassed; again: "We do not have a high priest who is unable to sympathize with our weaknesses, but we have one who in every respect has been tested as we are, yet without sin" (Heb. 4:15). God may ask us to do some very tough things, but I doubt we will ever sweat blood.

Second, in the midst of this conflict *Jesus is completely free*. He can do as he pleases, and if he stays it is only because he freely chooses to obey. He consciously embraces his Passion as a free man, an obedient son, not as a slave to fate. Earlier Jesus had declared: "I lay down my life in order to take it up again. No one takes it from me, but I lay it down of my own accord" (John 10:17–18). It is not that Jesus had no way out. He could have walked away. He could have just said no. When the guards arrive and the disciples move to defend him, Jesus stops them, saying: "Do you think that I cannot appeal to my Father, and he will at once send me more than twelve legions of angels?" (Matt. 26:53).

Third, *Jesus doesn't bargain with God*. In his distress, he entreats God as Son to Father: "My Father, if it is possible, let this cup pass from me; yet not what I want but what you want" (Matt. 26:39). In all simplicity, he lays out his request and we are given to understand that he received the Father's answer. Jesus doesn't rationalize or debate, he doesn't put forward persuasive arguments or make counterproposals. He asks, and once he receives an answer, he obeys.

Fourth, throughout this turmoil, Jesus makes it perfectly clear that *God's will enjoys absolute supremacy for him*. It is the sole determining factor of his decision. His request that the cup pass him by is made conditional on it being his Father's will. "Not my will, but thine be done," he hastens to add to his petition. He has a strong personal preference but it is completely secondary; more than that, it becomes irrelevant. His moral conscience has a single point of reference and all he needs to know in order to act is what his Father desires from him.

Fifth, the entire scene of *spiritual combat takes place in the context of prayer*. To reach his decision Jesus does not wander off by himself to think things over. He works through the entire struggle in loving, albeit anguished, dialogue with his Father. He emerges from the ordeal strengthened in his resolve, ready to face his Passion. Like Jesus, it is in prayer where we discover God's will and reaffirm our unconditional commitment to it.

Though Jesus' conscience was active throughout his life, nowhere is it more in evidence than in these two moving scenes. We have already discovered some important lessons about how Jesus' conscience worked and his prompt, unconditional obedience to it. Now it is time to lay out the distinctive qualities of that conscience that Christians are called to imitate.

THE STRUCTURE OF CHRIST'S MORAL LIFE

Saint Paul exhorts us to "put on the Lord Jesus Christ" (Rom. 13:14). We are to take him as a model, clothe ourselves in him, grow to resemble him. "Putting on Christ" refers especially to his inmost being, his heart and mind. It doesn't mean letting our hair grow, sporting a beard, or trading in our blue jeans for tunics. It means, rather, learning to think like Christ, act like Christ, and love like Christ.

At the beginning of this chapter we acknowledged how difficult this is, both in theory and in practice. Many of Jesus' actions and decisions stemmed from his unique identity and his singular mission as the Redeemer of mankind. Some things Jesus did we are *unable* to do, such as performing miracles or reading people's souls. Other things we are not *called* to do, such as itinerant preaching or throwing money changers out of the local temple. Where we can and must imitate Jesus is in the *structure* of his moral life.

As we have seen, structure here refers to the way Jesus approached the moral life, that is, how he went about making choices. Jesus was free. What were the motivations that drove him or the criteria for determining one course of action over another? How did he use his freedom, in deliberating and weighing his options? In short, we imitate him as regards *conscience*.

The fact of the matter is that we learn less from the *content* of Jesus' decisions than from the *way* he goes about making them. The specific decisions Christ made are not normative in themselves but reveal a normative principle. For example, Christ preached "only to the lost sheep of the house of Israel" (Matt. 15:24). This principle was not normative for all Christians, as evidenced in Acts, when the apostles began to preach to the Gentiles. Yet from another angle Christ's decision *is* normative, in that it represents loving obedience to the mission that the Father entrusted to him. What we learn, therefore, is not that we are called to preach only to the house of Israel, but that we are called to be faithful to the specific mission we have received.

Before we look, however, at the moral criteria for Jesus' decisions, we should first consider his *purity of conscience*. Prior to all his "little decisions" of every day, Jesus had made a big, decisive choice: he would serve God no matter what. He did not place his freedom at the service of his own well-being, of the pursuit of fame or fortune, but of God. Remember the words of Moses' successor, Joshua, who led the Israelites into the promised land. He gathers together all the tribes of Israel at Shechem and declares to them: "If you are unwilling to serve the LORD, choose this day whom you will serve, whether the gods your ancestors served in the region beyond the River or the gods of the Amorites in whose land you are living; but *as for me and my household, we will serve the LORD*" (Josh. 24:15, emphasis added). In other words: choose your treasure, your god, your life's ideal, and be true to it.

Like Joshua, Jesus chose faithfulness to God. That was his ideal—not only for judging right from wrong, but for guiding his every step. Given this fundamental orientation of his existence, everything else followed as a logical consequence. So what were these consequences? What were the specific dimensions of Jesus' conscience? What were the distinctive notes of the moral structure of Jesus' life and how can we imitate them today?

AN INTERPERSONAL RELATIONSHIP

Everyone has a conscience. Everyone has standards of right and wrong behavior. For many people these consist in principles or a code of conduct. For Jesus, right and wrong were not functions of an abstract *law*, but of an interpersonal *relationship*. It was never a question of a Kantian "duty for duty's sake," following a set of rules, or even the "good" thing. Morality was interpersonal. The Father loved him, and he loved the Father, and in his actions he strove to respond faithfully to the Father's love. Jesus sums up his moral life without affectation in the beautiful expression: "I always do what pleases him" (John 8:29 NIV). There is, of course, an immense difference between a child who tries to *please* his parents and one who strives only to *avoid displeasing* them. Jesus didn't tiptoe through life trying to avoid stepping in moral doo-doo. He lived striving to please the Father in everything. That is the nature of love.

This decisive interpersonal tone should flavor the moral life of all Christians. We are called to go through life aware that God is with us, that he loves us, and that in the end we are answerable only to him for our conduct. True, we should strive to do "the right thing" in every situation, but what does this mean and why do we do it? The right thing is not sought in isolation, through abstract moral calculation, but in the company of God our Father whom we strive to please in all things.

God's Will

Nothing was clearer in the examples of Jesus' moral struggles than this: loving God means doing his will. The Father's will was Jesus' normative point of reference. "My food is to do the will of him who sent me and to complete his work" (John 4:34). His way of loving the Father was to faithfully carry out his will and keep his commandments.

As we saw earlier, God's will was not for him *one* factor in his decisions; it was the *only* factor. Jesus didn't follow God's will *except when it conflicted with other plans, seemed illogical, unproductive, or simply too hard*. He followed it as the true lodestar of his entire existence. By his own admission, that is what he was here for. "I have come down from heaven, not to do my own will, but the will of him who sent me" (John 6:38). Nothing could be clearer than that.

We may think that here Jesus did have an advantage over us. He knew God's will perfectly, whereas we often feel clueless about what God wants from us. Yet if we look carefully, we find that Jesus knew it because he looked for it. He spent hours in prayer, drawing light from his conversation with his Father. He read the Scriptures and took the prophecies about himself as a map for his conduct.

We, too, have many ways of knowing what God is asking of us, as we will see further along. We have prayer, God's Word, and the living tradition of the Christian community guided by the Holy Spirit. God always reveals his will to the person who earnestly and sincerely wants to know what he wants. He may not reveal his whole plan to us, but he will tell us what we need to know to take the next step.

Obedience

Knowing God's will is extremely important, but obeying it is more important still. It does us little good to understand our marching orders if we turn around and do something else. At the Last Supper, after Jesus washes the disciples' feet and explains to them the importance of humble service, he says: "Now that you *know* these things, you will be blessed *if you do them*" (John 13:17 NIV, emphasis added). Jesus associates the blessing not with knowledge alone, but with carrying out what one knows.

We are accustomed to the expression "Jesus saved us by dying for us on the cross." Yet remember that Jesus didn't save us by the quantity or intensity of the suffering he underwent, but by the unconditional loving *obedi-ence* to the Father's will. "For just as by the one man's disobedience the many were made sinners, so by the one man's *obedience* the many will be made righteous" (Rom. 5:19, emphasis added). Jesus didn't choose suffer-ing; he chose the Father's will. If God's will had been a beach in the Baha-mas, that's where we would have found him, swinging in a hammock.

Obedience is very important to God, not because he likes to see us lined up like tin soldiers, but because it is the most convincing sign of love. "If you love me, you will keep my commandments" (John 14:15), Jesus said. And again, "Those who love me will keep my word" (John 14:23). Jesus' love for his Father wasn't just a sentimental bond but some-thing he expressed by actively pleasing him in all things. As we have seen, the process of submitting to the Father's will was not easy or painless but involved suffering. Son though he was, Jesus "learned obedience through what he suffered; and having been made perfect, he became the source of eternal salvation for all who obey him" (Heb. 5:8–9). He was, in a very real way, the first martyr, the true witness unto death of faithfulness to God.

We, too, are called not only to discover what God wants from us but to obey. When our conscience prods us, we have three options: follow it, ig-nore it, or reject it. Sometimes it calls us to more prayer, sometimes to greater generosity with our time, sometimes to forgiveness of someone who has wronged us. If we are able not only to hear, but to "put it into practice," blessed will we be!

THE MISSION

Jesus is conscious of having a "mission," a specific task for which he was sent by God, and his conscience spurs him on to fulfill it. We already men-tioned that Jesus stayed within the boundaries of Israel, since that was what he was sent to do (see Matt. 15:24). In fact, the expression "what I was sent to do" crops up over and over again in the gospel. In Capernaum, the crowds were so pleased with Jesus that they wanted to prevent him from leaving them. And as much as Jesus would have loved to stay, he an-swers, "I must proclaim the good news of the kingdom of God to the other cities also; for *I was sent for this purpose*" (Luke 4:43, emphasis added). Jesus had an acute sense of being on earth for a reason, to accomplish something specific. He was, for instance, sent to "seek out and to save the lost" (Luke 19:10). He pushed himself because he had work to do, something important to carry out.

From the cross, Jesus exclaims, "It is accomplished" (John 19:30). According to Saint John's account, these are Jesus' last words before his death. What a beautiful ending of a life: to look back on our lives and say, "Mission accomplished. I have done what you sent me to do"! Jesus' clean conscience at the point of death testifies to his fidelity to everything God asked of him.

We, too, are sent. "As the Father has sent me, so I send you" (John 20:21), Jesus says. Granted, our mission is not the salvation of the world, but it is a specific parcel of the mission of the Church. Each of us is entrusted with a particular mission for us alone. Our mission is nontransferable, like an airline ticket. We cannot pass it off to someone else. If we don't do it, no one will. The commandments set a universal minimum for our moral lives and mark out what *everyone* must do, or not do. A Christian must not steal, commit adultery, or take God's name in vain, for example. Yet above and beyond these negative precepts, we are summoned to give something to the world. Conscience calls us to rise to the occasion and to answer with generosity and a loving sense of responsibility.

The Poor

Speaking of why Jesus was sent, he says that he came "to bring good news to the poor" (Luke 4:18), citing the prophet Isaiah. He identifies with Isaiah's messianic description and proclaims the liberation of captives, returns sight to the blind, and offers freedom to those imprisoned by sin. He shows compassion for the suffering and oppressed, and a predilection for the little ones, for children and the underprivileged. His love extends in a special way to those who suffer from moral poverty: sinners. He declares that he would leave ninety-nine sheep in the wilderness only to seek out the one that was lost. This, of course, did not mean he didn't love the rich. Numerous examples in the gospel attest to the universality of Jesus' love. But he did give special, preferential attention to those most in need.

Was this just an aspect of his particular mission, or is it meant as a quality of all Christians? Let's see. Jesus tells us that whatever we do to the *least* of his brethren, he considers as done to himself. He encourages us to welcome *little children* as he did, since they are near the Father's heart. And he recommends that when doing good for others, we choose *the indigent*, those who are unable to give us anything in return.

From the very first centuries of the church, the Christian community embraced a particular love for the poor as something essential to her mission. Almsgiving marked the life of the early church and continues to this day as one of the most important works of mercy we can perform. Just as Christ's heart spontaneously reached out in compassion to the most needy, Christians have always understood this to be the way of the Church.

Our consciences, too, are called to be especially attentive to the needs of the poor. This means, on the one hand, the materially poor: those who don't have enough to eat or drink, the homeless, those who lack the most basic material goods. It also means reaching out to those who suffer other forms of poverty: illiteracy, loneliness, depression, betrayal, and their own weakness and sinfulness. Jesus could always be found in the company of sinners and the poor, and that is where Christians are called to love in his name.

We have answered two of the three objections that we posed at the beginning of this chapter. We have seen that Jesus *did* have a human conscience, and an active, razor-sharp conscience at that. We have seen that things were no easier for him than for us—they were harder. He wasn't playacting. We have also seen that though Jesus' situation differed radically from our own, and though many of the specific choices he made derived from his particular mission, still the structure of his moral life serves as a pattern for our own.

We must, however, still answer the first objection. As a model of humanity, doesn't Jesus set the bar a little too high? The answer is yes, he does. The bar is *extremely* high. But this is because God has high hopes for us. He dreams of us as we don't dare dream of ourselves. He knows what we are made of, what we were made for, and what we are capable of. He wants us to "have life, and have it abundantly" (John 10:10). Sure, he knows better than anyone that we carry a treasure in vessels of clay. He knows that without him we "can do nothing" (John 15:5). But he also knows that with him "all things are possible" (Matt. 19:26).

We think that by lowering the bar we are being "realistic." Rather than set ourselves up for disappointment, we recast God's plan according to the measure of our small-mindedness. Yet "God did not give us a spirit of cowardice, but rather a spirit of power and of love and of self-discipline"

(2 Tim. 1:7). Indeed, we have "the Spirit of God" (Rom. 8:9). We do not realize what the Spirit is capable of doing in us. We do not believe enough; we do not trust enough. We see our own poverty, our own weakness, but we fail to see the infinite power of the Holy Spirit. Do we imagine that the great saints, the outstanding Christian witnesses of times past, were members of a race of superhumans? They were flesh and blood, as we are. Yet they combined an acute awareness of their own frailty with an overflowing confidence in the power of God.

Weakness is no impediment to moral and spiritual greatness. If you feel weak, join the club. Paul writes: "Whenever I am weak, *then* I am strong" (2 Cor. 12:10, emphasis added). This conviction imbues the Christian with courage, with holy audacity to undertake great challenges that far surpass our pitiful human capabilities. We never expect too much from God; we always expect too little. We don't fail because we are weak; we fail because we put our trust in our own efforts instead of finding our strength in him.

Having thus explored not only the biblical teaching on conscience but also Christ's own witness as our model, we can turn to other, less-satisfactory theories of conscience. We live in a secular society that draws much of its "wisdom" from intellectual trends and cultural fashion. Knowing where people are coming from when they refer to conscience will help us bridge the gap between Christ's teaching and a more worldly mentality. Moreover, and more importantly, it will help us clean up our own understanding of conscience, which may be more than a little stained by the world around us.

Questions for Study and Discussion

1. What evidence do we have from Scripture that Jesus had a conscience?
2. In what way is Jesus a true model for Christian behavior? Isn't that putting the bar a little high?
3. Did Jesus have to struggle to do the right thing? Give examples.
4. What can we learn from the way that Jesus faced the devil's temptations in the wilderness?
5. In what way is Jesus' agony in the Garden of Gethsemane a model for the Christian moral life?

6. What are the outstanding characteristics of Christ's moral life? Give examples from Scripture to back up your assertions.

Questions for Personal Reflection

1. Do you find Jesus to be an attractive ideal for your own life? Is he your hero? Why?

2. Do you sometimes find yourself tempted to take shortcuts rather than do things God's way? In what areas? How do you respond?

3. How important is God's will for you in your decision-making? Do you resemble Jesus in this aspect?

6

ANGELS AND DEMONS

Modern Attempts to Explain Away Conscience

Since humans are moral beings, everyone experiences the "prick" or "prod" of conscience. This can be uncomfortable, and many have striven to explain—or explain away—conscience. A modern illustration of conscience, typical of animated cartoons, takes the form of two small figures perched on either shoulder, one decked out in a white satin gown, golden wings, and a shimmering halo; the second outfitted with trident, horns, red leotard, and a naughty expression on his face. The proverbial scene involves each taking turns presenting his case for doing the right or wrong thing, thus illustrating the moral tug-of-war between good and bad.

As simple as this illustration is, it reveals some important dimensions of conscience. First, the dimension of *internal conflict* emerges as typical of ethical decision-making. We often feel torn between two courses of action. If there were a single "voice" within us, urging us in one direction, moral choice would be simple and immediate. As it stands, we experience contrary forces working within us.

Second, the two figures operate on different planes. The voice of the angel often expresses *moral* considerations, calling on the person to do the right thing. The little devil rarely says that his way is the "right" way but rather appeals to the baser arguments of amusement, revenge, or personal preference. Often his strongest argument is simply that his way is more "fun"! Thus we see that what is portrayed as an "angelic" voice manifests the demands of conscience, while the demonic voice speaks not for conscience but for passions, emotions, and feelings.

Third, this identification of the small angel with conscience effectively reveals that the moral conflict going on is not internal to conscience but takes place at the level of *personal decision*. The person is no longer deliberating over right and wrong. The judgment of conscience has already been made and is expressed by the angelic figure with its demands. The only matter left for deliberation involves obedience: whether the person will follow conscience or not.

Though these whimsical illustrations can be useful, people have sought for deeper understanding as well, searching for more theoretical explanations to describe the origins and workings of conscience. Alongside the Christian understanding of conscience, others have formulated alternative accounts of conscience. Many such explanations exist, but here we will examine two thinkers who have had a particular impact on modern attitudes toward conscience: Sigmund Freud (1856–1939) and Friedrich Nietzsche (1844–1900).

THE ORIGINAL FREUDIAN SLIP

Perhaps the modern idea of conscience owes more to Sigmund Freud than to any other source except the Christian tradition. Freud was an Austrian neurologist and the founder of the psychoanalytic school of psychology. Given the volumes of literature generated around Sigmund Freud and the psychoanalytic method, there is no need here for a thoroughgoing critique of his theories. For our purposes, it will suffice to examine his theory of *conscience*, with special emphasis on the underlying assumptions that led him to see things as he did. One key factor, whose importance has only recently been sufficiently appreciated, is Freud's *atheism*.

Dr. Freud was a keen observer of the human condition. His study of psychological pathologies furnished those dedicated to understanding the human mind and its infirmities with an entire lexicon, including such well-known terms as *neurosis, psychosis, the unconscious,* and *the Oedipus complex*. Nonetheless, Freud also suffered from deep-seated prejudices that conditioned his theories and diminished the objectivity of his psychological observation. The central premise that dogged all of Freud's work was the nonexistence of God. Freud was not an *agnostic*, unconvinced by theism but open to the possibility of the divinity; he was a militant *atheist*, for whom the nonexistence of God was axiomatic, a personal dogma. In structuring his own science, Freud took the very *unscientific* approach of systematically excluding the very possibility of God's existence.

According to Freud, since God could not exist, the nearly universal belief in God must respond not to an external reality, but to some other internal cause. He formulated this cause as an unconscious projection of the paternal figure. For Freud, religion becomes a response to man's childish needs of protection and security. A person's belief in God springs from his need to overcome his vulnerability, which leads him to the idea of a higher power, which he calls God. Made in man's image, God becomes the "ultimate wish-fulfillment" of man's desire for a loving father (see Freud, *The Future of an Illusion*). This explanation is based on no clinical evidence whatsoever, yet it forms the backdrop to Freud's understanding of the human mind and reality itself.

In 1999, Dr. Paul Vitz of New York University published an important study on the psychology of atheism titled *Faith of the Fatherless*. In it Vitz showed the strong degree of correlation between the phenomenon of virulent atheism and absent, abusive, and weak father figures. Contrary to the conventional Freudian wisdom that religiosity was an unnatural condition in the human person that required explaining, Vitz's study found that the opposite was true: theism tends to correlate to a healthy psychology whereas atheism arises disproportionately among those with problematic relationships with their fathers. Obviously atheism is not *caused* by disdain for one's father, and many other factors contribute to the rejection of God; what Vitz's study suggests, rather, is that such a relationship may *predispose to unbelief*.

Even if one applies Freud's own methodology of seeking the causes for certain psychological pathologies in repressed childhood experiences, the phenomenon of atheism emerges as an unconscious response to a problematic relationship with the father figure. Strangely, Freud's own atheism fits this pattern. His father, Jacob Freud, was a weak man and a poor provider. Moreover, in two of his letters Sigmund describes his father as a sexual pervert, noting that his children suffered because of this. In an essay on Leonardo da Vinci, Sigmund would universalize his own experience, writing that "psychoanalysis, which has taught us the intimate connection between the father complex and belief in God, has shown us that the personal god is logically nothing but an exalted father, and daily demonstrates to us how youthful persons lose their religious belief as soon as the authority of the father breaks down" (*Leonardo da Vinci and a Memory of His Childhood*). Yet as Vitz's study helps demonstrate, Freud had it exactly backward. Atheism is the pathology that needs explaining, whereas theism is the natural state of a healthy psychology.

FREUD'S THEORY OF MIND

Understanding Freud's atheism proves invaluable for understanding his notion of *moral conscience*. Since conscience could not have God as its author, it must have evolved as an internalized expression of the father figure, and of societal norms generally.

According to Freud's structural model of the human mind, first discussed in his 1920 essay *Beyond the Pleasure Principle*, and fully elaborated in *The Ego and the Id* (1923), three key elements combine to form personality: the *id*, the *ego,* and the *superego*. These elements surface in the very first years of a child's development. We are born with the *id*, a primitive, instinctual drive based on the "pleasure principle." Located in the irrational and emotional part of the mind, the *id* drives a person to satisfy basic needs and urges, such as food and sleep, heedless of their consequences.

According to Freud, in the next three years, the *ego* emerges. The *ego* or I is based on the "reality principle" and is capable of discerning one's true good from a mere impulse of the moment. Located in the "rational" part of the mind, the ego deliberates on the best course of action by weighing short- and long-term goals.

Finally, by around the age of five, the *superego* develops as an internalization of the ethical constraints placed upon us by our caregivers. Located in the "moral" part of the mind, the superego assimilates ethical limits received from society and becomes an ethical overseer of our conduct. A child fears incurring his parents' displeasure with the resulting loss of their love, and this fear instills a moral compass. Many identify Freud's superego with conscience as a sort of parental voice within us that chastises us when we do wrong.

In point of fact, Freud posited two subsystems to the *superego*, the *ego ideal* and the *conscience*. The *ego ideal* pushes us toward perfection and the attainment of our aspirations to excellence. *Conscience*, on the other hand, provides negative norms regarding bad behavior to be avoided. It enforces its rules by its ability to create anxiety and guilt. Conscience comprises all those actions the child is reproved for doing, while the ego ideal embraces those things the child is praised for doing. The conscience makes the individual feel guilty and the ego ideal makes the individual feel proud, thus directing the striving for perfection.

In a healthy person—still according to Freud—the ego dominates the other two components of personality, which do battle with one another. The ego acts as a sort of arbiter between the impulses of the id and the moral demands of the superego. If the id gains the upper hand, one tends toward a life of irresponsible self-gratification, and the inability to sacrifice a present desire for a long-term greater good. If the superego takes over, however, a person becomes unbending and judgmental toward self and others. A proper balance must be struck, and this is provided by a strong ego. At the same time, the ego should draw from the energy provided by the id and the superego rather than supplant them, which would result in an overly rational and unfeeling personality.

PROBLEMS WITH FREUD'S THEORY

Like the cartoon version of the struggles between an angelic and demonic "mini-me," Freud's creative description of the workings of conscience bear some resemblance to reality. Once again we see the conflictive nature of moral choice, the impulsive character of deep-seated passions and urges, and the irreducible moral voice that judges our actions. At the same time, Freud's explanation of conscience suffers from serious flaws. Of the many problems with Freud's view of conscience and superego, three stand out as particularly unsettling.

First, for Freud, conscience is an *unconscious* and *irrational* assimilation of societal prohibitions rather than the mind thinking morally. According to Freud, these prohibitions may or may not correspond to true human flourishing. The assimilation and/or rejection of received moral norms would not be a personal, rational choice, but an unconscious, involuntary process. Freud writes: "Their parents' prohibitions and demands persist within them as a moral conscience." Moreover, Freud declares, this entire system of rewards and punishments is assumed "unaltered into their religion" (*New Introductory Lectures*). From the outset, conscience is suspect and unreliable. It must be tempered by the rational ego to avoid a dictatorial moral outlook leading to rigidity, scrupulosity, and feelings of guilt. True freedom and maturity, therefore, imply a liberation from conscience. The rational ego does not and *should not* simply obey the dictates of conscience any more than it should obey the irrational impulses of the id.

Though our parents often were our first *teachers* of morality, it doesn't follow that they are its *authors*. They taught us many things—manners, speech, and the multiplication tables—without having concocted them themselves. Moreover, much of this learning process takes place at the *conscious* level. Freud employed the model of an iceberg when describing the relationship and proportion between the conscious and unconscious in the human mind. He deserves credit for drawing attention to the importance of the unconscious and its influence on human psychology. Nonetheless, it now seems clear that Freud attributed an exaggerated significance to the unconscious. As a child develops he compares what he has learned from parents with his own experience and information gleaned from other sources and develops his own view of the world and of his own moral responsibility. Conscience is not only conscious, it is *rational*, and a mature person learns to distinguish between mere social custom and moral truth.

Don't think that these are merely academic questions. Freud's theories of conscience have seeped into the modern mentality in unsuspected ways. How often we, too, look at our consciences in this way! How often in our popular culture passage into adulthood takes the form of throwing off the childish strictures of moral conscience! Just take the example of Hollywood films. A stock character, especially of teen films, is the "good" boy or girl who still does things by the book, and who is not yet ready to break the rules. This is portrayed not as admirable, but rather as a problem to be overcome. The person in question does not yet think for himself, is unwilling to cross moral boundaries, and does not express his or her freedom in creative ways. The most recurrent example, perhaps, is the character who is "still a virgin." Entire films are constructed around the theme of the loss of virginity, and the resulting victory over conscience! Undergirding this trite plot is the unspoken belief that conscience holds us back from our true destiny as mature adults.

Second, as we have seen, Freud was a convinced atheist closed to the possibility of the existence of God. He began his theorizing with the premise that God *could not* exist, that he must be the projection of our own needs and desires. Since Freud ruled out *a priori* the possibility of God as the author of conscience and a moral code, he was compelled to provide another explanation. He postulated that the human person confuses the historical moral development of *society* with rules given and enforced by *God*, and thus confers a divine value on merely human moral traditions. The internalized teachings of his parents and culture become mandates of God: "You shall not murder," "You shall not commit adultery," "You shall not steal," etc.

In *The Future of an Illusion* (1927), Freud wrote that "it would be an undoubted advantage if we were to leave God out altogether and honestly admit the purely human origin of all the regulations and precepts of civilization."

Once God is eliminated, conscience becomes a question of social convention and loses all moral authority. Having postulated its origins on a mechanical process of assimilation, Freud likewise stripped conscience of any real moral worth, even at the level of human reason. Morality itself ceases to be important and we are left with a pragmatic, amoral "reality principle" as the true guiding light of human conduct.

This aspect of Freud's theory lives on in the modern mentality. For many, conscience possesses no real authority and thus ought to be tamed by the ego. Since there is no objective moral referent for which conscience speaks (only social convention), people are justified in manipulating their consciences at will. The moral norms that we take to be of divine origin are really just historical expressions of an evolving culture. "Right" and "wrong" become subjective expressions of a particular social milieu and cannot be said to possess any intrinsic value.

Christians are not immune to this relativization of conscience. We, too, often fall into the trap of making conscience superficial and shallow. Each person has his or her "values," and no one's scale is necessarily better or worse than anyone else's. In our eagerness to be nonjudgmental, we sometimes jettison the entire moral law as well.

Third, Freud thought that to overcome repression and inhibitions we need to eliminate *shame*, often by exposing shameful things in the open. He thought that shame led to psychological problems and useless inhibitions. Yet the loss of shame is not necessarily a good thing. Shame is a proper response to what is shameful, and bolsters our moral conscience. Where shamelessness reigns, immorality of all sorts—cowardice, lying, envy, and unchastity—are easily assimilated and accepted. Much of the American experiment in ethically nondirectional sexual education has demonstrated this.

On the other hand, Freud was right that certain things do need to be brought out into the open. True neuroses can emerge from unacknowledged sin, or an attempt to justify what we know is wrong. Unacknowledged sin, like gangrene, festers and cries out for excision. Getting things out in the open effectively leads to mental health and peace of soul when it involves admitting our sinfulness, asking pardon, and sincerely proposing to do better. Awareness of sin, shame, and guilt exist as a goad to move us to repentance and the joyful experience of God's forgiveness.

CONSCIENCE AND GUILT

The question of sin and shame brings us to a final consideration. Freud was fixated on the removal of guilt. To do so he gutted conscience of any real moral authority. There can be no moral obligation to a purely conventional, irrational conscience. Freud saw the experience of guilt as the cause of a number of psychological maladies. The only way to overcome these maladies—he thought—was by eliminating the guilt that provoked them.

Freud's antipathy toward guilt was way off the mark. Guilt plays an essential role in a healthy psychology. It is rather the habitual *absence* of all guilt that gives serious cause for concern. Modern studies have shown that the critical distinguishing trait of psychopaths is precisely the *inability* to experience guilt (See McCord and McCord, *The Psychopath: An Essay on the Criminal Mind*). As George MacDonald wrote: "She was sorely troubled with what is, by huge discourtesy, called a bad conscience—being in reality a conscience doing its duty so well that it makes the whole house uncomfortable" (*George MacDonald: An Anthology*).

Guilt is to the conscience what pain is to the body: an indicator that something is amiss and needs attention. No one likes to feel physical pain, but it serves a basic purpose. Perhaps you have heard of the rare disease called "congenital insensitivity to pain with anhidrosis," referred to as CIPA. Babies born with this disease cannot feel pain, so they do all sorts of damage to themselves without realizing it and without letting anyone else know. What may seem like a blessing (no pain) is actually a curse. Think of how important pain is in your life and how difficult things would be without it. If you accidentally put your hand on a hot burner, pain makes you recoil in haste rather than nonchalantly continuing your conversation as your fingers char. Or suppose you were to break your leg and feel no pain. You would continue going about your business but the injury would grow worse; perhaps the bone would set, but in a distorted position. In the same way, a guilty conscience tells you that damage has been done, that you are off course, so you have the chance to do something about it.

A healthy response to guilt mirrors a healthy response to physical pain. A good doctor addresses the *cause* of the pain, not only the pain itself. It would do little good to treat a cancerous tumor by simply prescribing morphine. The tumor would continue to grow unhindered, while the person lived in blissful oblivion to his worsening state. A guilty conscience needs to be treated, not by anesthetizing it so it no longer registers right and wrong, but by repentance and a sincere effort to do what is right. Any "therapy" that only caresses our misdirected egos instead of encouraging us to moral improvement does a deep disservice to our true good.

NIETZSCHE MARKETING

If you really want to explain something away, begin by speaking about its "origins." Focus not on what it *is* but how it *came to be.* That way you will make clear that such a phenomenon is not natural but only developed "later," as a sort of human appendage we could just as well do without. If you can set the origins beyond the reach of empirical observation, such as the unconscious, all the better. That way if anyone questions your theory, he will not be able to appeal to any hard data. Another similar method is to place something's "origins" in prehistory. By definition, prehistory refers to a time from which we have no written records. Thus, like the unconscious, it falls beyond the reach of your critics and will allow you to speculate freely.

These methods were employed, with limited success, by the enthusiastic German philologist (one who studies the meaning, origins, and evolution of words) Friedrich Nietzsche, especially in his book *The Genealogy of Morals* (1887). Here Nietzsche explains away not only conscience, but conventional morality itself, as a Judeo-Christian plot to bring down the great. For Nietzsche's overactive imagination, the original human society—the "State"—refers to "a herd of blond beasts of prey, a race of conquerors and masters." These great warrior artists "are ignorant of the meaning of guilt, responsibility, consideration" and are "born organizers." Such—writes Nietzsche—is the origin of the "State."

Both in *Genealogy* and a prior work, *Beyond Good and Evil* (1886), Nietzsche claimed that the moral categories of "good" and "evil" are inventions of the weak to control the independent brilliance of the strong. Nietzsche contrasted a Judeo-Christian "slave morality," based on resentment, with a "master morality" deriving from great races of warrior-aristocrats and artists, especially the Aryans. The masters are those with the physical and imaginative strength to get things done in the world. Master morality self-consciously embraces the universal human will to power and so produces superior human beings. Since the strong, the masters, define their own place in the world, they provoke the envy of the small-minded. Morality would be a kind of revenge of the weak and helpless upon the strong, since they cannot fight them on their own terms.

Historically (according to Nietzsche's "second sight"), the slaves, ever jealous of the freedom of the mighty, sought to bring them down through the weapon of morality, by the "transvaluation of value" (*Genealogy of Morals*). They demonized the activity of the strong, calling it "evil" and blameworthy. In this way, the slaves effectively wrought their revenge on the holders of power. The slave morality glorifies weakness, self-discipline, and pity as virtues, deforming the natural inclinations of the person. As Nietzsche imagined it, this work was brought about principally by the Jews and finished by the Christians, who brought Jewish weakness to its pinnacle in the humiliating death of Jesus Christ on the cross.[1]

In *Genealogy*, Nietzsche writes that everyone has a will to power, a primal desire to dominate and inflict pain on others. Nietzsche praises the master manifestation of this instinct as a "beast-of-prey conscience," ever unremorseful, exuberant, free, and powerful. When this will to power is suppressed by the herd mentality, it needs an outlet, and thus we try to inflict pain on ourselves instead—and this is "bad conscience" or the guilt of the weak. Man, writes Nietzsche, "invented the bad conscience so as to hurt himself, after the *natural* outlet for this will to hurt, became blocked." Conscience, then, is a deformed will to power, turned against oneself and expressed as moral masochism.

THE DANGER OF NIETZSCHE

Since most people rightly dismiss Nietzsche's fanciful speculations on the origins of morality for what they are, why bother including them in our discussion of conscience? Like many theorists, Nietzsche has continued to influence people well after his day. His radical, unconventional theories, expressed with passion, conviction, and poetic ardor, have captivated many, and he is a favorite among the young and disenfranchised. In fact, his influence has only increased with time. He is, in fact, the source of what we call "postmodern thought." Not only do we see his hatred for the Judeo-Christian ethic and his exaltation of the Aryan race with its "blond beasts" incarnated politically in Adolf Hitler and German National Socialism, we also find remnants of it where we would least expect it, trickling into the popular mentality of liberal democracies.

Though few of us are tempted to Nietzsche's racism and elitist morality, many are tempted by his idealization of primal instincts. For Nietzsche, self-discipline and the restraint of passion stem from Judeo-Christian vindictiveness, as a slave's tool to control the master. Passion should be given free rein. The "tame man" produced by Christianity is a "wretched, mediocre and unedifying creature" and rightly does the higher man despise him for his "excess of deformity, disease, exhaustion, and effeteness" (*Genealogy*).

Think back for a moment to those cartoon angels and devils that we mentioned earlier in this chapter. There we find not a little of Nietzsche's legacy. How often the angelic figure strikes us as unbearably self-righteous, boring, irritating, effeminate, and cowardly! The little devil, on the contrary, exerts greater appeal, instigating adventure, fun, excitement, and good-natured naughtiness. Our popular culture has accepted the proposal that conscience, or at least faithfulness to conscience, is the lot of the fearful and weak-minded.

How winsomely Nietzsche paints the "higher men," whose only conscience is that of a beast of prey!

> The knightly-aristocratic "values" are based on a careful cult of the phys-
> ical, on a flowering, rich and even effervescing healthiness, that goes
> considerably beyond what is necessary for maintaining life, on war,
> adventure, the chase, the dance, the tourney—on everything, in fact,
> which is contained in strong, free, and joyous action. (*Genealogy of
> Morals*)

We, too, may be tempted to see the Christian virtues of humility, compassion, and self-mastery as unnecessary restraints on our creative power,
or even as signs of weakness. Who has not felt the Nietzschean urge to
throw off the fetters of morality and give free rein to our baser instincts?
The Christian proposal of freedom proposes a more arduous task than
simply allowing our primal instincts to run wild.

Yet more insidious still is Nietzsche's reversal of the moral order. Evil
becomes good and good evil. No longer is it a question of "giving in" to
evil, but of willingly embracing evil as the true good. How often we see
that in our contemporary society! How tempting it can be to follow the
age-old siren song of being our own gods, autonomous and answerable to
no one but ourselves!

As extreme as they are, the theories of Freud and Nietzsche do not
exhaust the possibilities of error regarding moral conscience. Many of
today's errors are more subtle, and for that reason more tempting and attractive. Perhaps the most insidious of all is the temptation to moral relativism, or the belief that there is no right and wrong. In the next chapter
we will look more closely at this modern-day conscience trap.

Questions for Study and Discussion

1. What is misleading about the typical representation of conscience as
   a little angel and a devil perched on either shoulder giving moral advice?
2. What was Sigmund Freud's view of conscience? Why is it important to
   study this?
3. How can atheism cloud one's ideas about conscience? Where does
   moral authority lie if there is no God?

4. How would you answer Freud's claim that we irrationally assimilate our parents' and society's moral norms?
5. What is the role of guilt in the Christian moral life, and how does it differ from Freud's notions of guilt?
6. How did Friedrich Nietzsche understand the moral life? In what ways was he mistaken?

Questions for Personal Reflection
1. Do you sometimes wish you could throw off conscience in order to be free of its demands? How do you react to that desire?
2. How important is your Christian faith in your own moral choices?
3. Do you think Christian morality makes you weaker or stronger? In what ways?

7

WHAT WE KNOW AND
WHAT WE DON'T

Certainty, Humility, and Good Judgment

If conscience is meant to guide us to right conduct, it must offer more than *opinion*. It must offer moral *truth*. Otherwise "right" conduct wouldn't be *right* at all. It would simply be a question of perspective, preference, or social convention. Yet what happens when two people—or two cultures—disagree on fundamental questions of good and evil? Who is to say who is right and who is wrong? Are both right? Is neither? Or is morality more a question of consistency with one's own values—whatever they may be—than of conformity with a universal standard of goodness?

Let's say, for example, that one culture permits polygamy or wife-swapping, and another insists on monogamy. Who is to say which is better? If a given tribe advocates human sacrifice, or punishing adultery with death, is there anything necessarily wrong with that, or must each culture be judged on its own standards? Aren't there just as many systems of morality as there are cultures? And if this is the case, is judgment of conscience nothing more than an expression of cultural differences rather than universal norms or moral truth?

This was the theory advanced by the American Anthropological Association. In 1947, on the occasion of the United Nations debate about universal human rights, the Executive Board of the AAA issued a statement expressing opposition to the United Nations' attempt to formulate a universal declaration of human rights. Written by leading members of the AAA, the statement argued that individual cultures and societies must be evaluated on their own terms, and not by universal standards. "How can the proposed Declaration be applicable to all human beings," the authors asked, "and not be a statement of rights conceived only in terms of the values prevalent in the countries of Western Europe and America?" The Statement added that "standards and values are relative to the culture from which they derive" and "what is held to be a human right in one society may be regarded as anti-social by another people."[1]

For those who see morality as a question of cultural convention, one moral code is no better than another, any more than driving on the right side of the road in America or Italy is better than driving on the left side of the road in England or Australia. We may prefer one way over another, but it is not morally superior to the other.

The view that morality has no absolute standard (such as human nature) is called *moral relativism*, since it understands moral principles to be relative to a given reference point (one's culture, historical period, individual scale of values, etc.). The version of moral relativism we have been examining here is commonly called *cultural relativism*. It sees a moral code simply as a part of a given culture, with no touchstone outside of the culture.

As fashionable and seemingly "tolerant" as moral relativism may be, it runs up against serious shoals. The problem with moral relativism, in fact, is threefold. First, it wipes out not only a particular moral principle or system, but the very idea of morality itself. Unlike the social sciences, which are essentially descriptive and statistical, ethics is a *normative* science. In other words, while the social sciences tell us how people generally *do* behave, ethics tells us instead how people *ought* to behave. If it is unfair to hold human behavior up to any universal standards, then our own standards lose their moral authority as well. If justice and injustice are equally tenable, the only thing left is brute force. If there was no moral difference between Nazi Germany and democratic England, we would live in a world of moral chaos. By this reasoning a society can enforce its laws, but with no claim to moral authority or rectitude. In the end, there would be no right and wrong, but only *your* right and *my* right.

Second, moral relativism clashes with human experience. When we say that rape and child abuse are morally wrong, we are not merely expressing our personal distaste for these activities, the way we express our dislike for lima beans or the music of Marilyn Manson. *I don't engage in rape myself, but who am I to impose my moral values on others? I am personally opposed, but socially open-minded.* Hardly! When we say that rape and child abuse are wrong, we are saying that these sorts of behavior are reprehensible, and that no one should engage in them, since they violate personal dignity and are unworthy of human beings. When the United Nations endeavors to spread the idea that every human person possesses an inherent dignity, that women are entitled to the same fundamental rights as men, that certain ways of treating children are always and everywhere wrong, it is proclaiming the existence of *universal moral truths.*

Let's take the case of slavery. To the moral relativist, we can make no universal moral judgment on the practice of forcing human beings into servitude. It would depend—they would say—on the historical moment and cultural environment in which we find ourselves. Therefore we cannot evaluate the institution of slavery *itself* in universal terms. Yet does anyone really believe that, deep down? Is our aversion to slavery simply a product of a Eurocentric cultural ethos, or does it reflect something deeper about human nature itself?

Third, moral relativism is not only wrongheaded, it is also impossible. In practice, no one is a complete moral relativist. Imagine, if you will, that a Namibian signed a contract with the American Anthropological Association for the exclusive publication of his memoirs. Imagine further that the Namibian made simultaneous agreements with four or five other publishers and collected a fine sum from each one. If—when found out—he were to fall back on the claim that "in my country, honoring one's contracts is not morally binding," does anyone really think the AAA would shrug its collective shoulders and say, "Indeed, we mustn't impose our Western value of honesty on this other culture. After all, 'what is held to be a human right in one society may be regarded as anti-social by another people....'" I don't think so.

More damning still, however, is the inherent contradiction in this position. Those who say, "No one should impose a universal moral principle on others" are already contradicting themselves. After all, what is "Thou shalt not impose one's moral principles" if not a moral principle itself? Human beings cannot get along without universal principles any more than mathematics can get along without axioms or physics can get along without formulas.

Besides these three insurmountable obstacles, cultural relativism also faces a fourth hurdle. If morality were really just a question of cultural conditioning, with no basis in human nature, we would expect to find radical differences in moral codes from one culture to another. We would expect murder to be condemned in one culture and praised in another, or that somewhere in the world gratitude would be considered a vice just as we consider it a virtue. We would also expect there to be amoral cultures, where the categories of right and wrong simply couldn't be found. Yet this doesn't happen. Despite the myth of moral diversity, anthropological studies show a remarkable consistency in basic moral norms. Nowhere is betrayal venerated or courage scorned. Nowhere are disrespect for one's parents and dishonesty esteemed as qualities to aspire to. Despite the very real differences in specific moral norms from culture to culture, an astounding similarity exists.

C. S. Lewis, an attentive student of the human condition, pointed out in *Mere Christianity* that the moral law is essentially the same in all cultures, and that existing differences are not nearly as great as they are made to appear. "If anyone will take the trouble to compare the moral teaching of, say, the ancient Egyptians, Babylonians, Hindus, Chinese, Greeks, and Romans," he wrote, "what will really strike him will be how very like they are to each other and to our own." To take one example, he wrote: "Men have differed as regards what people you ought to be unselfish to—whether it was only your own family, or your fellow countrymen, or everyone. But they have always agreed that you ought not to put yourself first. Selfishness has never been admired."

Moral relativism falls flat on so many fronts, it is surprising that people continue to espouse it. Yet they do. In fact, though its forms may vary, moral relativism continues alive and well to our day.

DIFFERENT FORMS OF MORAL RELATIVISM

Cultural relativism, in fact, is only one strain of moral relativism. Alongside the belief that morality is a product of individual cultures, other species of moral subjectivism flourish as well. Let's look at four versions of relativism.

1. "EVERYBODY'S RIGHT"

A classic scene in Norman Jewison's film adaptation of the stage play *Fiddler on the Roof* involves Tevye intervening in an argument between two townspeople. One vehemently asserts that a peaceful life demands avoiding curiosity with the things that don't concern us. "Why should I break my head about the outside world?" he exclaims. "Let the outside world break its own head!" To this, Tevye observes, "He's right." But young Perchik of Kiev disagrees. "Nonsense! You can't close your eyes to what's happening in the world." To this argument as well Tevye concedes, "He is right." Noting a contradiction, another steps in and says, "He's right and he's right? They can't both be right!" And here Tevye ponders for a moment and then solemnly declares, "You know, you are also right."

Many moral relativists adhere to Tevye's logic: "Everybody's right. Let's just be peaceful. If it works for you, that is what matters." In this scenario, right and wrong are what you want them to be. Yet this doesn't work either. Many times, in fact, right and wrong are *not* what we would like them to be at all! How often we would like to rewrite the moral law at convenient moments to be able to do as we please, with no qualms of conscience. Yet we cannot do this. The moral law imposes itself. Conscience steps in and reminds us that the right thing is not always the most pleasant.

Moreover, the commonsense "principle of noncontradiction" states that two contrary propositions cannot both be true. If you and I hold contrary ideas as regards the existence of God or the morality of adultery, we simply can't both be right. In our day and age, no one wants to be an absolutist. No one wants to tell someone else he is wrong. Yet sometimes, *we cannot both be right.*

In reality, as we have seen, no one is a total relativist. No one believes that one way of thinking is just as good as another. Though many today love to label others as "dogmatic" and "absolutist," while they claim to be "open-minded" and "tolerant," no one is totally open-minded. Some people may challenge you to be more open on questions of sexual ethics or abortion, and then turn around and insist on the absolute moral obligation to recycle your bottles or sign the Kyoto Protocol. Everyone holds to some moral absolute, even if it is only: *You must be tolerant!* We simply cannot live without some moral framework.

2. "It Doesn't Matter Who Is Right"

Others, however, would say that even if there is one moral truth, it doesn't really matter. A good person isn't the one who does the *right thing*, but the one who does *what he believes to be the right thing*. What matters is to be true to your own convictions, whatever they may be. Good and evil are determined by the correspondence between one's choices and the hierarchy of values one has personally embraced. Sincerity would be the sole moral standard.

One of the definitions of conscience offered by *The American Heritage Dictionary of the English Language* would seem to back this up. The dictionary describes conscience as "conformity to one's own sense of right conduct." According to this definition, conscience would be about self-consistency, or integrity with one's personal scale of values. This definition jibes nicely with a tendency of modern society to exalt sincerity as the supreme virtue. Since we may never agree who is right and who is wrong—the logic runs—at least be true to your own convictions.

Sincerity is indeed the indispensable starting point of a good conscience. Without sincerity we lack the fundamental requirement for acting well—being true to our principles, and honest with ourselves and others. An insincere person easily falls into duplicity and deceit and lacks the integrity of a mature person.

Yet sincerity alone is insufficient. Moral consistency is an admirable trait, but it does not guarantee good moral choices. One could make the case that Joseph Stalin and Pol Pot were sincere and consistent in their endeavors, but this quality hardly justifies their objectively bad actions. While the words of Shakespeare's Polonius—"This above all: to thine own self be true"—make for splendid rhetoric, they miss one of the most essential elements of morality. We are not merely accountable to ourselves but to others as well and, ultimately, to God. The measure of the goodness of our choices is not our own "scale of values," but moral truth. As we have seen, John Henry Newman lucidly remarked that conscience is not a long-sighted selfishness, nor a desire to be consistent with oneself, but a messenger from God.

3. Celebrating Diversity: "The More Opinions, the Better"

For others, morality is a question of lifestyle choice. One universal moral code would be boring, just as it would be boring for everyone to wear the same clothes or listen to the same music. The world is richer and more interesting because of the variety of moral systems that exist. Here moral pluralism would not merely be a *fact*, it would be an *imperative*: "Moral diversity is a good to be pursued. The more moralities, the better!"

In many things, diversity is indeed a good to be pursued; in others, it is not. In art, literature, and music, the loss of specific cultural traditions would mean a genuine loss for humanity. Imagine if we could listen only to ragtime piano tunes! No folk music. No classical or jazz. No big bands. This would be a real loss. On the other hand, no one calls the loss of belief in a flat world an assault on scientific "diversity." No one calls for more diversity in mathematics, rather than admitting only one possible answer for each equation. Education surely reduces the diversity of beliefs as people come to know the truth, but who would consider this a setback?

The same is true in the case of morality. Society is not made richer by mixing injustice with justice, dishonesty with honesty, or treachery with loyalty. The discovery of universal moral truth may lessen diversity, but it makes the world better, not worse.

4. "We Can't Know Who's Right"

Another more subtle form of relativism might say the following: "Yes, there may be objective moral truth, but if there is, it is unknowable. You are convinced and I am convinced, and there is no objective point of reference to tell us who is right and who is wrong. In the end, God will judge. Live and let live."

This reminds me of the famous story from the Buddhist Sutra that speaks of six blind men trying to describe an elephant. Since one touches the side, another the tail, another a leg, another a tusk, another the trunk, and another the elephant's ear, their perceptions of the elephant vary considerably, and each captures only a part of the overall reality. Obviously someone describing only an elephant's tusk or trunk doesn't do justice to the whole elephant. Many nowadays use this analogy to describe how different cultures, religions, and moral codes approach reality. Each would have a part of the truth, and no one the whole truth.

At first blush, this story makes good sense. No one can know everything, and we are enriched by others' experiences. The problem with the story, however, is that the narrator of the story (who is not blind) *does* claim to have the whole picture, which explains how he knows that the others have only a partial knowledge. Someone needs an idea of the bigger picture in order to critique the reductive descriptions. Even moral relativists claim to know something about moral truth, if only to criticize it.

For a Christian, there are two further problems to this scenario. First, it assumes that the blind men do not communicate with each other or compare their experiences. They live an isolated existence and have nothing to go on other than their individual sensory experience. Yet with human morality this is not the case. Western civilization in particular has at its back more than two millennia of serious moral reasoning. Discussion about what constitutes the good life and what it means to live according to right reason has been the bread and butter of moral philosophers and theologians since the time of Socrates. We benefit not only from our discussion with one another, but also from the great thinkers of the past who have wrestled with these topics.

Second, the story not only assumes the absence of *horizontal* communication (between human beings); it also assumes that there is no *vertical* communication (between God and human beings). To continue with the proposed scenario, what if the Maker of the elephant were to describe his creation to the blind men, explaining not only what the elephant looks like, but everything else about it as well? This is what divine revelation is all about. Christians believe that the Creator of the universe revealed himself to human beings, especially through his own Son, who became man and lived among us. In so doing, he not only revealed himself, he also revealed to us what it means to be a human being. The Christian moral life corresponds to the blueprint that God has for his human creation. Therefore the moral norms that we embrace bear the seal of both the best of human reasoning and also the revelation of God himself.

Many today, thinking they are practicing intellectual humility, refuse to take a firm position on moral questions that are empirically unverifiable and prefer the comfortable stance of "open-mindedness." A clear moral stance would leave them in the awkward position of saying, or at least tacitly implying, that other people are wrong. We think it judgmental and discourteous to proclaim our moral beliefs as absolutely *true*, since we think that moral convictions could only be the fruit of pride.

Yet humility doesn't mean moral ambivalence. While self-questioning has its place, we cannot wake up every morning and wonder whether our most closely held beliefs and understanding of the world are correct. We can be convinced of our position without thinking that we are therefore better than others. And even when we are convinced we are right, and that another person's beliefs are one hair short of ludicrous, we must be gentle and understanding, taking the other *person* seriously, even when his *opinions* don't merit it.

Some do, however, arrogantly trumpet their beliefs before others and make no effort to understand why others think the way they do. They use the truth as a billy club with which to beat other people down. This is an error and slows down the work of evangelization. It doesn't compromise our own beliefs to try to understand others better. In fact, we can learn something from everyone. Even disagreement itself can be carried out in a civilized—indeed in a Christian—way.

As we have seen from these different arguments, moral relativism always favors the subjective element of moral decision-making over the objective element. A little further examination is needed here.

Paving the Road to Hell

Our actions have two sources of moral value: one subjective and the other objective. Both are important. First, we must always follow our consciences. That is, we must do what we *believe* to be right. Second, what we believe to be right must coincide with what *truly* is right. In other words, the goodness of our action also depends on the correctness of our moral judgment. We must choose truly good things. A person of good conscience wants to do the right thing and not just to feel complacent about "trying" to do the right thing. Conscience looks for real answers, and for these it must look beyond itself and its own sincerity for the objective truth.

Many people seek ethical advice. They turn to a friend or a religious leader to receive counsel for hard decisions. Unfortunately, some counselors merely respond, "Follow your conscience." Yet to tell someone simply to "follow your conscience" is to tell him nothing at all. It is often equivalent to saying, "There is no right or wrong answer in this case. Do whatever you please. Whatever you choose in conscience is fine." In fact, such advice is often an invitation to take the low road of what is easiest. To declare that, in a given moral sphere, "It's a question of conscience" sends a clear message that a right moral answer simply doesn't exist. This is a sad betrayal of a person's trust.

A person seeking moral advice above all needs *content* for his or her moral decision-making. What he needs is not just *encouragement*, but moral *principles*. The reason he has come seeking counsel is because he is *already* following his conscience, which has impelled him to get better information, precisely because he realizes that he lacks the necessary moral reference points to make a good moral decision.

It's said that the road to hell is paved with good intentions. This means that when people do evil things with good intentions, they still do evil things. If you eat rat poison thinking it is cheese spread, you are still eating rat poison. The knowledge that you subjectively "acted in good faith" will be cold comfort as you are rushed to the emergency room to have your stomach pumped.

Our intentions don't change the essential goodness or badness of our choices. Intentions are undoubtedly important. Acting with a good intention far surpasses acting with a bad intention. But for a truly good person, it isn't enough. Acting with a good intention, in its deepest sense, means wanting to really know and do *the right thing*. We desire the objective assurance that what we are doing *really* is good. Let's say a person suffers from gangrene in her right leg, and there is no solution but amputation. We would hardly excuse a doctor who amputated the woman's *left* leg just because he had "good intentions." With the best intentions in the world, the poor patient would still wind up losing a perfectly healthy leg.

We all make mistakes, and a vague appeal to "acting in conscience" cannot justify wrongdoing. Sometimes we do wrong because we don't listen to our consciences; other times, however, our consciences themselves are mistaken in their judgments. Therefore, along with our duty to *follow* conscience comes a duty to *form* our consciences, so that their judgments will guide us according to moral truth rather than subjective whim.

Conscience is a tool for knowing the truth, but what matters most is the *truth* we are seeking. Conscience is important because moral truth is important. A good conscience does not seek arguments to justify doing what one feels like, or what most gratifies one's immediate desires. By its nature it seeks moral truth, as much as that may cramp our style and pinch our desires. When a good husband decides to follow his conscience and not proposition the cute intern at work, he does so despite his baser inclinations. Conscience doesn't serve our urges and pleasures; it serves the truth.

Christian ethics has consistently held that the end doesn't justify the means. That is to say, some things should never be done, even if we expect all sorts of good to come from our bad action. To take a contemporary example, what could be better than finding a cure for Parkinson's disease? Yet does this good end justify the creation of human embryos in order to harvest their stem cells—killing them in the process—in the hope that one day their death may benefit others? Does a noble goal justify absolutely any means to get there? Nazi doctors in World War II concentration camps conducted all sorts of vile experiments on their prisoners, and through them medical science gained useful new knowledge about the human condition. Yet do any number of medical advances justify the abuse of those prisoners? Of course not. They became innocent victims of medical progress, and the conduct of the doctors was unconscionable.

There is a certain asymmetry to morality. Bad intentions can corrupt good actions, but good intentions cannot rehabilitate bad actions. Everything needs to be in place for an action to be good. Therefore, if I ostentatiously give money to the poor in the hopes of being esteemed, my objectively good action is vitiated by my bad intention. But if I commit adultery even with the best of intentions, it is still wrong. Good acts done for the wrong reasons are bad, but so are bad acts done for the right reasons. To be truly good, an action must be *totally* good. In other words, the action must be good in itself *and* done for the right reasons. This is what ethicists mean by the Latin saying *"Bonum ex integra causa, malum e quocumque defectu"* ("An action is good when good in *every* respect; it is wrong when wrong in *any* respect"). If any of these factors is missing, the action will be bad.

What fundamentally makes an act bad or good is its conformity with moral truth, not with subjective moral perception of that truth. We strive as far as possible to adjust our moral perceptions to the truth, since the goal is not a subjectively "clean conscience" but truly *good actions*, which correspond with right reason and are pleasing to God. An "honest" mistake is still a mistake and, whenever possible, must be avoided. When we make no effort to correct or avoid "honest mistakes," then we must begin to wonder whether our mistakes are really "honest" after all. When they are accepted, they become at least to some extent deliberate.

JUDGING OTHERS

One of the best-known sayings of Jesus is his injunction to abstain from judgment. "Judge not, that you be not judged" (Matt. 7:1 RSV). The moral law is first and foremost a rule of life *for me*, not a yardstick to measure others. That is why Jesus also invites us to remove the wooden beams lodged in our own eyes before trying to remove the speck of dust from our brother's eye (see Matt. 7:3–5).

The choice to avoid judging another person involves acknowledging our ignorance as to their *intentions*. There are many aspects of other people's behavior, motivations, and personal responsibility that we simply cannot know. It's hard enough to understand our own motivations and intentions without having to get inside someone else's head or heart! We don't know what temptations they struggle against. Nor can we know what efforts they are making. We must leave judgment up to God.

Humility and meekness go together. When we recognize that it is not our place to judge others, we grow gentler in the way we treat them. This gentle approach often helps people more than an angry condemnation of their behavior. Jesus himself bore this out on many occasions during his public life.

I had the privilege of visiting the Holy Land at Eastertime in 2007. When I visited the town of Jericho, I saw what the locals claim to be the actual sycamore tree climbed by Zacchaeus to see Jesus. Maybe you remember the poignant scene described by Saint Luke in his gospel (Luke 19:1–10). Though he was a Jew, Zacchaeus was one of the senior tax collectors and a collaborator with the occupying Romans. He had grown rich by his trade and was hated by the people. Still, he was curious and wanted to see Jesus, about whom he had heard so much. Since he was a short man, he couldn't see Jesus passing by through the crowd, so he climbed up a sycamore tree to get a better view. Jesus saw him there and came over to the tree.

Now Jesus could have taken a harsh approach. He could have shaken his finger at Zacchaeus and said, "Come down, you rascal! It's collaborating scum like you who give Jews a bad name!" He didn't. Rather, he looked up and said, "Zacchaeus, come down. Hurry, because I must stay at your house today" (see Luke 19:5). Jesus didn't demand a series of conditions. He simply reached out. And Zacchaeus was overjoyed. He was used to being ostracized and couldn't believe that Jesus actually wanted to come to his house. When others complained that Jesus was going to a sinner's house, Zacchaeus spontaneously responded, "Look, sir, I am going to give half my money to the poor, and if I have cheated anybody, I will pay him back four times the amount" (see Luke 19:8). The gentle approach had won his heart.

This prohibition of judgment must be understood correctly, however. It doesn't mean a refusal to call good and evil by their names. An old adage sums this up quite nicely: *Hate the sin, love the sinner.* We can, and sometimes must, judge *actions* as good or bad, but we can never judge the *person.* We can never know the state of another person's soul, even when he or she has done very bad things.

Jesus' example bears this out. Jesus welcomed prostitutes, but he never welcomed prostitution. He was soft on adulterers, but unyielding on adultery. After forgiving the adulterous woman, he adds, "Go and sin no more" (John 8:11 NKJV). This is not just a matter of semantic hair-splitting. Jesus came to call sinners but to condemn sin, much as a doctor loves sick people but hates sickness. In fact, when Jesus tells the chief priests and elders that "the tax-collectors and the prostitutes are going into the kingdom of God ahead of you" (Matt. 21:31), he is not winking at thievery and prostitution. He is responding, rather, to their willingness to acknowledge their errors and to change.

Even on the social level, moral tolerance can go only so far. To tolerate child abuse or rape is a sign of cultural degradation, not moral enlightenment. A just society must always draw a line somewhere between what will be tolerated and what will not. Though we still should avoid judging abusers and rapists, we cannot hesitate to condemn the activities they engage in.

One of the best ways to avoid judging others is to cultivate a deeper understanding of why others think the way they do. Many factors enter into people's moral convictions, and it is not easy to sift through the many layers of influences that condition one's ethical code. It will be helpful here to examine more closely some of the elements that come into play in forming moral convictions. This will help us to understand others better and also to understand (and fine-tune) our own moral beliefs.

WHY PEOPLE THINK THE WAY THEY DO

Even though many *apparently* differing moral codes turn out to be more similar than different, real differences do exist. People do espouse differing moral systems. What causes such differences? Where do they come from? If God has indeed written his law on the human heart (the natural law), why don't we all think alike? To answer these questions, we can begin by examining what factors enter into the formation of our moral understanding.

This brief exploration is not meant to be merely a sociological exercise in understanding others. There is practical value in examining the sources of moral views. It helps us discover the roots of certain prejudices and to develop a self-critical attitude. Part of the moral life involves examining our own suppositions and prejudices and constantly confronting them with the gospel. *Is this really what Jesus wants from me? Is my way of thinking and acting truly Christian?*

UPBRINGING

The first and most incisive source of our moral outlook comes from upbringing. We naturally assimilate our parents' values and moral code. How many times do we hear a person, in a moment of moral decision-making, quote his or her mother or father? "Dad used to say that we should always help those down on their luck, because we never know when we will find ourselves in a similar situation." "Mom always said that lies are for liars, but not for the Johnsons."

We often see that children mimic both their parents' virtues and their defects. Where parents are attentive to the needs of those around them and generous in sharing their own things, children often follow. When parents are racist or sexist in their judgments, children readily pick up the same traits spontaneously. It is rare to find cases of child abuse where the perpetrators didn't suffer something similar in their own lives.

True, there comes a time—usually around adolescence—when children begin questioning their parents' values and criteria. They may even go overboard, criticizing *everything* their parents do. This is a natural part of growing up that allows young people to spread their intellectual wings and form their own convictions. Many times, following a rebellious stage, young people return to the core values they learned in their families.

Though parents' words and teaching are important, their example is even more so. It is one thing to tell your children that going to church on Sundays is important, and quite another thing for the kids to see Mom and Dad personally making church attendance a priority. Actions do indeed speak louder than words.

A mature adult learns to sift through the examples and teachings received in the family and to make his own those that are worthwhile. A Christian especially is called to form an objective judgment of right and wrong, to adjust his moral standards to those of the gospel. In the end, Jesus and the Church he founded is our final and sure point of reference for right and wrong.

The Law of the Land

We live in a legalistic society, where legality is often identified with morality. When questioned on the quality of their conduct, many people spontaneously justify their choices with the words, "Hey, it's not against the law!" The implication is that if it's not illegal, it cannot be immoral. The law not only tells citizens what they can and cannot do, it also educates them in morality. It outlines for a given society what sort of behavior is permissible, and what sort is not. For many, civil law is a point of reference for morality.

But the identification of morality with legality can easily go too far. First of all, the civil law doesn't try to legislate *all* morality, but only the most basic principles of justice for the sake of the common good. The law may forbid stealing another's car, but it can't forbid ingratitude, pettiness, or selfishness. The law can offer tax credits for charitable donations, but it cannot make us generous or others-centered. The law, in short, can go only so far. Morality must go farther. It calls us to an excellence that can never be legislated.

Second, we suppose the law to be good, and fortunately most laws are. Yet not all are. Civil laws reflect the moral sense of the majority. In general, we are right to trust them. This reflects a healthy confidence in the

basic goodness of our legal system. On the other hand, our confidence in
the law can make us lose our critical judgment. Not all laws are just laws,
and not everything permissible by the law is morally permissible. Just because the law of the land once permitted slavery, it was never morally
right. Just because assisted suicide may be legal in some states doesn't mean
that somehow it is morally okay to practice it.

As a good citizen, a Christian must respect the civil laws of his or her
country without abdicating his critical sense. Laws must be evaluated according to their conformity with the natural law and with the gospel and
judged as good or bad. By themselves, they are insufficient for educating
our moral sense.

Religion

A third factor in the formation of our moral principles is religion. Unlike
upbringing and the civil law, religion plays a much more mottled role in
people's lives. For some, religion is hugely important for inculcating a
moral sense. Those who are taught from an early age that God created
them and will eventually judge them learn to live with an eye to his will
and his commandments. Others, however—especially in today's secular
society—grow up with little or no religious sense. For some, their accountability goes no further than the civil law, with its incentives and sanctions.

Religion reinforces the *transcendence* of the moral law. That is, it helps
people to understand that their choices always have consequences, both
here in this life and also in the life to come. Granted, religions vary, and
some hold no belief in resurrection and judgment. Most, however, do relate our earthly actions with eternal consequences. As is often said, even
when no one else sees you, God sees you. In the end, that's what matters.

Religion also explains that behind the natural moral law, which each
of us perceives, there stands a divine Lawgiver or Legislator. The natural
law didn't arise in human beings as a mere offshoot of an evolutionary roll
of the dice. It is a necessary part of what it means to be human beings,
made in God's image and likeness. God created us as free beings, responsible for our actions, and he makes his will known to us in various ways.
Again, religions vary, and we cannot overgeneralize. At the same time, the
three major monotheistic religions—Judaism, Christianity, and Islam—
resemble one another fairly closely in these basic points.

Despite some modern assertions to the contrary, religion exerts an overwhelmingly positive influence in the moral lives of individuals and societies. Reams of historical and sociological evidence back this up. Historically it was atheism that was suspect. How can a person who doesn't believe in a Creator, judgment, or eternal life—it was said—possibly be trusted? At the same time, religion, too, must be purified by reason. A religion that commands its adherents to commit acts that violate the natural moral law—such as the killing of innocents—must be questioned. Civil law should promote religious practice in general as a true good for men and women but disallow those practices that clearly jeopardize the common good.

PUBLIC OPINION

A corollary to our upbringing as children is the role that public opinion—or peer pressure—plays in our moral lives. Our social and cultural milieu has a deeper effect on our moral thinking than we sometimes realize. We unconsciously adopt many of the ethical assumptions and sensibilities that course around us. Who of us wants to be out of style, out of touch, culturally backward, or unfashionable? How much effort do we expend paying tribute to public opinion, often without knowing it? This is why Saint Paul enjoins believers, "Do not be conformed to this world, but be transformed by the renewing of your minds, so that you may discern what is the will of God—what is good and acceptable and perfect" (Rom. 12:2). This means an active and critical reevaluation of the principles that rule our culture. Especially in a democratic state, where even moral truth seems to be determined by majority opinion, it is especially difficult to hold on to one's moral convictions. Since all of us are, in a certain sense, products of our particular environment, from time to time we need to take a step backward to consider which of our moral opinions need revisiting.

In his 1995 encyclical letter on the value of human life, Pope John Paul II issued a strong warning against this cultural conformism and its threats to Christians and human life itself. He spoke with great concern about the profound changes in the way in which contemporary society considers life and relationships between people. He wrote:

> Choices once unanimously considered criminal and rejected by the
> common moral sense are gradually becoming socially acceptable. Even

certain sectors of the medical profession, which by its calling is directed to the defense and care of human life, are increasingly willing to carry out these acts against the person. In this way the very nature of the medical profession is distorted and contradicted, and the dignity of those who practice it is degraded.[2]

The effects of these shifts in ethical thinking can be terrible.

The end result of this is tragic: not only is the fact of the destruction of so many human lives still to be born or in their final stage extremely grave and disturbing, but no less grave and disturbing is the fact that conscience itself, darkened as it were by such widespread conditioning, is finding it increasingly difficult to distinguish between good and evil in what concerns the basic value of human life.[3]

PERSONAL PREFERENCE AND NATIVE SENSITIVITY

Along with these various external factors, our moral sense is also influenced by our temperament and natural moral sensitivity. Often such differences can be noted from a very early age in children. Some are more "tuned in" to the feelings of others and to their well-being. Others seem coarser. Some have a native tendency to be nurturing and caring, while others seem less empathetic. Some, too, have an acute sense of justice and fairness, while others seem more inclined to take advantage of others.

These natural tendencies can be further modified by our personal experiences. When we have suffered a certain sort of wrongdoing in our own lives, we are often more sensitive to others who suffer similarly (and less tolerant of those who cause such suffering). In other cases, suffering can make people *less* sensitive, or even sadistic. Many times serial killers and other sociopaths were themselves mistreated as children.

Studies have been done, furthermore, noting differences between the way males approach moral questions as compared to the way females reason morally. Men, it seems, tend more often to relate to moral *principles*, and hold up *justice* as the moral ideal, while women more often see moral questions in terms of *relationships* and pay greater attention to *caring*. None of these factors is determinative or removes our moral freedom. They may, however, affect the way we approach moral issues and our response to them.

HABITS OF SIN OR VIRTUE

A final factor in the formation of our moral sense is our own history. Sin not only affects our moral state; it also affects the way we perceive reality, especially moral reality. All of us have experienced this. The first time we commit a particular sin, we can feel broken up and profoundly sorry for having offended our Lord in this way. After a while, however, when we have committed the same sin over and over, we no longer react so acutely. Repeated sin often brings with it a softening of our ethical criteria. After a while, what once seemed morally repugnant no longer strikes us as so terribly bad. Since we no longer *feel* so bad, we begin to *think* that certain actions really mustn't be all that serious. *Who knows—we think—maybe they're not wrong at all?*

What is true of vice is also true of virtue. Though we can never recover lost innocence, we can re-form the habit of doing the right thing. The more we focus on pleasing Christ, for example, the more sensitive our consciences become. We notice things we would never have noticed before. Soon we find that even slight failures to love put us out of sorts. We have recovered what was lost.

To continue fine-tuning our understanding of the true nature of conscience, we need to look more closely at the relationship between *moral knowledge* and *action*. What is the connection between the *judgments* of conscience and the practical *decisions* we make? Is it enough to *know* what is right in order to always *do* what is right? Do we do wrong only out of ignorance, or are there other factors in play? A look at the Christian doctrine of original sin will provide a refreshing, cool shower of realism.

Questions for Study and Discussion

1. What is moral relativism? Give some examples from contemporary society.
2. What are some of the problems with moral relativism?
3. If different people have different moral standards, how can we be sure who is right? Could everyone be right? Or no one? Does it matter?
4. How important are one's intentions in the moral life? Is one's intention all that matters? Why or why not?
5. What did Jesus say about judging others? What does it mean to hate sin and love sinners? Give some practical examples of how this could be lived out.

6. What are some of the factors that influence people's moral norms? Why is it important to understand this?

Questions for Personal Reflection

1. Are you convinced that objective standards of right and wrong exist? Do they give you stability and a sense of security?
2. Are you ever tempted to relativize your own moral conduct? Why? In what areas?
3. What have been the principal influences on your own moral principles and beliefs? Do any need readjusting?

8

WHERE SOCRATES WENT WRONG

The Difference Between Knowing What Is Right and Doing It

Knowledge of right and wrong makes us accountable for our decisions. A totally ignorant person would have no moral responsibility at all—for good or for ill—like a little child before the use of reason. But is moral knowledge everything? If we were perfectly instructed, with full knowledge of good and evil, would that be enough for us always to choose the good?

Permit me to recap here an old but important philosophical debate. The opinion we just described—that we always choose the good when we know it—was articulated by one of the most eminent philosophers of all time, one whose name is almost synonymous with philosophy itself: Socrates. Socrates, and Plato as well, thought that virtue consisted in knowledge, and that moral faults were the result of ignorance of the good.[1] Whoever knows what is good, Socrates surmised, will do it. Perhaps this sanguine reading of human nature stemmed from a projection of his own goodness onto others. Be that as it may, there is a serious problem with this theory.

Let's go back for a moment to the angel and the devil perched on our shoulders. As good and bad duke it out for our allegiance, we already know what we *ought* to do (represented by the voice of the little angel), and all that remains is for us to *do it* or not. In our moral deliberation, two separate actions are involved. The first is the *judgment* of conscience itself, which evaluates the goodness or malice of a given action, like helping your mother with the dishes (good), or stealing a bicycle (bad). The second act involves not a moral judgment, but a *decision* to obey or disobey what conscience dictates. These two acts are distinct and do not necessarily agree with one another.

No doubt about it: bad conscience leads to bad choices. If we judge incorrectly, our actions will not be truly good. If my conscience mistakenly judges that stealing a bicycle is a morally good thing to do, following it will lead me to do something that is objectively evil. But bad conscience isn't the only source of wrongdoing. Our free choices don't always follow what our consciences command. All of us make some immoral choices, knowing full well that what we are doing is wrong. Otherwise, in a sense, there would be no blameworthiness or praiseworthiness to our actions. Everything would be a result of correct or erroneous moral calculation, and the smarter a person is, the more virtuous he would be.

ARISTOTLE TO THE RESCUE

It was Plato's student, Aristotle, who eventually set things straight. He realized that people are free to embrace or reject the good they know. You and I make good choices and bad choices. After looking at Socrates' doctrine that moral action depends solely on knowledge, Aristotle wrote: "This theory is manifestly at variance with plain facts." It seemed obvious to him that people sometimes choose to do the wrong thing, even though they *know* it is wrong.

Aristotle devised a very helpful outline to understand and categorize people's relationship with moral goodness. He broke states of moral character into four categories. Two of these groups—the "virtuous" and the "vicious"—are either so good or so bad that they experience relatively little interior conflict. Those who possess *virtue* do the right thing spontaneously and happily, whereas the *vicious* (Aristotle also calls them "profligate") do what is evil without thinking twice.

The other two groups, to which the vast majority of humanity belongs, he calls the "restrained" and the "unrestrained." The *restrained* know what is good and do it, but only with much huffing and puffing. Their consciences judge rightly, and despite their contrary desires, they choose the good. The *unrestrained* also know what they should do, but they are weaker-willed and give in to their passions rather than obey their consciences. Graphically, these categories could be portrayed as follows:

Like any breakdown of persons into groups, these categories are not absolute, and there is plenty of overlap between them. We can be, for instance, very restrained in certain areas (control of our unruly temper) while unrestrained in others (our weakness for junk food). Still, our relationship to our consciences and their dictates often follows a pattern. We are either very faithful to them, moderately faithful, or simply negligent.

Going back to our example of stealing bicycles, we could say that the virtuous person never really thinks of stealing a bike as an option and doesn't have to struggle. The restrained person may see a beautiful bike, realize how easy it would be to steal it, and even want to steal it, but in the end he follows his right conscience that tells him stealing is wrong. The unrestrained person sees the bike, desires it, wrestles with conscience that is telling him *not* to steal it, but then steals it anyway. The vicious person sees the bike, and, without thinking twice, steals it with no remorse at all.

Clearly the group we would like to belong to is the virtuous, who not only know and do what is right, but do so happily and even "naturally." Such is the nature of virtue: those who possess it not only do good, they do so *spontaneously*, as if by second nature. Forming virtue—good habits—means a sort of reeducation of our hearts and our free will to choose the good. A truly humble person unhesitatingly reacts in a humble way, without having to deliberate and consciously choose the "humble thing to do."

This makes sense when we remember how habits work. Let's take an example from sports. When we train our muscles to work in a certain way by repeating the same movements over and over again, after a while they automatically follow the same pattern. A golf swing is like that. Beginners have to remember countless details: how to position their feet, how to hold the club, to keep their heads down, the proper path for the back-swing, to keep their left arms straight, etc. After long hours at the driving range, however, things start to improve. The golfer can relax a little more because his or her body starts naturally following through correctly, and he or she develops a good swing. What once required total concentration and discipline slowly becomes second nature. Our good moral habits—virtues—work in a similar way.

The middle two groups have more difficulty than the virtuous. According to Aristotle, members of both these groups correctly discern right from wrong, so conscience is working. Still, as with the person with the angel and devil on his shoulders, many decisions still entail a struggle. Even the restrained person who eventually does the right thing does so with great expenditure of effort. He does not yield to his evil desires, but they assail him and leave him worn-out. How typical this struggle is for most of us! We strain not only to know what is right but, perhaps even more so, *to do it* once it is clear to us. Most of our moral failures do not proceed from a lack of knowledge, but from a lack of goodwill, self-discipline, and generosity.

The unrestrained person deliberates but ends up doing the wrong thing, and then feels remorse afterward. Sometimes his failures stem from the impetuousness of passion, where he is caught up in the moment and later regrets his conduct. How many times we blurt out hurtful comments in anger, only to regret them once we have calmed down! Other times he succumbs out of weakness of will and simply cannot bring himself to carry out the good he knows he should do. Think especially of the good things we know we should be doing but never get around to because of the effort required. More than any other group, the unrestrained feel internally divided, since they abandon their good judgment in favor of their lower inclinations.

Despite the conflict involved, these two middle positions share a huge advantage over the person in the grip of vice. Conscience is working! The judgments it emits are correct and the person knows what she should be doing, whether she does it or not. Like a hiker with a good compass, she sees where she has to go, though it may be uphill through thorns and brambles. With God's grace, even the unrestrained have the tools they need to pull themselves out of the moral swamp into which they have stumbled.

Yet the states of self-restraint and unrestraint (some translate Aristotle as saying "continence" and "incontinence") are also more volatile than the states of virtue and vice. It is hard to stay there forever, and we tend to get either better or worse. Therefore our moral choices in these states are decisive for the future of our moral character. Let me give two examples. The restrained person, if he keeps following his good conscience, will eventually become a virtuous person. The repetition of good actions—acts of charity or generosity or forgiveness—will eventually lead to *habits* of virtue. If you are an impatient person but continually bite your tongue, you learn to be patient. It becomes almost instinctive. When evil desires are resisted and kept in their place, they lose some of their vehemence and gradually become less of a nuisance.

Unfortunately, our bad choices also have consequences. The worst of these is the corruption of conscience. When an unrestrained person continually gives in to wrong actions, he gradually starts to believe that they must not be so wrong after all. If you often criticize people behind their backs even though you know it is wrong, backbiting easily becomes a habit, and gradually your conscience stops registering it. The old adage says that when we don't live according to what we believe, we end up believing according to the way we live. This corruption of conscience leads to the horrible situation of no longer discerning right from wrong. Once a person falls into this state of vice, it is very difficult to escape from it, since the one instrument that would have alerted him to the error of his ways—conscience—has become perverted.

REINING IN WILD HORSES

Why all this struggle? If God made us good, why don't we more naturally do what is right? Are we a defective product, tending not to good but to evil? Is all of this somehow God's fault?

There are two important answers to that question. The first refers to man's composite nature of body and soul. If we were angels, things would be relatively simple. Angels don't get tugged in seven different directions at the same time. They are *simple*. Human beings, on the contrary, are anything but simple. Many different forces act within us at any given moment, on many different levels. We have urges, sentiments, passions, intelligence, will, conscience, and plenty of outside influences as well. We are not wholly rational, any more than we are wholly emotional, instinctual, or willful. We are all of these things, and they combine in our decision-making.

The human being is endowed with different faculties, different capabilities of body and spirit. A faculty is simply the capability to carry out a particular type of action. If we observe a car going up a hill, we can be sure that there is a motor inside. Every action requires a capacity, the *power* to bring it about. If you and I can see, it follows that we must have the faculty of sight. If we can think and reason, we must necessarily have the power to think. This power is the faculty of intelligence or reason. We become aware of human faculties by observing the actions people perform.

We can distinguish between what is true and what is false through the use of our intelligence. We can likewise differentiate between various sounds, sights, and tastes—loud and quiet, bright and dim, sweet and salty—by the use of our five external senses. Not all faculties are on the same level. The ability to smell is definitely not as sublime as the ability to reason. Since the human person is a unity, all our faculties work together and all are important, but they work together according to a certain order or hierarchy. As we have seen, among all our capabilities, the ability to recognize good and evil holds a special importance.

Yet again, conscience doesn't act in a vacuum. Discerning between good and evil, and knowing that we should do good and avoid evil, doesn't mean that all our other appetites and desires simply fall in line. If I am envious of a friend because of her incessant good fortune, it may not be enough just to *know* that I shouldn't feel envious. The bad inclination doesn't go away so easily. All of us recognize in ourselves a whole gamut of urges and appetites that pull us in many directions. Since many of these appetites are irrational, sometimes they pull us in the right direction, but often they require harnessing.

Passions are strong, natural tendencies that drive us toward or away from something. There are bodily passions (sexual desire, appetite, comfort, pleasure) and passions of the spirit (love, ambition, fear, pride, envy, anger). Sometimes they assist us by providing needed drive to accomplish our objectives. Other times they may be unhelpful, or even destructive, and require reining in. Self-mastery—what Aristotle called "self-restraint"—is a necessary condition to grow in virtue. It allows us to discern between appropriate passions and inappropriate ones, to pick and choose which we will follow. Otherwise, conscience is swept away by blind forces that often take us where we ought not go.

In the mastery of reason over instinct, the human being shows himself to be superior to animals and reaches his true dignity. *Channeling* our passions is not the same as *repressing* them, however. To channel means to redirect or to harness. As we have seen, our passions provide energy and drive and shouldn't simply be rejected. If we have a spirited horse, we can let it run wild or lock it up in a barn, but we have a third option as well. We can *harness* it so that it serves our purposes.

An example from the gospel may help here. At one point we find the twelve apostles quarreling about who is the greatest. When Jesus confronts them about this petty argument, he doesn't merely scold them for their small-mindedness and worldly ambition; he *redirects* it. He says: "Whoever wants to be first must be last of all and servant of all" (Mark 9:35). In other words, *Your ambition is misdirected, but I don't ask you to repress it, but to seek true greatness rather than a cheap substitute. I will show you where true greatness is to be found.* Harnessing our passions lets them serve us rather than enslave us.

Along with our passions, other forces at work in us are our *feelings* and our *moods*. Like passions, our feelings are irrational and don't always coincide with what we really want. Sometimes I feel like doing what I know I ought to do, but often I don't. Sometimes I wake up in a good mood, ready to conquer the world; other times I have to force myself just to get out of bed in the morning. Feelings are subjective, spontaneous, psychological reactions to stimuli. Since they are reactions, they are blind, passive, and outside our control. We cannot just *decide* to feel happy or sad, excited or down in the dumps. It happens *to us*.

Once again, harnessing is required. Reason must govern feelings. Feelings can be wonderful allies when they happen to coincide with our objectives. But when they conflict with our goals and the directives of our consciences, they need to be kept in their place. Otherwise we end up like dry leaves tossed about by the wind. In order to impose a direction on our lives, passions and feelings need channeling.

ORIGINAL SIN

The complexity of human nature helps explain why *knowing* right from wrong doesn't always mean *doing* the right thing. Right conscience pulls in one direction, but often our passions, feelings, and inclinations pull us elsewhere. Yet this multiplicity of urges tells only part of the story. Why don't these different inclinations work together in harmony? Why this interior struggle?

Everyone experiences the effects of this internal conflict, even if they do not recognize the cause. We have all witnessed the universal human proclivity to self-deceit, greed, selfishness, and evil. Humanity's experience of evil doesn't allow us to make an ingenuous appeal to human goodness and purity of judgment, unstained by self-interest or egoism. Some have tried, of course, but the results have been disastrous. The French Enlightenment philosopher Jean-Jacques Rousseau, for example, developed an entire theory of education based on his belief in the natural innocence of human beings, or the *bon sauvage*. According to Rousseau, people are naturally good and corrupted only by their interaction with society. In a state of nature, men are pre-social animals who do not know good and evil, but their independence, along with "the peacefulness of their passions, and their ignorance of vice," keep them from doing ill (*A Discourse on Inequality*). For Rousseau, the natural moral state of human beings is to be compassionate; civilization has made us cruel, selfish, and bloodthirsty.

Anyone who has spent time with little children sees the error of Rousseau's thought (Rousseau didn't, since he deposited his five illegitimate children in an orphanage shortly after birth). As endearing as they are, children are naturally selfish and must be taught to think of others and to share. They learn self-control; they are not born with it. Virtue is acquired rather than innate. As life continues, the struggle against our natural selfishness does not entirely disappear, though it may take different forms. We need self-discipline until the day we die.

Saint Paul—no novice at serious moral combat—describes this interior division with great dramatic flourish. Thankfully, when someone of Paul's moral stature confesses to having such difficulties, we realize that we are not alone, and if he turned out okay, so can we! These are Paul's well-known words:

I do not understand my own actions. For I do not do what I want, but I do the very thing I hate. Now if I do what I do not want, I agree that the law is good. But in fact it is no longer I that do it, but sin that dwells within me. For I know that nothing good dwells within me, that is, in my flesh. I can will what is right, but I cannot do it. For I do not do the good I want, but the evil I do not want is what I do. Now if I do what I do not want, it is no longer I that do it, but sin that dwells within me. So I find it to be a law that when I want to do what is good, evil lies close at hand. For I delight in the law of God in my inmost self, but I see in my members another law at war with the law of my mind, making me captive to the law of sin that dwells in my members. (Romans 7:14–24)

Paul here offers not only a detailed description of the moral struggle, but also a hint as to its cause. Christians refer to this internal division as a consequence of *original sin*. God created us good, but something happened. Through his disobedience, man lost God's friendship, which resulted in a deep internal rift at the core of man's being. How eloquently Saint Paul sums this up by saying, "With my mind I am a slave to the law of God, but with my flesh I am a slave to the law of sin" (Rom. 7:25).

The Judeo-Christian doctrine of original sin helps us to better understand why we must wage war on our baser instincts. We understand that God created the human being with interior harmony and order among the faculties. Sin disrupted God's plan for man. It brought disorder to the original harmony existing in man's interior and in his relations with his Creator and his fellows. This disorder among the faculties produces a dislike for goodness. Moral rectitude no longer seems attractive or worthy of pursuit but often weighs us down like a burden imposed from outside us. As a result of original sin, all of human life, whether individual or collective, appears as a dramatic struggle between good and evil, between light and darkness. In this regard I cannot help thinking of Oliver Wendell Holmes's quaint limerick:

> *God's plan made a hopeful beginning*
> *But man spoiled his chances by sinning*
> *We trust that the story*
> *Will end in God's glory*
> *But at present, the other side's winning.*

Perhaps the most significant contribution of the doctrine of original sin to our understanding of the moral life is the bracing *realism* it offers. The moral life is posited on man's ability to know good and evil and to freely pursue them. Yet both our knowledge and our freedom were darkened by the sin of our first parents. We know imperfectly, and even when we know, our wills are weak and we have difficulty pursuing the goodness we see. Man is still good—indeed very good—yet he is not Rousseau's *bon sauvage*, corrupted only by the external influence of society. We bear the seeds of corruption within ourselves. Because of original sin, we tend toward inordinate self-love and need education, socialization, instruction, character formation, and, above all, God's grace.

Thus Christian moral thought must come to grips with our condition as fallen creatures, taking inventory of strengths and weaknesses. We cannot behave or theorize as if we were not fallen or did not tend "naturally" to sin. A program of diet and exercise designed for a healthy person will differ substantially from a regimen drafted for the ill or infirm. Therefore a good conscience must be backed up by moral virtue, so that we are able to carry out the good that we perceive and desire.

All this talk about the "conditioning" effects of original sin and the corresponding need for self-restraint gives rise to important questions about freedom. How free are we, really? Does conscience merely point to an unreachable norm that we are incapable of attaining? Doesn't self-discipline stifle free expression and spontaneity? Let's look more closely at this elusive concept of *human freedom* as it relates to conscience.

Questions for Study and Discussion

1. What did Socrates say about moral knowledge and moral action? Where was he mistaken? Is knowledge of good and evil all we need to do good and evil?
2. Give some examples that clearly differentiate errors of conscience (moral judgment) from disobedience to conscience (free choices).
3. Aristotle broke moral character into four categories. What are they? Describe the characteristics of each one.
4. Jesus once told a parable about two brothers, who were both told by their father to work in the vineyard (Matt. 21:28–32). One said no but later went. The other said yes but did not go. How does this parable relate to our subject?

5. Why is it sometimes difficult to do the right thing, even when we know what it is?

6. How does original sin affect our own moral lives today?

Questions for Personal Reflection

1. When you make bad decisions, is it usually because you didn't know what the right thing was, or because you simply preferred some other path?

2. How do you motivate yourself to choose well? Where do you get your strength?

3. Do you sometimes get discouraged with your moral struggles and failures? Do you trust in God's power to win the moral battle, even in your life? Do you willingly accept his forgiveness?

9

How the Truth Sets You Free

Real Freedom and Its Counterfeits

In a 2006 article, Oxford scientist Richard Dawkins, a passionate atheist, made what he claimed to be a "scientific" argument against free will and personal responsibility. Since our behavior is determined by our genes and our cultural conditioning, he contended, surely we are not responsible for our actions, and thus punishment is nonsensical.

"Doesn't a truly scientific, mechanistic view of the nervous system make nonsense of the very idea of responsibility?" queries Dawkins. "Any crime, however heinous, is in principle to be blamed on antecedent conditions acting through the accused's physiology, heredity and environment." In other words, human accountability is a fiction, since our actions are simply the result of earlier conditions outside our control and cannot be attributed to us. Dropping to a more practical level, Dawkins asks rhetorically, "Isn't the murderer or the rapist just a machine with a defective component?"[1] The nice thing about Dawkins's theory, I suppose, is that it would allow us to charitably imagine that even his silly arguments must somehow flow from factors foreign to his will. Perhaps that first protozoan to emerge from the primeval slime millions of years ago is really to blame for his bizarre theories!

On the more serious side, however, the denial of free will is neither scientific nor sensible. Science takes as a premise that every effect has a cause, and it endeavors to search out those causes. Yet those causes need not all be empirically measurable. A modest scientist would immediately concede that science says nothing at all about free will as a spiritual reality, any more than it can deny the existence of God. A mechanistic, materialistic view of the universe that leaves no room for the possibility of spiritual realities is not a scientific proposition at all, but a philosophical one. There is nothing scientific about denying spiritual realities.

Unfortunately Dawkins is not alone in his deterministic understanding of human behavior. Many modern psychological schools of thought are premised on the assumption that human conduct is caused by factors outside of free will. According to these theories, if somehow we were able to know *everything* about a person's genetic makeup and environmental conditioning, we should be able to perfectly explain—and predict—a person's actions. That is why much psychological counseling delves into a person's past in an attempt to explain why we are the way we are, instead of challenging personal freedom to *become* the sort of persons we are called to be.

These mechanistic assumptions spill over into popular culture with alarming frequency. How many modern movies go to great lengths to show that criminals' behavior is always linked to a terrible childhood? Contemporary wisdom holds that people never *choose* to be bad; they are somehow *made* bad by their environment. If this is true, then Dawkins is right: punishing a criminal would be as foolish as beating your car with a stick when it breaks down.

Such absolute determinism flies in the face of a Christian view of human existence. Personal freedom and responsibility are part and parcel of a Christian understanding of life and allow for the possibility of rewards and punishments. As Saint Paul wrote to the Romans, "For he will repay according to each one's deeds: to those who by patiently doing good seek for glory and honor and immortality, he will give eternal life; while for those who are self-seeking and who obey not the truth but wickedness, there will be wrath and fury" (Rom. 2:6–8). Such talk of the eternal consequences of our actions would be deeply unjust if we were not *free* to choose one way or the other. Of course our genetic makeup and environment do affect us, but they do not *determine* who we are or what sort of choices we make.

Conscience, too, makes sense only if humans are truly free. We reflect on our past actions not as passive observers, but as the free *authors* of our actions. We acknowledge our personal responsibility and render an accounting. Conscience also urges us to avoid evil and perform good actions in the present and future. Again, it spurs us on to *choose* well, which presupposes the freedom to choose.

Since conscience is so closely tied to the idea of human freedom, a closer look at what we mean by *freedom* will help us better understand how conscience operates.

THREE LEVELS OF FREEDOM

In essence, human freedom is the ability to choose from within. It means that we are the *authors* of our actions, of our moral character. Since our actions belong to us, we are responsible for them and rightly deserve the credit and blame that accompany them. When I freely choose to skip work in order to go to the pub, I must be able to account for my actions. When I help a friend in need, it is I who make that choice, and not my genes or my cultural milieu.

Yet *freedom* is a word with many meanings, and it is necessary to distinguish and clarify three different dimensions.

1. FREEDOM FROM
The most typical definition of freedom is the absence of external constraints. When we are unfettered and without outside interference in our personal activity, we are said to be free. Here freedom means autonomy as opposed to outside control. A teenager may seek more freedom from her parents in terms of curfew, bedtime, and choosing her friends. Industries look for freedom from governmental restrictions. The prison inmate longs for the day when he will rejoin society and taste freedom once again.

Freedom from external constraints means more than the absence of physical locks and chains. Sometimes other psychological pressures shackle us more completely than cold steel. How many people do you know who are confused, unsure, and unable to think for themselves? How many are unable to escape the barrage of noise, images, and subtle messages generated by society, and particularly by the mass media? Though we may think we are free, in practice, many of our actions, choices, and preferences are defined for us by fashion, public opinion, and political correctness. What others think becomes more important than what we think.

Though freedom from outside restrictions is implicit to freedom, it isn't everything. Freedom means more than the *absence* of external constraints. True, we say that a released convict is now a "free man," or that a mother of six whose last little cherub marches off to kindergarten is finally "free" to pursue other activities. Yet human freedom must mean more than the removal of outside boundaries. An imprisoned man will always be freer than an emu or kangaroo grazing freely in the Outback. A person retains his interior freedom even when he is in a cage or slaving away in a forced-labor camp, whereas an animal isn't free even when soaring through the air or roaming unrestrained about the Serengeti Plain. Freedom is an *internal* quality related to choice, and choice is made from within.

Let's look at another dimension of freedom.

2. Freedom To

We have said *freedom* means you are the *author* of your actions. When you go to the grocery store, speak with your neighbor, or visit a friend in the hospital, you are exercising your freedom in a series of conscious acts. Right now, you and I are freely writing our own history by the deliberate choices we make. This dimension of freedom is *possibility*, as opposed to *necessity*. Necessity is that which could not be otherwise. Human actions are never subject to necessity, because every truly *human* action is a free action. Persons are free. Things are necessary. Seen in this light, freedom is the degree to which a person's actions depend on the person himself.

"Freedom to" also means *indeterminism* as opposed to *determinism*. We have many different options and alternatives at any given moment. When we wake up in the morning, we are faced with a panoply of possibilities. True, some of these alternatives (like skipping school and going to the movies) will inevitably result in unpleasant consequences, but these consequences do not determine us—they merely become factors in our eventual free decision regarding how we will act.

In addition to our actions, we are also free to be the *type of people* we choose to be. An honest person is honest by choice, not by compulsion. We are not only the efficient cause of our actions, but also of our moral character. When I choose to tell lies, my choice does not stop with the action but affects me more deeply as a person. I become a liar. When I choose to help people in need, I become a helpful person. Our free choices determine the sort of person we are.

We have seen how some people deny free will, claiming that the human being is completely conditioned and incapable of free choice. Some assert a biological determinism—our decisions are already present in our genes. Others speak of cultural and social conditioning that determines our way of thinking and choosing. Some—like Richard Dawkins—assert that a mixture of both elements determines our choices. There is a modest dosage of truth in these statements. We are, indeed, affected by both biological and social factors. But in the final analysis, we are free beings and, despite outside influences, our decisions are our own. It would be easier to blame someone else for our failings, but we know that ultimately the responsibility is ours. In the same light, good actions deserve praise, because in the face of different possibilities, goodness was freely chosen.

Yet freedom is not just possibility or indeterminism either. It is the *ability* or power to carry out that desire. Let's look at this third sense of freedom.

3. FREEDOM FOR

True freedom is more than clearing away rubble from life's runway or removing the chains that hold us captive. We clear the runway in order to take off in a plane. We unchain a person so he can live out his life and fulfill his dreams. We seek to be free from constraints so we can be free *for* action. Freedom suggests activity, a desired goal. "I'm free Friday night" already implies that I'm free *for* something—it is understood that there is something we want to accomplish.

Freedom begs for commitment and realization. If I am free on Friday night but wind up staying home doing nothing, my freedom becomes nothing more than a wasted opportunity. *Finally I have a couple hours free so I can . . . work on that model airplane, finish that book, write to Aunt Sarah.* This aspect of freedom involves decision and activity as opposed to indecision and passivity. Freedom is freedom when it is actualized, when it is exercised.

Freedom is like money. It serves no function while sitting around collecting dust, but only when it is used. A rich man who never spends any money out of fear of becoming poor ends up living as a pauper—the very result he was trying to avoid. The same thing happens with our freedom. When we systematically avoid commitment out of fear of losing our freedom, we live as slaves. The person afraid to commit his life to a cause, an ideal, or another person lives as if he had no freedom at all, for fear that, should he commit himself, he would lose what freedom he has.

Nowadays there is a widespread fear of commitment. Many decide not to decide because they are afraid of choosing badly. This type of person winds up as a prisoner of his own insecurity and fear of the future. By desperately trying to leave all his options open, he effectively closes himself off from his fulfillment as a human being. He wants to have his cake and eat it, too, without sacrificing anything. The modern syllogism of non-commitment could be formulated something like this:

1. The most important thing is to be free.
2. If I exercise my freedom (commit myself) I will limit my options and become less free.
3. Therefore, I will not commit myself.

Yet commitment is part and parcel of freedom. Freedom is *ordered* to commitment and only makes sense when we use it. Without the ability to commit ourselves, we are not free in any meaningful sense. Has Silvia, mother of six, lost the freedom she once had? Has Brad, swinging bachelor at fifty-three, discovered the key to perpetual freedom? Obviously not. People do not find true fulfillment or freedom by disconnecting themselves from other people or by avoiding all bonds of love, friendship, and responsibility. It is precisely in this self-giving that a person is actualized and fulfills his human potential.

Freedom, moreover, means the ability not only to elect an alternative in the present moment but to guarantee our choices in the *future*. Commitment is, in fact, the pinnacle of human freedom, and a society or culture unable to commit is far less free than one where commitment is embraced. Man's ultimate calling is not to be as free as possible, but to use his freedom well.

In every choice, especially the basic choices in life, you accept a certain degree of uncertainty. How will you feel five years from now? How do you know that So-and-So won't change? How can you be absolutely sure it's your vocation? The beauty of fidelity is precisely this—that a mature individual commits himself without knowing all the consequences of his pledge. The faithful person proves his worth by hanging tough even in trying times.

THE LIMITS OF HUMAN FREEDOM

For all its greatness, human freedom is not absolute. It runs into numerous limitations that circumscribe and contain it, and many options are not open to us. This fundamental limitation of human freedom and choice can be expressed in four dimensions.

1. LOGICAL LIMITATIONS
There are certain things you and I cannot choose to do simply because they cannot be done. This is due not to human weakness but to the unbending nature of reality. You cannot make, design, or even conceive of a circular triangle; it is a logical impossibility. You cannot write a five-line Elizabethan sonnet or a twenty-line haiku. These limitations apply to any inherently contradictory situation.

2. PHYSICAL LIMITATIONS
We can do many things, but always within the potential of our nature. You and I cannot choose to fly out of the window because, despite our best intentions, we would come crashing to the ground. We cannot stop a locomotive, outrun a speeding bullet, or leap tall buildings in a single bound. Our bodies and our control over physical matter are subject to some very real *physical* limitations that condition the extent of our choices.

3. INTELLECTUAL LIMITATIONS
No human person is omniscient. For every piece of data we know there is a nearly infinite amount of information of which we are ignorant. In fact, the more we learn, the more we realize how little we truly know. Our understanding of things is never complete, and our brains are limited in what they are able to absorb and process. This, too, limits the range of our real choices.

4. Moral Limitations

The most important limitations to our freedom, however, are our moral limitations. In a proper sense, this refers to our incapability to always choose good, without a special supernatural grace. Often we recognize what we *ought* to do but find ourselves too weak or undecided to carry it out. We depend on God's help to become truly free. His grace is not an "extra"—it is essential to our ability to choose well. In this sense, the better we cooperate with God's grace, and the more virtuous we become, the freer we are, because we are more able to carry out the good we would like to do.

In a secondary sense, moral limitation means that man is *subject* to the moral law, and not above it. Man is free to choose *to do* good or evil, but he cannot *make* something good or evil simply by willing it. He is free to steal, but he cannot convert theft into an act of virtue by judicial fiat. It will remain an evil act whether he likes it or not. Right and wrong are not human inventions. Morality corresponds to objective good and evil, which man is free to embrace or reject.

These limitations on human freedom are not a curse; in fact, freedom *requires* some constraints. The presence of restrictions allows us to exercise our freedom. I am free to play baseball as long as there are limits to my freedom—that is, provided there are rules that I must follow. If I can put an unlimited number of players on the field (thirty-four, say, instead of nine), it spoils the game; I'm no longer *free* to play baseball. Arbitrarily bending the rules along the way would make the game ridiculous.

Freedom without constraints would be like a body with no bones or a game with no rules. Everything becomes pointless when there is no structure, no clear objective or direction. Freedom needs limitations as a river needs its banks, or a rifle its barrel. Otherwise freedom dissolves into meaningless indeterminism.

In this regard, although conscience can seem like a limiting agent on our freedom, it actually makes us *freer*. The better we know right from wrong, the more informed and free our choices are. I can be a good person only if I know what goodness entails. Just as a scientist is empowered by knowledge and is able to construct more accurate hypotheses, so, too, the human person is morally empowered by conscience. When conscience enjoins us to act in a certain way, it appeals to our freedom and higher aspirations to goodness. It does not physically compel us but morally obliges us. It points to the high road and encourages us to follow it. When we obey conscience, our freedom is not diminished but perfected. Rather than be tossed about by our passions and baser desires, we learn to do what we most deeply want to do.

GROWING IN FREEDOM

It sometimes seems that the freest people are those who know no rules but simply do what they feel like doing. They are spontaneous, happy-go-lucky and carefree. Yet strange as it may seem, freedom depends on self-mastery and discipline. Blindly following our impulses results not in freedom, but in a subtle sort of slavery. Remember Jesus' words that anyone who commits sin is a slave (John 8:34). We may believe we are free while in reality we are slaves to irrational forces: our appetites, our passions, our feelings, public opinion, fashions, or peer pressure. Saint Peter, when writing to the early church, pointed out the contradiction of those who proclaim liberty through abandonment to bodily desires: "They promise them freedom, but they themselves are slaves of corruption; because people are slaves to whatever masters them" (2 Pet. 2:19). Slavery of the body is just one kind of bondage; slavery of the will is worse.

Freedom is like being in shape. Everyone is "free" to run a marathon, but many are *unable* to do so because they are out of shape. There are no external restrictions, but there is an internal one. You are truly "free" to run a marathon only if you train vigorously and are able to run twenty-six miles. Freedom is the empowerment that comes through discipline. Self-control means willpower, and willpower is necessary for freedom. As we have said, freedom is more than wanting; it is the *power* to bring about what we want. If I want to quit smoking but cannot because of my lack of willpower, I am not free. My will is out of shape.

Human freedom is freedom of the whole person, not just freedom of a particular part. If your passions pull you in one direction while your reason pulls you in another, you experience interior anarchy. Without self-control and self-governance, there is no real freedom. Imagine the case of a race car driver. He is free to drive only if he has total *control* over his vehicle. He has to be able to stop, to accelerate, to turn at a moment's notice—all these maneuvers demand strict control over these different parts of the car and are necessary to be free to drive. If the steering wheel wanders freely and the brakes have a mind of their own, the poor driver is no longer free to drive. Similarly, if I am going skiing, I sharpen the edges of my skis. They are no longer "free" to slip back and forth, but now I am free to turn and to stop. Control of the parts under a common direction is necessary for freedom of the whole.

True freedom is the ability to direct our feelings, passions, tendencies, emotions, desires, and fears under the government of reason and will. When the dictates of conscience reign over the impulses of the flesh, we are truly free. Thus understood, freedom requires us to be masters of ourselves, determined to fight and overcome the different forms of selfishness and individualism that threaten our maturity as persons.

A virtuous person has attained a level of freedom that those in the grip of vice can only dream of. Think of the times that someone you know— maybe even you—set forth on a diet program only to break it at the first opportunity. Often it is our lack of virtue (in this case the virtue of temperance or moderation) that keeps us from carrying out our good proposals and resolutions. It keeps us from being free. Growing in freedom, therefore, means growing in *virtue*. It is no accident that the word *virtue* comes from the Latin word meaning "power" and "strength." The more virtuous we become, through our good choices, self-discipline, and cooperation with God's grace, the freer we become to achieve our goals.

FREEDOM AND LOVE

Christians believe that God made us free so we could love. Love is impossible without freedom, since love cannot be taken; it must be given. Of course, this was a very risky thing for God to do. If we are free to love, we are also free *not* to love. This has been the sad story of humanity from the beginning, and often our own stories as well. Still, apparently for God the risk was worth it. Though he knew how many people would misuse his gift, he gave it anyway because he wanted us to be like him. He wanted persons with whom to share his own love and who could know the joy of loving him in return.

A well-formed conscience reminds us over and over again that we were put on earth to love, and when we fail to love, we fail in life's central and most important enterprise. When we speak of conscience judging our actions according to the *law*, we must remember that the central precept of the law is love of God and love of our neighbor. Jesus, in fact, said that the commandment to love God and our brothers and sisters *sums up* the law and the prophets (Matt. 22:40).

Freedom, then, finds its fulfillment in love. It is ordered to love and makes love possible. In and of itself, freedom is directionless and indeterminate. Love gives it a course, an ideal, a sure path to follow. Our consciences push us onward to use our freedom well. They encourage us not only to be free, but to be responsible in love. Like a good compass or a road map, conscience makes sure that our freedom moves us in the right direction toward our final destination, which is love of God and neighbor.

Freedom, then, makes both conscience and love possible. Without free choice, we are no longer the authors of our actions, and conscience loses its meaning. Similarly, without freedom our "love" would be the mere expression of irrational forces working within us.

A further question remains to us. Is this selflessness really the best way to use our freedom? In the end, does goodness really make us *happy*, or is it a formula for frustration and angst? Is the Christian moral life—of which conscience is an essential part—a recipe for sadness or for joy? Let's take a closer look.

Questions for Study and Discussion

1. Why is free will necessary for the moral life? How are freedom and love related?
2. Distinguish between three different levels of freedom. How do they complement one another?
3. Why are people so afraid of commitment? Does commitment lessen our freedom or enhance it?
4. Give some examples of how human freedom is limited.
5. Is freedom something we are born with, or do we acquire it? In what ways can we become more free?
6. What did Jesus mean by saying that the truth will make us free (John 8:32)?

Questions for Personal Reflection

1. How do you conceive of freedom in your own life? Are you a free person? How could you become freer?
2. Do you find that your Christian faith is liberating? In what ways?
3. Do you accept the limitations of your freedom and lean on God's strength and grace?

10

GIRLS (AND BOYS) JUST WANT TO HAVE FUN

Good Conscience and Christian Joy

In his 1977 song "Only the Good Die Young," Billy Joel declared he'd rather hang out with sinners than with saints, because the sinners are "much more fun."[1] He sums up the popular notion that Christians are somehow missing out on life because they are bound by a moral code. Sin seems more attractive, more "fun" than righteousness. How many times have we felt a similar pang of wistfulness for sin! Since goodness often means saying no to our immediate desires, we find it hard to believe that this is the road to happiness. So many times we may think: *I would love to do such and such, if only my conscience would allow me!* William Faulkner remarked that "A man's moral conscience is the curse he had to accept from the gods in order to gain from them the right to dream."

Indeed, conscience often seems more a curse than a blessing. At least if we were ignorant of right and wrong, we may think, we wouldn't be *responsible*, and we could do whatever we please. Sometimes we reluctantly drag our consciences along like a heavy burden—like taking our little sister along on a date. We obey conscience out of obligation, perhaps out of fear of eternal retribution, all the while wishing we didn't have to. We may even envy those who seem to have no qualms of conscience and do things we wouldn't dare.

In truth, we don't want to be *evil*, but we don't want to be "too good," either. We are convinced that a healthy human life necessarily includes some sin, which we term as "mischief" or "sowing our wild oats." We may secretly agree with Freud that conscience must be tempered, reined in, and listened to only *some of the time*. A healthy balance of goodness and naughtiness makes for a rich human existence, we think. In December of 2005, Pope Benedict XVI offered these illuminating thoughts:

> We have a lurking suspicion that a person who does not sin must really be basically boring and that something is missing from his life: the dramatic dimension of being autonomous; that the freedom to say no, to descend into the shadows of sin and to want to do things on one's own is part of being truly human; that only then can we make the most of all the vastness and depth of our being men and women, of being truly ourselves; that we should put this freedom to the test, even in opposition to God, in order to become, in reality, fully ourselves. In a word, we think that evil is basically good, we think that we need it, at least a little, in order to experience the fullness of being.[2]

The ties to conscience here are clear. If morality is good, conscience is a gift; if morality is bad, conscience is a curse. This is a question of capital importance. We have said that conscience is a guide, meant to take us *somewhere*. But if we don't like where it takes us, then better to have no guide at all. If a moral life isn't also a happy, fulfilling life, then we might as well abandon it altogether. Conscience is helpful only if it leads to a truly good and happy existence. A person who would rather wander off doesn't need a guide at all.

WHY DOES GOD GIVE US GUIDELINES?

This brings us to an even more fundamental question: What is Christian morality, anyway? Why does God ask certain things of his sons and daughters? Why doesn't he leave us alone to do what we feel like doing? The answer is equally direct: *because he loves us*. As much as popular culture insists to the contrary, sin doesn't make us happy and God isn't a spoilsport. Immorality leaves deep human sorrow in its wake and leaves people's lives in absolute shambles. God forbids sinful practices not because they violate some cosmic code, but because they aren't good for us, the way a good mother or father forbids overindulgence in junk food or playing with firearms. Self-indulgence in sin doesn't help us to be *happy*.

God is a good Father, the best of fathers, and wants only the very best for us. But good fathers make their children study and clean their rooms and sometimes give them foul-tasting medicine when they are sick. All of this doesn't manifest *less* love, but *more*. A father who lets his children vegetate in front of the television for hours on end because it is an easy way to keep them occupied, or who allows them to eat junk food all day to keep them from complaining, isn't a very good father. The moral code God lays out for us is a road map to a happy life.

Our secret longing for naughtiness and the suspicion that we are some-how missing out reminds me of a scene at junior-high school parties. The "good kids" know that the "bad kids" are doing something mysterious and wonderful in the back room of the party—and they aren't invited. They ache with envy. Yet a closer look at what was actually going on in the back room—smoking, a surreptitious experiment with drugs, giggling over a *Playboy* magazine—reveals that it was hardly worth all the fuss. Sin is, in two words, cheap and tawdry. It never delivers. It promises to enrich us but ends up impoverishing us. We do not become more, but less. That is why Jesus calls Satan "the father of lies" (John 8:44)—because he sells a faulty product (sin) that doesn't do what it claims to do, much like snake oil salesmen of the past.

SIN'S LURE

Jesus is not silent about the attractiveness of sin. In his parable of the prod-igal son (Luke 15:11–31), there are actually *two* sons: the younger one who leaves home with his share of the inheritance and the elder brother who sticks around faithfully working for his father. When the younger son finally returns to the father's house, the elder son is incensed that his father welcomes him back and even throws a party for him, and he refuses to join the celebration.

His reaction to his younger brother's return reveals much about what was going on in his heart and about how we look at sin, even when we choose not to commit it. The elder brother evidently felt *envy* when his brother left home for a dissolute life—something that the elder brother would probably have liked to do, if it hadn't meant giving up the security of his father's estate. He suspects that his brother was off having a marvelous time while he was at home "working like a slave" (his words!) for his father (Luke 15:29). He desires to see his brother punished in compensation, not realizing that the sin itself and the separation from the father was a terrible experience worthy of pity rather than anger or envy. The father feels compassion, the brother only envy and a desire for vengeance, as if *he* were the one offended by his brother's conduct.

Many times self-righteousness conceals a hidden envy for the sinful life that others allow themselves and an implicit acceptance of the lie that a sinful life is somehow better and happier. The self-righteous can feel bitter that they cannot sin the way others do. Thus, when they see others fall, they demand that severe justice be administered. They delight in the thought that one day sinners "will get what is coming to them." The proud cannot accept the goodness and indulgence of God. How different this attitude is from God's, who longs for the sinner's salvation!

Christians have nothing to envy of those who allow themselves every indulgence. If we look at the world around us, we can see that evil is always poisonous. It does not uplift human beings but degrades and humiliates them. It does not make them greater, purer, or nobler but harms and belittles them. It separates people from each other and from God as well. The truly rich and wonderful activities of human existence happen not in the shadows but in the *light*.

For this reason, ignorance of moral truth is no blessing. Ignorance may excuse us from guilt, but it won't save us from the consequences of immoral action, any more than not seeing an oncoming vehicle saves us from the effects of an accident. Dr. Janet Smith offers an illuminating expression of this:

> Doing wrong innocently is much like drinking poison in one's orange juice. Moral innocence does not save one from bad consequences. The 14-year-old girl who gets an abortion in good conscience is going to suffer because of that abortion. She's not going to walk away scot-free. Even though subjectively she's not culpable, she's going to have nightmares, or all sorts of psychological problems, or difficulty relating with men, or difficulty with her self-esteem.[3]

Our suspicion that morality may be a curse affects the way we evangelize others as well. Nobody passes along a curse, unless it is out of a petty desire to make others "suffer the way we do." Even well-meaning Christians occasionally come to the conclusion that the kindest thing to do for others is keep them in the dark about moral truth, for fear that they won't be able to live it and, in the end, it will only provoke frustration with no change in behavior.

This attitude, for all the good intentions behind it, carries with it two worrisome implications. First, it reflects a devastatingly pessimistic view of the human person and his capacity for goodness, with God's grace. Second, it buys into the myth that morality has little to do with happiness and human flourishing and is rather an expression of God's arbitrary will. Doing right or wrong doesn't matter—we may think—unless we *know* we're doing right or wrong. Only when we know it does it become a problem. Meanwhile, have fun.

HAVING FUN

Cyndi Lauper's hit single, "Girls Just Want to Have Fun" (1983), became something of an iconic feminist hymn. Yet as rebellious and feisty as the tune seems, the message contained in the lyrics offers a false portrait of what women—and men, for that matter—really do want. To her mother's entreaties to "live your life right" and dad's concerns of "what you gonna do with your life," Cyndi answers that all girls want is "some fun."[4]

Sorry, Cyndi, but it isn't true. Nobody *just* wants to have fun. Adolescents, maybe—but even young people possess ideals and usually recognize that life means more than a string of good times. To have meaning, life needs a purpose. It needs connection and goals. A "fun" life is not necessarily a happy life. Some of the happiest people I know think relatively little about "having fun" per se, and a lot about honor, faithfulness, duty, and friendship. They are dedicated to their families, to their work, to God, and to causes greater than themselves. Fun, by definition, is a self-referential category. That is, fun revolves around self and can only be determined by self.

In reality, girls—and boys—just want to be *happy*. This includes, surely, a good dose of fun. All work and no play makes Jill a dull girl. But fun doesn't equal happiness. Fun is one ingredient in a much richer recipe.

Pure fun is like a diet of whipped cream and maple sugar. In small amounts, it is wonderful, but after a while it becomes cloying and fails to satisfy a deeper hunger. In human life, this deeper hunger translates into meaning and transcendence, something that lasts.

Fun and entertainment are an escape, often a very good and worth-while escape. They break up the routine of work and responsibilities. But their value is found there, in the "break from" other meaningful activities. Fun is not the stuff of meaning. Wanting to have fun all the time is a Peter Pan–esque dream of not wanting to grow up. But even in Neverland, Peter Pan wasn't happy. Following our lowest urges with no check by reason does not yield a happy life.

HAPPINESS REQUIRES REALITY

Happiness doesn't come in escaping from reality, but in embracing it. Truth and joy go together. We need to know that what we are thinking, feeling, and experiencing is *real*. We don't just want to *feel* all right; we want everything to truly *be* all right. Try this thought experiment. What if you were offered a drug that allowed you to always *feel* good but left you completely out of touch with reality? Would you really want it? You might *feel* like a success when in reality you were a failure. Would it be worth it? Is ignorance *really* bliss?

Few of us would agree. To be truly happy, we must find meaning *in reality*. Above all, we must find the love of God. After experiencing all the horror of Nazi concentration camps in World War II, the Austrian psychologist Viktor Frankl wrote a wonderful book titled *Man's Search for Meaning*. Frankl insists over and over that what human beings most need is a sense of meaning behind what they do, what they suffer, and what they labor at. When our efforts *mean* something and fit into a bigger picture, we are able to achieve great things.

MAKING HAPPINESS LAST

Sometimes we are misled into thinking that there is a whole gamut of material elements without which we can never be happy. *I can never be happy without a lot of money, power, assorted pleasures, sex, personal achievement, friends, "experiences. . . ."* One organization once went so far as to formulate a twelve-point list of requirements for being happy that included a radio, a bicycle, and a set of kitchen utensils per family.

Linking happiness to material possessions and good fortune is disconcerting. These conditions are external to us and, to a certain extent, beyond our control. More importantly, none of them is permanent or secure. If I can't be secure in my possession of these conditions for happiness, then I can never be truly happy. I will always live in the anguish of knowing that my happiness is as precarious as a house of cards, liable to collapse at a moment's notice. Moreover, human experience does not support this theory. There are materially poor people who are extremely happy, just as there are wretched millionaires.

In many ways, modern man is like a spoiled child—inundated with things, but deeply unsatisfied. Civilization offers him a cornucopia of consumer goods that his recent ancestors never dreamed of. Yet he lives more anguished and miserable than people in past decades. He knows how to make an airplane, how to go to the moon; he knows how an automobile and a computer work. But he feels immensely unhappy because he doesn't know how he himself "works," what the human person is *for*, what the meaning of his existence is. Technological progress provides him with ever more answers to his *whats, hows,* and *whens,* but his *whys* go unanswered.

If it is to last, happiness must not depend on the winds of fortune. It cannot depend merely on *what happens to us.* As the philosopher Boethius described so eloquently in *The Consolation of Philosophy*, happiness cannot depend on health, riches, or prestige, or indeed anything subject to the volatility of chance and circumstance. It must rise above good fortune or any external variable.

HAPPINESS AND PAIN

Neither is happiness merely the absence of pain. You remember the story of the man hitting himself on the head with a hammer. When asked, "Why are you hitting yourself on the head with a hammer?" he answers, "Because it feels *so good* when I stop." For many, happiness seems to be an escape from the monotonous *un*happiness of a senseless, hollow life. It is a momentary pause in the midst of sadness. Yet true happiness—joy—is not a respite from a painful life, but *life itself*, animated by meaning, purpose, and love. Joy is a living thing, not a numbness or oblivion. Joy is dynamic, colorful, rich, and even sometimes painful. Where sadness is empty, joy is full—fullness itself.

Christian happiness does not consist in silencing our passions and beating them into submission so we no longer desire anything. The Buddhist "nirvana" of the gutted, unfeeling person has little in common with the Christian ideal of passionate love for God and neighbor. Jesus was anything but a wet blanket or an escapist. Rather, he ardently desires "that my joy may be in you and that your joy may be complete" (John 15:11 NIV). Let's look a little more closely at the Christian proposal.

CHRISTIAN JOY

The announcement of the Christian message is called the gospel—"good news." Contrary to popular legend, it is not the "bad news" ("The boss has arrived. Everybody get back to work!") but rather the good news of salvation and liberation ("Our Savior is here. Captivity is ended. Rejoice and be glad!"). In speaking about the coming Messiah, Isaiah has this to say:

> The people who walked in darkness
>   have seen a great light;
> those who have lived in a land of deep darkness—
>   on them light has shined.
> You have multiplied the nation,
>   you have increased its joy;
> they rejoice before you
>   as with joy at the harvest,
>   as people exult when dividing plunder.
> . . . For a child has been born for us,
>   a son given to us;
> authority rests upon his shoulders;
>   and he is named
> Wonderful Counselor, Mighty God,
> Everlasting Father, Prince of Peace. (Isaiah 9:2–3, 6)

This message of joy is echoed over and over again in the New Testament. Remember the events surrounding the birth of Christ. The angel Gabriel greets the Virgin Mary with the words: *"Rejoice*, you who enjoy God's favour! The Lord is with you" (Luke 1:28 NJB). When pregnant Mary visits Elizabeth, the baby John the Baptist *leaps in her womb for joy* (Luke 1:44). And at the birth of Christ the angels proclaim *"good news of great joy* for all the people" (Luke 2:10). Everything about the Incarnation speaks of joy and redemption.

This Christian joy is not a liberation from morality, but from sin. In fact, Jesus explicitly ties the moral life to joy. It is not in wandering away from God that you experience the happiness you long for, but in following him. Look how Jesus links obedience to joy: "As the Father loves me, so I also love you. Remain in my love. If you keep my commandments, you will remain in my love, just as I have kept my Father's commandments and remain in his love. I have told you this *so that my joy may be in you and your joy may be complete"* (John 15:9–11).

In other words, Jesus doesn't tell us these things in order to make life difficult or to put us to the test, but so that his joy may be in us! He enjoins us to love one another so that we may experience the intense and lasting joy of remaining in his love.

Saint Paul goes further still. He doesn't just suggest that we put on a happy face; he "commands" Christians to be joyful! "Rejoice in the Lord always. I will say it again: rejoice!" (Phil. 4:4 NIV). His last instructions to the Thessalonians repeat the same message: *"Rejoice always*, pray without ceasing, give thanks in all circumstances; for this is the will of God in Christ Jesus for you" (1 Thess. 5:14–18).

THE IMPORTANCE OF SELF-DENIAL

"Ha!"—you are probably saying at this point—"but Jesus preached the *cross*! He said we have to *deny ourselves*. What does that have to do with joy?" Yes, Jesus also preached the cross. But for Jesus, joy and the cross are not mutually exclusive. In fact, one leads to the other. *Per crucem ad lucem* ("Through the cross to the light"), as medieval Christians used to say. Christians are not masochists, and no sane person seeks abnegation for its own sake. Self-denial is a means to an end and not an end in itself. Without some measure of self-denial, we can never be happy. There are three reasons this is so.

First, self-denial is necessary for *freedom*, and freedom is necessary for happiness. Over and over again, Saint Paul had recourse to examples from the military and competitive sports when referring to the spiritual life. Following Christ is a true battle, and battles require rigorous training, discipline, courage, and mettle. The athletic expression "No pain, no gain" holds true for every aspect of our lives: personal, professional, and relational. As we saw in the last chapter, freedom comes through self-mastery. And ultimately there is no one sadder than the person who is not in control of himself.

Man is divided. Saint Paul described this as the "flesh" warring against the "spirit." This interior conflict—fruit of original sin—can be satisfactorily resolved only through self-denial. If the spirit doesn't subjugate the flesh, the flesh will end up dominating the spirit. All of us experience conflicting tendencies pulling us in different directions. If we cannot say no to ourselves—to our baser passions—we will always follow the path of least resistance. We are not truly free unless we are able to do as we *choose* to do, not as we *feel* like doing! And if we are not truly free, we cannot be truly happy.

Second, self-denial is important because it allows us to choose *whom we will serve*. We cannot be true Christians unless we dethrone the little tyrant that reigns in each of us. Jesus' words allow for no compromise: "No one can serve two masters" (Matt. 6:24). Curiously, the statement is not a command but a declaration. Jesus doesn't say: "Thou shalt not serve two masters" nor "I don't want you to serve two masters" but simply "No one *can* serve two masters." It doesn't *work*. His words articulate an inescapable fact: it is impossible to serve two masters. A heart divided between love of self and love of God represents an unstable and precarious situation that cannot endure.

Perhaps you have seen children playing "King of the mountain" on a mound of earth or a snowbank. One alone stands on the top of the mound and the others rush to depose him and take his place. The human heart is a mound of that sort and there—as in real life—biumvirates and triumvirates are doomed to fail. One alone will remain, jealously guarding his position, and will brook no opposition, no power sharing. Saint Augustine famously expressed this using the metaphor of "two cities"—one devoted to the love of self, up to disdain for God, and the other devoted to the love of God, up to disdain for self.

The odd thing is that the person who rapaciously seeks himself really doesn't find himself. In other words, he fails at the very endeavor to which he is most dedicated! Happiness is not found in a narcissistic quest for self, but in losing oneself, in selflessness. The more we grasp at fun, the more true happiness eludes us. Jesus said that only the one who loses his life will truly find himself. Again, Jesus' words do not so much represent a command as an explanation of how human life *is*. He was describing a fundamental truth of the human condition. It is the one who loses himself in service of God and others—forgetful of self—who truly finds himself. It is the seed that falls to the earth and dies that bears much fruit.

Third, self-denial is a necessary expression of *love*. Advertisers would have us believe that the solution to unhappiness is the elimination of pain. "Take a pill." "Take a vacation." "Take a drink." If we are entrenched in this mentality it will be hard to understand the logic of love. Love doesn't circumvent suffering. It doesn't see sacrifice as the greatest evil, always to be avoided. The mystery of love is a mystery of sacrifice, of dying to oneself, of pouring oneself out for the good of another. This is why our couch therapy/feel-good culture is incapable of happiness: because we are incapable of love. And we are incapable of love because we are incapable of forgetting ourselves.

How do you best show others that you love them? How can you *prove* your love? Only by doing something hard, something costly—that you wouldn't possibly do if it weren't for love. A young man trying to prove his love for a young woman dedicates time, money, ingenuity—as much as he can of himself. It's the only way he has to *show* her that he loves her.

A true lover wants to prove his love by doing something difficult. Maybe you saw the 2001 film *A Knight's Tale*. At a certain point in the movie, the talented young knight named William Thatcher enters a jousting competition. He wins over and over again and tells his Lady Jocelyn that he is doing it *for her*. She suspects that he is winning because he likes to win and only *claims* he is doing it for her. To test his love, she asks him—of all things—to start *losing*. In other words, she asks him to deny himself, to do something difficult. In this way she will know that he loves her. It is only when we do something for the other that we wouldn't do for ourselves that we realize that we truly love.

Because of our acute self-love, we find it hard to love others. We can even become enslaved to our self-love, which can become like a ball and chain. In other words, selfishness is always getting in the way. Only by denying ourselves can we truly love another. We seek to remove the obstacles that keep us from loving—especially our selfishness.

The Paths to True Happiness

If this is the nature of happiness, how is it to be found? What are the stepping-stones to a happy life? We cannot simply choose to *be* happy. We can, however, choose *other things* that will lead us to happiness. Then one fine day we realize that we are happy as a result. What are these other things, these conditions for happiness? What do they have to do with conscience?

Humility

As surprising as it may be, the first path to happiness is humility. For the humble, everything is an unexpected, undeserved gift of God. When we think we deserve everything, that life owes us the moon, we can never be happy. We will always be unsatisfied with the hand we are dealt. This helps explain another paradox. Often the people who seem to have the *least* are happier than those who seem to have *everything*. Look around you. Think back over your own life and the people you have known. Many times the poor, the handicapped, and the underprivileged are more joyful than those who have everything.

Humility and gratitude go hand in hand. The person who thinks he has merited nothing will be thankful for every little thing that comes his way. I have seen wealthy children lying on a heap of toys in their bedrooms, crying their hearts out because they want *more*. I have seen poor children laughing over the simplest pleasures. The more aware we are of God's gifts and his immense love for us, the happier we will be.

Generosity

The second condition for happiness is generosity. The frenetic quest for "fun" actually leads us further and further from the deeper happiness we yearn for. The self-centeredness this quest implies is the sworn enemy of true happiness. The person full of himself can never be truly happy, because happiness comes through self-giving, and self-giving is possible only when we let go of self-taking.

Here, too, Jesus' teaching sheds much light on this mystery. He tells us that "there is more happiness in giving than in receiving" (Acts 20:35 NJB). Remember, too, the dual gospel parables of the treasure in the field and the pearl of great price? In both of these parables, a man discovers something wonderful—a treasure buried in a field, or a priceless pearl. In both cases, the man must *sell* all he owns to buy the field or the pearl. In other words, it is worth so much to him that he sells everything else he has in order to possess it. It is only by giving up our attachments to other things that we can possess true happiness. Yet in both these parables, Jesus describes the sacrifice as a joyful one. The man goes off rejoicing and sells all that he owns.

We spoke earlier about conscience resembling either a coach or a referee. As simple as this distinction may seem, it exerts a great influence on our personal happiness. For those that see conscience as a referee, as a restraint, moral choice will always tend toward negotiating the most "liberty" possible from a demanding conscience. The questions that will most often arise will take the form of: *Is this really forbidden? How far can I go? Is this a serious sin?* When we see conscience as a coach, we allow ourselves to be pushed out of our comfort zone. The questions then become: *Is this the best I can do? How can I love better? Where can I give more?* And these are questions that lead to a happy life.

TRUST

A third stepping-stone to happiness is trust in God. Letting go of other securities means trusting God will deliver. It means confidence in his faithfulness. But trust is perhaps the hardest Christian virtue to practice nowadays. It seems that everyone has been let down by someone, and the more we feel betrayed, the less we are willing to trust the next time.

Who knows us better than anyone? Who loves us more than anyone and wants only to see us happy? The answer to both of these questions is, of course, God, our Creator and Redeemer. But do we believe it? Do we trust him enough to do things his way, or would we rather shore up our position with a back-up plan in case God falls through? He charts out the path and asks us to trust him unconditionally.

LOVE

A fourth condition for happiness is love. Love is the gift of self. The odd thing about this sort of giving is that we don't lose what we give. When we give money, we have less money. When we offer our time, we have less time. When we dispense food or clothing, we have less of these. But when we give of ourselves, we wind up with more (not less) self.

Among O. Henry's numerous excellent short stories, one of the best is "The Gift of the Magi." It is a tale of a young married couple—James Dillingham Young and his wife, Della—who barely scrape by on the meager income James brings home. They reside in a tiny flat in the city and struggle to make ends meet, but they are happy. As winter is coming, each saves up to buy the other the most splendid Christmas present possible. James's one prized possession is a gold pocket watch handed down to him by his father. Della decides the best gift she can offer him is a chain for his watch. Since the price of the platinum chain she likes is well beyond her means, she decides to sell her long, dark, beautiful hair.

Meanwhile, James has his own plans. After scouting all over town, he finally comes upon the perfect gift for his darling wife: a set of tortoise-shell combs for her hair. Since they come to a price he can't nearly afford, he decides—yes, you guessed it—to sell his pocket watch to pay for the combs.

This is what love is: Ridiculous. Illogical. Foolish. But what is life without love? What sort of meaning will you try to artificially tack onto life if you try to live without love? You and I are made to love, and we find our fulfillment and happiness in this most sublime human activity.

Solitary confinement is considered the severest of punishments. This makes sense, when we think about it. No man is an island. The human person is made in God's image and likeness, and God is love. God is a loving communion of persons. Without love we become freaks of nature, strangers and puzzles to ourselves. Yet some people subject themselves to a sort of self-imposed solitary confinement. They armor-plate their hearts to make them invulnerable to pain. Though it is understandable (it usually follows after having been hurt), this approach cannot but mutilate our humanity. Whether others put up the walls to keep us inside or we erect them to keep others out is of little consequence. Our smallness and powerlessness are never so evident as when we are all alone. Happiness is found in giving, in loving, in trusting. And that is precisely where a good conscience leads us.

God

At the risk of stating the obvious, I propose that a final condition for true happiness is God himself. Perhaps it is not so obvious. There is much debate today about the possibility of a totally "secular" ethics, apart from any reference to a Supreme Being. Is happiness possible apart from God? Many people desperately assert that it is. And I say "desperately" because they are scared to death that in order to be truly happy they will have to recognize God.

Since we are spiritual beings, we go beyond what is finite and limited to seek the Absolute. The human spirit looks to the Infinite, never satisfied with any quantity of finite goods. After gorging ourselves on all the pleasures, adventures, and possessions the world has to offer, our unsated spirits look further and inquire: *Is there nothing more?*

We seek and do not find because we seek right, left, around, and under us but fail to seek above us. The only thing capable of filling man is God, because only God is infinite. The infinite cavity within us can only be filled by an infinite being. Blaise Pascal, in his *Pensées*, offers a similar diagnosis of man's search for happiness: "The infinite abyss can only be filled by an infinite and immutable object, that is to say, only by God Himself."

Another thinker closer to our own day, C. S. Lewis, in his masterpiece, *Mere Christianity*, explains why happiness without God is nothing but a pipe dream:

> What Satan put into the heads of our remote ancestors was the idea that they could . . . invent some sort of happiness for themselves outside God, apart from God. And out of that hopeless attempt has come nearly all that we call human history—money, poverty, ambition, war, prostitution, classes, empires, slavery—the long, terrible story of man trying to find something other than God which will make him happy.
>
> The reason why it can never succeed is this. God made us: invented

us as a man invents an engine. A car is made to run on petrol, and it would not run properly on anything else. Now God designed the human machine to run on Himself. He Himself is the fuel our spirits were designed to burn, or the food our spirits were designed to feed on. There is no other. That is why it is just no good asking God to make us happy in our own way without bothering about religion. God cannot give us a happiness and peace apart from Himself, because it is not there. There is no such thing.

The key to finding things is to look where they are. Happiness is in God, so we shouldn't expect to find it elsewhere. The good things of this earth are but signposts that point to the Supreme Good. The trick is not to confuse the signposts with the point of arrival. As long as we realize we are on a journey, we will have a traveler's joy. A traveler—a pilgrim—has the happiness of hope, the certainty of possessing in the future what he does not yet fully possess in the present. One day not too far off, when the journey is done, we will know the happiness of arrival.

If happiness consists in having fun, in pleasure, possessions, and power, then conscience will always be a spoilsport. If, on the other hand, the paths to happiness are found elsewhere—in humility, generosity, trust, love, and God—then we have a good friend in conscience. Conscience will always lead us by these sure paths.

As we saw earlier, however, conscience is not infallible. It sometimes makes mistakes. How does this happen? How does good conscience go bad? And if we need a good conscience in order to become good and happy people, how can we keep our consciences in shape and avoid having them lead us astray? This will be the topic of our next chapter.

Questions for Study and Discussion

1. Do sinners have more fun than saints? If not, why do so many people think they do?
2. In what way does morality seem to be a curse? What is wrong with this idea? What is God trying to achieve by giving us a moral law?
3. What does Jesus say about the attractiveness of sin? What means does he offer us to see things more clearly?
4. Is "fun" the greatest human aspiration? How can "fun" be distinguished from a deeper sense of Christian joy?

5. Are joy and sacrifice incompatible? If Jesus wants us to be happy, why does he ask us to take up our cross and follow him?
6. What are some of the conditions for true happiness to flourish? How can we become more joyful people and make others happier as well?

Questions for Personal Reflection

1. Deep down, do you consider your Christian faith to be a gift? Are you ever tempted to see it as a curse? Do you long to pass it on to other people?
2. Looking back over your life, when were you the happiest? What things make you deeply joyful? What things make you sad?
3. Have you accepted Jesus' invitation to take up your cross in your own life? Do you trust him to make you happy?

11

ALTERED STATES

The Wearing Down of Moral Sense

The corruption of conscience is a terrible thing. Perhaps you remember a fairy tale written by Hans Christian Andersen in 1845 called "The Snow Queen." A very wicked hobgoblin devises a looking glass "which had the power of making everything good or beautiful that was reflected in it almost shrink to nothing, while everything that was worthless and bad looked increased in size." In this distorting mirror "the most lovely landscapes appeared like boiled spinach, and the people became hideous, and looked as if they stood on their heads and had no bodies."

The looking glass was shattered into a million pieces, and the shards flew about and lodged in people's eyes, without their being aware of it. As a result, their way of seeing reality became that of the warped mirror. They no longer saw reality as it really was.

A bad conscience produces a result like the hobgoblin's looking glass. It perverts reality and makes us see things differently than they really are. And since everything one sees is crooked, there is no way out of the mess unless someone from outside sets us straight.

In this way, a bad conscience illustrates the terrible words of the prophet Isaiah:

> Ah, you who call evil good
> and good evil,

who put darkness for light
and light for darkness,
who put bitter for sweet
and sweet for bitter! (Isaiah 5:20)

Sin is a horrible moral evil, but perhaps it is not the worst. The most dangerous crisis that can afflict the human person is the inability to correctly discern between good and evil. Even the worst of sinners has hope as long as conscience is working, since it can lead him to conversion. Forgiveness is always available for those who want it. But what happens when the light of conscience goes out? Who can save us when we no longer perceive the difference between right and wrong?

THE DEADENING OF CONSCIENCE

Conscience will only impose itself for so long. Wars of attrition against conscience sooner or later take their toll and, like a beaten dog, conscience retires whimpering to a corner of our souls. A quotation attributed to the English novelist Samuel Butler (1835–1902) sums this up nicely: "Conscience is thoroughly well-bred and soon leaves off talking to those who do not wish to hear it." In other words, after a while not only do we become deaf to the voice of conscience, but for all intents and purposes it ceases to speak. Unfortunately this is often the case.

In the fourth chapter of *The Adventures of Pinocchio*, Carlo Collodi graphically illustrates the deadening of conscience. Pinocchio orders the Talking Cricket to leave, but in response the Cricket replies: "I refuse to leave this spot until I have told you a great truth."

"Tell it, then, and hurry," says Pinocchio.

"Woe to boys who refuse to obey their parents and run away from home!" the Cricket declares. "They will never be happy in this world, and when they are older they will be very sorry for it."

He encourages Pinocchio to go to school or at least to learn a trade so he can earn an honest living. To this advice Pinocchio responds, "Of all the trades in the world, there is only one that really suits me. That of eating, drinking, sleeping, playing, and wandering around from morning till night."

"Let me tell you, for your own good, Pinocchio," replies the Talking

Cricket, "that those who follow that trade always end up in the hospital or in prison."

Fed up with the Cricket's nagging, Pinocchio picks up a hammer and hurls it across the room, killing the Cricket on the spot.

Such is sometimes the case of the human conscience. At times our moral judgment may be obscured in a particular area, but it may also be deadened in general. Sometimes the moral sense itself—the importance we attach to right and wrong as criteria for our decisions—loses practical force in our lives. We simply *don't care* whether something is right or wrong; we may not even habitually consider the moral character of our conduct. Our concerns become more pragmatic. Our intentions focus on success, on the practical outcome of our actions and whether they afford us pleasure or pain, rather than their relationship with moral truth.

It has been said that the greatest sin of our times is the loss of the sense of sin. Sin seems to have diminished in importance for people of our generation, and we consider it impolite even to speak of it. It happens sometimes in history that the moral conscience of many people becomes seriously clouded, and that seems to be the case today. If we look around at our world, do we not sometimes perceive that modern men and women are threatened by an eclipse of conscience? Many basic moral truths that seemed self-evident to our forebears now are glibly dismissed as antiquated. Sin itself seems thoroughly passé.

Sure, maybe we placed too much stress on sin in the past. Maybe we accentuated the negative and undervalued the positive message of Christianity. Yet some are inclined to replace exaggerated attitudes of the past with new exaggerations. From seeing sin everywhere, they stop recognizing it anywhere. From too much emphasis on the fear of eternal punishment, they pass to preaching a love of God that excludes any punishment whatsoever. From severity in trying to correct erroneous consciences, they pass to a kind of naïve veneration for conscience that excludes the duty of seeking moral truth. Furthermore, many preachers and moral teachers add to the problem by minimizing the importance of sin or ignoring it altogether.

A *sense of sin* does not mean a neurotic fixation on sin, a scrupulous fear of fun, or a cynical distrust of human goodness. It is simply an awareness that sin exists, and that a fundamental part of the Christian life, as Saint Paul writes, means considering ourselves "dead to sin" and not to "allow sin to reign over [our] mortal bodies" (Rom 6:11–12 NJB). A *sense of sin* also means the ability to unmask sin in the thousand guises under which it conceals itself. A healthy sense of sin never loses sight of our condition as fallen creatures who, for all our best intentions, are prone to fall. Granted, a sense of sin does not exhaust conscience, since conscience importantly urges us to good and not merely to avoid evil, but a sense of sin most certainly sets at least a minimum boundary for human endeavor. It goes without saying that whoever disregards moral *evil* in his life will care even less for the pursuit of moral *goodness*.

One of the major forces behind a loss of the sense of sin is called *secularism*. Secularism is an overfocusing on the things of this world to the exclusion of eternity. It leads us to ignore transcendent, eternal truths and to give all our attention to the here and now. Like a man walking around staring at his feet, a secularist is unable to lift his gaze to see beyond the present moment to what lies ahead (and above). Thus a sense of sin is linked to the sense of God. The more aware we are of God's presence, the more attentive we will be to the way we treat him. The less we think of God, the less sin registers with us.

Many, while not denying God outright, live a practical atheism and organize their lives as if God didn't exist. The secularist advocates a humanism devoid of God, centered upon action and production, the pursuit of pleasure and the avoidance of pain, and blithely unconcerned with the danger of "losing one's soul." For the secularist, sin has no meaning since God has no meaning. If wrongdoing slows down our enjoyment of the present world, the solution is therapy, not conversion and forgiveness.

Except for a special grace from God, the corrupt conscience has lost the ability to recognize its own error. In this light, silencing our consciences is no victory. Though we may sometimes wish we could muzzle our consciences so that they would leave us in peace, we do not *really* want this. It is the greatest of tragedies. Though it may grant a temporary respite from the gnawing feeling inside, it also closes us off to the truth.

Fortunately, just as it is impossible to eradicate completely the sense of God, so, too, the conscience is never silenced completely. The spark of divine truth in us can never be totally extinguished. Let's go back to Pinocchio for a moment. After the dramatic and awful event of Pinocchio heaving the hammer against the Talking Cricket, that is not the last we see of him. Later Collodi has him reappear as the ghost of his former self, still importuning Pinocchio with his wise advice. How closely this mirrors the human drama of a deadened conscience! Even when we think we have extinguished it forever, it never truly dies but, by the grace of God, makes itself heard when we least expect it.

SIGNS OF THE SLIPPERY SLOPE

But life and death are not the only two options for conscience. Like any instrument, conscience can be sharpened or dulled. It can become more sensitive or coarser. Like a finely honed knife, a good conscience distinguishes our intentions, motivations, and inmost thoughts. It discerns right from wrong and impels us to do good. A lax conscience, on the other hand, detects only the gravest of faults and often errs in its judgments.

Rarely is conscience corrupted totally, and even more rarely does this happen overnight. The radical shifts between good and bad—*à la* Dr. Jekyll and Mr. Hyde—are the stuff of fiction. Conscience usually grows keener or blunter in a progressive way, by incremental and almost imperceptible changes. Moral collapse happens little by little, first by ceding in seemingly unimportant, innocuous matters, later with something slightly more serious ("But no one got hurt!"). Then one day we wake up and find ourselves unrecognizable and morally disfigured.

We may begin by reclassifying certain sins as "not sins for me, because my conscience is clear" (even though the Church, Christian tradition, or wise and holy people hold them to be sinful). This subjective reevaluation with no accountability except to one's own opinions next leads us to downplay the overall seriousness of sin itself. Consequently there is less and less to repent of or confess.

As we will see further on, frequent examinations of conscience are most helpful for catching signs of the slippery slope. This exercise helps to fine-tune our consciences and to adjust our behavior early on, before we get too far off track. When examining our consciences, there are a few warning signs that should set off red flares when we detect them. They are the beginning of moral corruption. If we can be aware of these little changes, we can better direct the way our consciences progress. Like early symptoms of a disease, if caught in time, they usually present no difficulty.

If we allow them to fester, however, they can grow into a serious problem, and we may no longer have the wherewithal to fight them. Let's look at some of the more common symptoms of deformation of conscience.

SNEAKINESS

The first such symptom is sneakiness. When we begin skulking around, doing things behind people's backs, something is probably wrong. The first question we should ask ourselves is: *What do I have to hide?* If what we are doing is on the up and up, we should have no reason to conceal it.

Here Jesus' words help immensely. He said that a wicked person hates the light, because his deeds are evil and he doesn't want them "to be exposed" (John 3:20). A good person, on the contrary, comes out into the light so that it may clearly be seen that he is acting correctly. A little further along in John's Gospel, as we've seen, Jesus calls the devil "the father of lies" (John 8:44). The devil himself loves sneakiness and avoids the light. What is sneakiness, after all, if not a sort of lie? We try to project an image of ourselves that does not correspond to the truth and to get away with less noble deeds in the shadows.

A person of good conscience isn't two-faced. He or she doesn't act one way in front of people he wants to impress, and another way with a different crowd. This transparency reveals a pure heart and a good conscience. Its absence should trigger a warning bell. We may need to dig deeper and set things straight.

MORAL PARENTHESES

A second early warning of a sick conscience is the presence of *moral parentheses*—pockets of our lives where our moral code changes or disappears altogether. Remember the famous scene from Francis Ford Coppola's 1972 film *The Godfather*, where Michael Corleone arranges the murders of the heads of other mafia families, all to take place during the baptism of a baby for whom Michael will be godfather. The juxtaposition of Michael's attendance at the holy rite with the brutal murders of his adversaries is enough to send chills down your spine. The mafia, in fact, is known for its moral double standards—one code for those on the "inside," and another for those on the outside. They pride themselves as being *uomini d'onore* ("men of honor") with one another, while committing the most heinous crimes toward those who stand in their way.

But these moral no-fly zones are not merely the stuff of mobsters. Many of us have areas of our lives where we adhere to a scrupulous moral code, and other areas where laxity reigns. We all have met those who make a show of being ethical while nonchalantly cheating on their taxes. Think, too, of honest family men who, once at work, check their morals at the door and become ruthless in their business practices—as if business ethics were not part of the same moral fabric of their lives. Sometimes the moral inconsistency doesn't reach the extremes, but it is inconsistency nonetheless.

Here, too, Jesus offers hard words. He berated the Pharisees for their moral posturing and for straining out gnats and swallowing camels (see Matt. 23:23–24). Jesus hated hypocrisy and praised the pure of heart.

A person who accepts immorality in one area of life sooner or later accepts it everywhere. Morality—the love of goodness and devotion to moral truth—is a *whole*, it cannot be broken into parts. A person willing to compromise in one area of his life, if pushed to it, will also compromise in other areas. We cannot compartmentalize moral goodness.

LOOKING FOR LOOPHOLES

Another sign of the moral slippery slope is a lawyerly way of approaching morality, whereby we jockey for as much ethical wiggle room as possible. When we start looking for moral loopholes, asking ourselves whether such-and-such a deed would really be *all that serious*, we are already moving down a bad road. When we fail to find loopholes, we start creating our own. A person who genuinely loves God and wants to be good doesn't try to walk as close as possible to the border between virtue and sin.

The search for moral loopholes reminds me of Satan's tricky question to Eve in the garden. "Did God really tell you not to eat of *any* tree in the garden?" Of course Satan knew that God hadn't commanded this (he had only forbidden eating of one tree), but he wanted to get Eve to start questioning God's command rather than accept it with simplicity. After all, what is one tree more or one tree less? When we are most anxious to do our own will, we look for excuses that make it look as if our will coincides with God's. We stretch God's will to make it match our own. But this is not the approach of a truly good conscience. Good conscience wants to know first of all *what God wants*, then adjusts its own plans to fit God's.

It is understandable that a person who doesn't want to pay his taxes will look for every possible loophole in the tax code to pay as little as possible. But a person of good conscience doesn't want to squirm out of moral obligations; he wants to fulfill them with as much love and perfection as possible. Again, it goes back to our understanding of morality itself as *a good thing*, worth pursuing, and not the enemy of our happiness.

FLIGHT FROM PRAYER

A fourth symptom that we are starting down the wrong path is the avoidance of prayer. Prayer is like looking God in the eye. When we no longer want to look someone in the eye, it is because we are ashamed of ourselves. We don't want him to see what is going on in our hearts.

It is very hard to pray with spontaneity and love when we are in the habit of offending God. If you offend your sister, you cannot just start talking about the latest political news as if nothing had happened between you. The problem between you would stand out like the proverbial elephant in the living room. No! When we have done wrong, we need to face up to it, tell God we're sorry, and get back to business. Yet when we have no intention of changing our ways, this becomes impossible. The only course left is to stop praying so as not to have to deal with God or "look him in the eye."

When we start finding any excuse to avoid prayer, it's a sure sign that something is wrong with our consciences. When Adam and Eve sinned, the first thing they did was try to hide from God and to cover themselves up. When we no longer look on God as our best friend but rather as someone to be avoided, something is wrong. When we no longer want to talk with him and listen to him, chances are that the corruption of conscience has begun.

RATIONALIZATION

No one likes acknowledging his own mistakes. It is never easy to say, "I'm sorry. I blew it. It was my fault." But this radical honesty is essential to a healthy conscience. The opposite tendency—to defend our actions at all costs, justifying our mistakes—leads quickly to a conscience that is no longer open to the possibility of personal error. All sorts of defense mechanisms come into play. We rationalize our own wrongdoing to ourselves and defend our actions before others. We tell others not to judge and excuse ourselves with complex arguments.

There are many ways of doing this. One typical way is to cover up our vices by changing their names. We can even make them sound virtuous! In this way, as Newman said, a civilized age is more exposed to subtle sins than a rude age, precisely because it is more fertile in excuses and evasions. A civilized age can make error plausible; it can make vice look like virtue. It dignifies sin by fine names. It calls greed "proper care of one's family," or "industry"; it calls pride "independence"; it calls ambition "greatness of mind"; resentment it calls a "sense of justice," and so on.

Another way to rationalize our own mistakes is by comparing ourselves to other people. We direct our attention away from our own faults by saying that everybody does it, or that at least we don't do more serious things, like So-and-So does! Our own vices don't look so bad when we compare ourselves to dictators and serial killers!

When we see this happening in our own lives, we need to be attentive. Rationalization is symptomatic of a conscience that is growing warped. Behind it is the vice of pride, which never wants to admit its errors. Good conscience depends on the virtue of humility and a real willingness to be corrected.

Where does all this take us? If these are some of the signs of the corruption of conscience, what is the ideal state of conscience that we should be pursuing? Let us now examine some of the different states of conscience we can face. We will first look at some temporary states of conscience and then discuss habitual states.

STATES OF CONSCIENCE

OBJECTIVE STATES OF CONSCIENCE
Objectively speaking, conscience can either be true or false. This refers specifically to the *judgment of conscience*: the moral evaluation of a particular action. Let's say you are in a music store and you feel the temptation to pick up the latest Rihanna CD and put it in your pocket. You are sure no one will see you. A false conscience will tell you that there is nothing wrong with this action (*Everybody does it; it doesn't cost the store anything*, etc.). A true conscience, on the other hand, will step in quickly and say: *Shoplifting is a sin. You have no right to take that. It isn't yours!*

When the judgment of conscience agrees with moral truth, it is a true or upright conscience. Like a compass that really points north when it says north, a true conscience indicates the real moral quality of our actions. A conscience telling you that stealing and lying are okay is a *false conscience*, since its judgments don't agree with moral truth.

A false (or erroneous) conscience is also an ignorant conscience. It doesn't correctly ascertain the moral value of a given action. This ignorance can be culpable or inculpable. That is, it may be our fault that our consciences judge badly. Maybe, for instance, we didn't form them well, or we didn't bother to learn the moral principles that should guide us, or we have tamed our consciences by habits of sin, etc. Other times the error of conscience may not be our fault. Maybe we have always been taught that a given behavior was morally correct (when in fact it is not), and we never had any reason to doubt what we were taught. In this case, we may have what ethicists call an invincibly ignorant conscience—we have no way of correcting the error.

As we insisted earlier, a conscience in error is always in error, and even when the error is not our fault, it harms us as persons. But we are not responsible for what we had no way of knowing.

SUBJECTIVE STATES OF CONSCIENCE
Along with the objective states of conscience—their correspondence to moral truth—there are also *subjective* states. Subjective states refer to our own perception of moral truth. For example, I may *objectively* be wrong (think stealing a CD is okay) while *subjectively* acting "in good conscience" (doing what I think is right). Since conscience is our best guide in the present moment, we must always follow it. But sometimes conscience itself isn't sure about what we ought to do. What happens then? Let's look for a moment at some different "subjective" states of conscience.

Certain conscience. A conscience is said to be certain when we have no doubts about what we ought to do. If I have the opportunity to speak badly about a colleague who has stabbed me in the back, I may feel tempted to do so while knowing in my heart (conscience) I really shouldn't. I know it wouldn't please God. It wouldn't be the Christian thing to do. In this case, my conscience is certain, not because it is right (which it also is), but because I have *no doubts*.

Maybe, for instance, a Moslem youth in Afghanistan is absolutely convinced that it is the will of Allah that he strap C4 to himself in order to blow up a bus full of western tourists. Though he is objectively wrong (God never wills the murder of innocent people), he may be subjectively *certain*—in that he has no doubts whatsoever.

From these examples we can see that one's subjective state depends on the degree of certainty of one's moral judgments. A certain conscience— even when objectively false—always obliges, since we have no reason to doubt it is correct. As soon as some doubt enters the scene, however, we must try to clear it up.

Probable conscience. A probable conscience is one step lower than a certain conscience. Perhaps we are quite sure that we ought to act in a certain way, but a lingering doubt remains. *Is this really the way I should behave? Is this truly what God wants?* In this case (irrespective of the objective truth of our moral judgment), our consciences are said to be *probable*, because we are almost sure—but not quite. Maybe you have always been taught to believe that blacks are inferior to whites, but when push comes to shove, you begin to wonder: *Is this really the case? Does skin color really matter? Should I treat this person in front of me in a disdainful way, just because her skin is a shade darker than mine?* Here conscience is probable, but not certain.

Again, the point here is not whether we are right or wrong in our judgment (the objective level), but how *sure* we are (the subjective level).

Doubtful conscience. A doubtful conscience takes us one step lower in the hierarchy of certainty. Here we really don't know what the best course of action is. We may have an inkling that it is one way rather than another, but we are basically *unsure*. Let's say, for instance, that doctors are proposing a very expensive treatment for my terminally ill father. They offer no guarantees that the treatment will help, but it could. Should I accept, even though my family finances are strained, just in case it could do some good? Here I may be at a real loss as to what the moral choice is.

Usually we are not obliged by a doubtful conscience. We are obliged, however, to do what we can to resolve the doubt. We should seek advice, explore other options, pray, find out what the Church says about such cases, etc. Many times we can clear up our doubts by *informing our consciences* regarding the moral principles in play.

Perplexed conscience. A perplexed conscience represents a particular case of doubt. Here, it seems that no matter what we do, we will act immorally. In other words, every option at our disposal seems to involve sin. This is impossible, of course, since no one is ever obliged to sin. There is always a moral option (even if it isn't always pleasant). In this regard, we see that a perplexed conscience is necessarily false (or erroneous), because it sees sin where there is none.

As in the case of a doubtful conscience, the person with a perplexed conscience has the duty to try to resolve the perplexity through the means I outlined above.

HABITUAL STATES OF CONSCIENCE

Along with momentary states of conscience regarding particular judgments, there are also *habitual* states of conscience, or conditions of conscience that are more or less permanent. When our consciences are healthy, they call a spade a spade; they recognize good as good and evil as evil—and do not confuse the two. But for different reasons our consciences can get maladjusted, like a scale that reads too heavy or too light. Most of us don't mind getting on a scale that reads light. It is nice to read "126 pounds" when you're really pushing 150. But if we want to know the truth, a faulty scale is a problem. Though we may read the scale correctly, we have no way of knowing what our true weight is.

To help distinguish a balanced conscience from one that's out of tune, we can use three adjectives to describe the degrees of sensitivity. Conscience can be habitually scrupulous, lax, or well-formed.

Scrupulous conscience. A scrupulous conscience is a sick conscience. Like the scale that reads too heavy, it makes everything appear worse than it is. It discovers sins where there are none and sees serious sin where there's merely imperfection. The scrupulous conscience is timid and fearful. A scrupulous person interprets temptations as sin, even when there has been no consent of the free will. Living with a scrupulous conscience is similar to driving a car with the parking brake on: there is constant friction, tension, and stress.

A scrupulous conscience is often a symptom of lack of confidence in the goodness and love of God. The surest cure for this moral sickness is to form one's conscience correctly, according to objective norms, and to take

counsel from someone with proven good judgment. We have to be strict
with ourselves and humble enough to take good moral advice from others. In this, too, C. S. Lewis offers some excellent advice:

> Remember what St. John says: "If our heart condemns us, God is stron-
> ger than our heart." The feeling of being, or not being forgiven and
> loved, is not what matters. One must come down to brass tacks. If there
> is a particular sin on your conscience, repent and confess it. If there isn't,
> tell the despondent devil not to be silly. You can't help hearing this voice
> (the odious inner radio) but you must treat it merely like a buzzing in
> your ears or any other irrational nuisance. (*Letters to an American Lady*)

Lax conscience. At the opposite end of the spectrum we find the lax
conscience—the scale that reads light. The person with a lax conscience
decides on insufficient grounds that an evil action is permissible, or that
something gravely wrong isn't so serious. He sees virtue where there is sin
and registers only flagrant deviations from the moral law.

The lax person has as his motto "To err is human" and convinces himself that either he is too weak to resist sin, or that it simply doesn't matter.
He is careless and makes light of wrongdoing with the excuse that "everyone does it, so it can't be so bad." This type of individual also tends to
undervalue responsibility for his actions.

A lax conscience is like a stretched spring that has lost its elasticity and
no longer returns to its original form. Through repeated concessions in
"little things," or by ignoring its judgments, the conscience becomes
dulled and insensitive. As G. K. Chesterton remarked, "One is tempted to
say that a man who has not got a troubled conscience is in danger of having no conscience to be troubled."

Well-formed conscience. The well-formed conscience falls at the mid-
point between the two extremes. It is delicate in the sense of attention to
detail, like a painter with a delicate brush stroke, who isn't satisfied with
general shapes and forms but insists on perfection. The well-formed conscience pursues excellence, but not in an anxious, sweated way. Based on
love, the good conscience is dynamic and joyful. A person whose conscience is well formed is aware that he stands before God at all times and
doesn't allow himself to rationalize or hide from the truth.

QUALITIES OF A GOOD CONSCIENCE

To recap some of the reflections we have made earlier, we could say that a well-formed conscience is distinguished by the following four qualities:

First, a good conscience is *active.* It doesn't leave us tranquil and complacent for long periods of time. It is a goad, an uncomfortable burr under our saddle. A good conscience is not a silent conscience that sleepily nods in approval at all our choices, like a traffic cop lackadaisically waving traffic along. A good conscience is exacting because love itself is exacting.

Second, a good conscience doesn't limit itself to our *actions* but analyzes our intentions, motivations, and underlying attitudes.

Third, a good conscience pushes us to our *best,* drawing the most out of us. It encourages, impels, suggests, and prompts. It doesn't simply register wrongdoing or reproach us for our failings but points us to the heights. "Good" is not sufficient. How about "better"?

Fourth, a good conscience turns us toward *God* rather than inward on ourselves. It makes us see our actions not just as credits or debits on our personal record, but as a generous or cold response to God's love. It pushes us to a truer love of God, because he loved us first.

If the well-formed conscience is our goal, how are we to get there? We have spent a fair amount of time considering how conscience gets *deformed.* Now it's time to look at the still more important question of how to *form* our Christian conscience. How does conscience help us become the sort of persons we want to be? What can we do to make sure that conscience leads us in the right direction? These are some of the questions we will address next.

Questions for Study and Discussion

1. What is meant by the "corruption" of conscience? Why is it so serious?
2. What does it mean to lose a sense of sin, or for conscience to become deadened? How does this relate to the biblical idea of being "stiff-necked" or "hard of heart"?
3. What are some of the warning signs that we may be allowing our consciences to be deformed? What can we do about this?
4. What is meant by *objective* and *subjective* states of conscience? What are they?
5. What should we do when we have a doubtful conscience?

6. What is a scrupulous conscience? How can we avoid becoming scrupulous?

Questions for Personal Reflection

1. Do you protect and defend your conscience from corrosive influences? If so, how? If not, how can you begin to do so?

2. Do you ever find yourself rationalizing your mistakes? Are you honest with yourself and with God? Why or why not?

3. Would you qualify your conscience as scrupulous, lax, or well formed?

12

GROWING INTO— OR OUT OF—CONSCIENCE

Human Maturity and Conscience Formation

We were often asked as children, "What do you want to be when you grow up?" We were expected to say "a firefighter" or "a lawyer" or "president of the United States." The question implicitly referred to a chosen trade or career path. An answer such as "When I grow up, I want to be responsible, kind, loyal, unselfish, and hardworking" would have drawn looks of surprise and bemusement. Still, as unexpected as this response would have been, it would have gotten to the heart of what adulthood—maturity—is all about. This is what it really means to "grow up."

Growing up means more than getting older. There are infantile octogenarians, just as there are mature fourteen-year-olds. Adulthood means more than finishing school and getting a job, finding a spouse and having children. It is a lifelong process of spiritual and moral development into the sort of human beings we are called to be. What role should conscience play in this process? How does a mature adult deal with conscience? What ideal are we looking for when considering the form our own conscience should take?

For some, maturity means leaving behind rules and regulations to become autonomous adults. How many times do we hear the declaration "No one can tell me what to do. I will decide for myself"? For those who conceive of conscience as a vestige of childhood, a mere "superego" of internalized societal mores, maturity means growing out of conscience and thinking for oneself. There is a modicum of truth in this attitude. As we grow older, we sort through the different values and principles that we have learned—some we jettison and others we embrace. We commit ourselves *personally* to a path, a worldview that explains for us what life is really about and what is expected of us. For Christians, this worldview entails accepting Jesus Christ as the way, the truth, and the life, and the conditions of discipleship.

Yet once we have reached an understanding of the meaning of life and committed ourselves to following Christ, we can no longer say, "No one can tell me what to do." Suddenly we find ourselves committed in freely chosen obedience to the King of kings and Lord of lords. Maturity for a Christian does not mean radical autonomy, but conscientious discipleship. Conscience itself takes on an exalted status as the interior voice that continually reminds us what it means to follow Christ and urges us always to choose the higher road.

We know that we are called to grow "to the measure of the full stature of Christ" (Eph. 4:13) and, like Paul, to become adults and put an end to childish ways (1 Cor. 13:11). At the same time Christ invites us to preserve our childlike simplicity, since "whoever does not receive the kingdom of God as a little child will never enter it" (Luke 18:17). How do we attain this harmony between human maturity and evangelical simplicity? How can we overcome childishness while holding fast to a childlike spirit?

THE FORMATION OF A MATURE CONSCIENCE

Perhaps the most important aspect of growing up takes place through the formation of conscience. Though the natural urging to do good and avoid evil is innate, some of the specific demands of morality are not. None of us is born with comprehensive knowledge of right and wrong, any more than we are born with knowledge of the multiplication tables. We do have a natural moral law written on our hearts, but because of original sin we see this law in a muddy and imperfect way, and conscience needs instruction and purification. Moreover, some of the demands of Christian discipleship surpass a mere natural ethics. We must learn to be humble, to share, to be pure or forgiving. Conscience doesn't come factory-ready—it requires education.

Aristotle—following Plato—understood that the rewards and punishments meted out to the young teach them to find pleasure in good things and displeasure in bad things. Education aims at making a student like and dislike what he ought. In other words, moral education endeavors to instill *virtue*. Children have a natural selfish streak. They naturally gravitate toward what is immediately pleasurable and resist what is hard. They think of themselves first, rather than others. Thus children must learn to appreciate goodness. Like ballet or opera or major league baseball, moral goodness is an acquired taste. The more you "get into it," the more you appreciate and enjoy it.

When I was a boy, my parents "made me" take swimming lessons. The water was cold, and I didn't like it one bit. I resisted, because it required discipline and hard work. But as I gained a certain degree of proficiency, I learned to love swimming and am forever grateful for this training. We never like things while we are going through the painful stage of *learning* them, but only once we have learned. Many others have had similar experiences with learning piano, or studying math, or playing sports. Often parents must *oblige* their children to stick with certain good things until they learn to like them. We are all thankful that we were obliged to master certain skills when young, which have proved invaluable as we have gotten older.

Morality follows a similar pattern. In a good family, a child slowly learns good conduct by imitation, by instruction, and by the application of rewards and punishments. This external input serves to condition behavior and reinforces a growing personal sense of right and wrong. The immature mind must be given external sanctions before it can reach the internal. In the end, however, conscience has little to do with rewards and punishment per se. Little by little, as a child matures, he or she learns to distinguish right from wrong and acts more and more out of personal conviction rather than external constraints.

How does this spiritual and moral growth come about? The maturing process involves the transformation of *external* norms and rules into *internal* principles and convictions. When a person consciously and freely assimilates moral principles, that person becomes more adult, more mature. Unlike the Freudian idea of irrational and unconscious assimilation, maturity demands a free acceptance of moral norms and the rational discovery of moral truth. As a person grows, he or she should gradually learn to recognize and appreciate certain values and to discard other proposals as unsuitable or false.

This internalization of one's moral compass also entails growth in self-mastery. A child has to be watched and reminded (in some cases even forced) to do his homework or go to church on Sunday. His parents have to regulate the amount of television he watches because he is not mature enough to discipline himself or to discern what is best. Any child, if he were the one to plan his diet, would sooner eat chocolate cake than green beans. Norms must be imposed from outside, because a child follows his natural inclinations and impressions and is not capable of thinking things through or sacrificing an immediate pleasure for a future good. These qualities are proper for an adult.

As important as these first stages are, moral education doesn't end in childhood. It demands ongoing work. As life progresses, our moral choices become more complex and our responsibilities to others grow as well. Just as our professional training continues through the years, so, too, our moral formation should not be static but should grow along with our changing circumstances. Our experience as moral beings—doing the right thing and sometimes the wrong thing—teaches us how to love God better and how to put others before ourselves.

The Formation of a Pure Conscience

This ongoing moral formation isn't merely a question of mastering moral conundrums. Earlier we spoke of three levels of conscience. At the first level was a general disposition to be good, to love God, and to do the right thing. The second level comprised knowledge of moral principles. The third level involved the application of moral norms to our concrete situation. To be effective, conscience formation must take place at each of these levels.

Growing in Love for God
The more we truly love God and desire to please him in all things, the better our consciences will react and the more their judgments will hit the mark. The first level of conscience formation, therefore, involves

growth in *love of God* and in a heartfelt *desire to do good*. A striving for moral excellence, for holiness and self-forgetfulness, leads us to make good moral judgments with less and less admixture of self-interest. The more we love goodness and hate sin in our lives, the more clearly we will see the path we are to take. But how does this come about? What practical steps can we take to get there?

Prayer. Surely the first and most important means we have at our disposal is prayer. A person who spends time alone with God, talking with him and listening to him, cannot help but grow in love for him. Prayer makes us more reflective, deeper, and more aware of what lies beneath our own behavior and choices. We get an ever-clearer sense of what life really means, of where we come from and where we are going. In short, we learn to know God and know ourselves. Prayer awakens religious fervor and gives courage and strength to achieve moral excellence. In prayer we find consolation and the power of God's grace.

Prayer demands silence and reflection. It allows us to retire from the noise and confusion of the streets to contemplate what is truly important. Just as a trek up a mountain grants the hiker a whole new perspective on the world below, so prayer grants us a whole new perspective on life. It allows us to see things as God sees them. In other words, we see things as they really are.

Single-heartedness. A second, closely related means of growing in love for God is being pure of heart. As we've seen, Jesus cautions us against falling into divided loyalties. He says, "No one can serve two masters; for a slave will either hate the one and love the other, or be devoted to the one and despise the other" (Matt. 6:24).

If we care more about what others think of us and our actions than about what God thinks, we will end up betraying him as often as a conflict of interests arises. Scripture assures us that "fear of the Lord is the beginning of wisdom" (Prov. 9:10). This "fear" does not mean an emotion of anxiety or apprehension, but a reverential awe before God. "Fear of the Lord" means taking God as a point of reference for our lives and decisions and caring more for his opinion than for public opinion. The virtue of singleheartedness helps us put God and his will in the first place in our lives.

Gratitude. A third way of growing in our love of God and of goodness is through thankfulness. The more aware we are of how good God is to us, the more we desire to love him in return. Just as realizing how much God has forgiven us makes us more merciful toward others, so, too, a deeper recognition of his gifts makes us more generous with him and others. How many children learn to really love their parents when they begin to understand how many sacrifices their parents have made for them!

So how do we grow more grateful? Gratitude begins by focusing more on the good things we have received than on life's difficulties. When we examine our lives with the eyes of faith, we become aware of God's presence and loving company at every moment, even in the most difficult times. Learning to see the "glass half full" rather than the "glass half empty" is more than an exercise in optimism; it is an exercise in thanksgiving. To spend our lives complaining about our pains and sufferings produces the unhappy effect of blinding us to God's gifts and his love. The less we feel loved, the less we feel inclined to love in return. The converse is also true, however. The more we experience God's love for us, the more we are empowered to love.

KNOWING MORAL PRINCIPLES

The second level of conscience formation involves *education in right moral principles*. We cannot make good moral choices unless our "moral compass" points "north." We all need objective principles, a yardstick against which our consciences can measure our actions. These principles articulate for us what God wants from us, what constitutes the right thing to do. In the first place, this means knowing universal norms, like love of God and neighbor, and the Golden Rule, which enjoins us to do to others what we would like done to ourselves. They also include the norm that we may never do evil in order to bring about good (the end doesn't justify the means), and the understanding that Christ is our moral model (*What would Jesus do?*).

All of us should know the Ten Commandments and their applications in our own lives and relationships. When Jesus was asked what we need to do to inherit eternal life, the first answer he offered was, "Obey the commandments" (Matt. 19:17 NIV). Norms like honoring one's parents and abstaining from adultery and murder have lost none of their moral relevance in the thousands of years since they were written.

Along with universal norms, conscience also needs more specific principles and standards that should govern our behavior. Each person should possess the degree of moral knowledge sufficient for him or her to live rightly in their own state in life. A doctor should be familiar with medical ethics; a married couple should know their duties toward each other and their children; a businesswoman ought to understand her ethical obligations toward employees, clients, and stockholders; and a politician should understand the moral obligations of integrity, honesty, and disinterested service that his office entails. An important part of the obligation of conscience is our duty to learn the specifics of God's will for our lives.

Where do we go to learn these moral principles? How do we find out what God wants from us in the concrete circumstances of our lives? God is just, which means he doesn't leave us in the dark regarding his will. He offers us the means of knowing the morally right thing to do.

God's Word. A first way of knowing moral principles is through the Bible: "a lamp to my feet and a light to my path" (Ps. 119:105). As we have seen, this Word includes the Ten Commandments, a compendium of universal moral principles that provide our consciences with a sure guide for our behavior. But God's self-revelation doesn't end here. The whole Bible, and especially the New Testament, offers numerous expressions of the attitudes and actions that please God and are worthy of human beings. Jesus summarizes these principles in his "great commandment": to love God above all things and our neighbor as ourselves (Matt. 22:36–40).

Christians should know God's Word and make it their daily bread. The Gospels especially furnish us with Christ's own example and teaching as a model to follow. It was Saint Jerome, the first translator of the Bible, who pronounced the important maxim "Ignorance of Scripture is ignorance of Christ." By his word and example, Jesus teaches us to be humble and generous, to embrace our crosses every day, and to seek poverty of spirit. For Christians, the principle of doing what Jesus would do in our place requires a knowledge of what Jesus did in *his* place and what moved him to do so. Formation of conscience here would entail a study of Jesus' life and teachings in order to apply them in our own lives. A very superficial knowledge of the gospel, for a Christian, could constitute culpable ignorance. Christ is, after all, the fundamental point of reference for Christian living.

Natural law. A second guide for knowing moral principles is the *natural law*, by which we discover the rule of right reason. All persons have access to moral truth through the use of their reason. We learn the demands of fairness and justice. We also discover what is good and bad for human beings and understand that people are always to be treated as ends and never used as means.

Even before the promulgation of the old law, as we've seen, the natural law enjoining good and proscribing evil was already written on the heart of man. To take just one example, look at the sacredness of human life. This was written from the beginning in man's heart, accessible to his conscience. After Cain kills his brother Abel, God asks him, "What have you done?" (Gen. 4:10). Cain cannot excuse himself by saying, "You haven't yet commanded us not to kill." He is responsible for his brother's murder, not under "the law," but because his conscience already testified that murder was evil. This passage interprets the experience of every person: in the depths of his conscience, the human person is always reminded of the inviolability of life—his own life and the lives of others—as something that does not belong to him, because it is the property and gift of God, the Creator and Father.

Since moral truth is one, and God doesn't contradict himself, the natural law never contradicts the divine law. Natural law, in fact, is an expression of God's eternal law written in our hearts. Similarly, God's revelation, which we find in sacred Scripture, confirms and completes what we know by reason and invites us to a higher standard based on Jesus himself—loving our enemies, praying for those who mistreat us, and serving our neighbor up to the point of giving our lives.

Church teaching. Christians are not moral islands, called to work out their moral dilemmas in isolation from others. We form part of a community, a body, and as a body we are called to profess one faith, one Lord, and one moral teaching. Paul's appeal to "one faith" implies not only doctrinal belief, but also to a common effort to live in accordance with the moral demands of the gospel. It implies, moreover, a common witness to a world that hungers for ethical certitudes and rightly expects moral consistency from Christians.

Modern Christians should be slow to abandon the moral beliefs held by the Christian community often for centuries. The moral wisdom handed down from generation to generation should not be simply tossed out because of pressures from popular culture or the reigning moral fashions.

Christians have wrestled with moral problems from the very beginning and, as Jesus promised, the Holy Spirit has continued to guide the Christian community to the fullness of truth (see John 16:13). The assistance that the teaching Church offers is especially necessary in these difficult times, where moral quandaries abound. New situations never contemplated in biblical times call for careful moral evaluation and purity of conscience. Many issues that are not explicitly described in the Bible—such as contraception, abortion, *in vitro* fertilization, and euthanasia—have been considered by the Church, which under the guidance of the Holy Spirit offers sure teaching for forming our consciences. We shouldn't take our Lord's words lightly: "Whoever listens to you listens to me, and whoever rejects you rejects me" (Luke 10:16). He gave his apostles and their successors authority to teach in his name, which includes moral teaching. He also said to Saint Peter: "whatever you bind on earth will be bound in heaven, and whatever you loose on earth will be loosed in heaven" (Matt. 16:19).

When moral decisions are clear, doing the right thing may be *difficult* because of the sacrifice involved, but it won't be *complicated*. In these cases, the teaching Church has little to do but confirm our correct moral insights. When, however, things become more complex, such that even good and intelligent persons disagree, that is when the teaching role of the Church and her pastors becomes indispensable. Newman put this beautifully when he wrote:

All sciences, except the science of Religion, have their certainty in themselves; as far as they are sciences, they consist of necessary conclusions from undeniable premises, or of phenomena manipulated into general truths by an irresistible induction. But the sense of right and wrong, which is the first element in religion, is so delicate, so fitful, so easily puzzled, obscured, perverted, so subtle in its argumentative methods, so impressible by education, so biased by pride and passion, so unsteady in its course that, in the struggle for existence amid the various exercises and triumphs of the human intellect, this sense is at once the highest of all teachers, yet the least luminous; and the Church, the Pope, the Hierarchy are, in the Divine purpose, the supply of an urgent demand. (*Letter to the Duke of Norfolk*)

Even where due diligence is employed, conscience will err sometimes. As a check on individual caprice, we ought to consult the best living authorities and the best traditions of the past. A healthy humility, with a keen awareness of the possibility of error, is a prerequisite for good conscience. Really unavoidable mistakes will not count against us, but many errors are preventable. Humility gives us a healthy mistrust of self and encourages us to often ask whether we could be doing a little better, even if it means personal sacrifice. Again, where our goal is to please God rather than choose the path of least resistance, we will look for moral truth above all else.

THE APPLICATION OF MORAL PRINCIPLES TO CONCRETE ACTS

The third level of conscience comprises the formulation of a concrete judgment regarding the morality of our actions. Here, too, conscience needs formation. Not only do we need a deep-seated *desire* to do God's will and *knowledge* of moral principles, we also need to know how to *apply them* to our real lives and to our moral decision-making.

Sometimes this application is extremely simple. For example, if you know that adultery is wrong, your conscience spontaneously urges you to abstain from sexual relations with someone other than your husband or wife. If you know that stealing is a sin, your conscience forbids you from shoplifting or rifling through your mother's purse for pocket money. Yet not all moral decisions are so simple.

Let me give three examples of where the application of moral principles grows much more complex. First we have the case of the "positive" moral precepts: love God, love your neighbor, be humble, honor your parents, etc. Here conscience has its work cut out for it. It is much harder to apply these open-ended moral precepts than it is to simply abstain from what is morally wrong. *What does it mean for me to love God here and now? How far am I to go in love for neighbor? How much of my time and money should I be giving to others?* Remember that conscience is much more than a moral "referee"; it also is a moral "coach," pushing me toward excellence and holiness. In other words, conscience doesn't limit itself to what is strictly obligatory but invites me to go further. A coach's job implies much more creativity than a referee's.

A second area where this process gets murky refers to our specific vocations and missions in life. One thing is to understand universal moral principles common to all persons, and another thing is to understand what God is asking of me *personally*. *What did God create me to do? What is my mission in life? Am I to get married and raise a family, become a missionary, dedicate myself completely to his service?* These moral questions demand a different sort of knowledge of God's will, and a greater attention to the voice of the Holy Spirit. Similarly, even within our particular states in life, many things that God asks of us on a daily basis cannot be reduced to general moral principles. *How much should I be praying? How much time should I devote to evangelizing activities? Should I take the higher-paying job that allows for a better life for me and my family, or another job where I will be doing more good for others?* These and many other questions demand a well-formed conscience.

A practical example may help. We know that we should cultivate the virtue of gratitude. Let's say a certain person has been especially good to you and recently did you a huge favor. How should you respond? What does it mean to be grateful in this instance? There is no moral principle that says *send flowers* or *make a phone call*. We have only the very general principle that we should be grateful. Here conscience will deliberate over the possible ways that gratitude can best be expressed to this particular person.

A third realm of difficulty involves the avoidance of occasions of sin. As Christians, we know that we should strive to please God in all things, and stay away from anything that could displease him. Here, too, conscience has an important task. Not only do we need knowledge of moral principles, we also need knowledge of ourselves: our strengths and weaknesses, our personal histories, our present state of mind. It also demands an almost ruthless honesty with oneself to avoid self-deception. Dr. Janet Smith offers the following example of just this sort of moral application.

Take a married man away from home for a few weeks of business training. He walks by the hotel bar. An attractive colleague sitting at the bar invites him for a drink. He thinks, "Would having a drink with her just be companionable? Would it just be a nice way to relax and unwind or am I putting myself in an occasion of sin?" Now the good person would consult his conscience. Having a drink might be perfectly all right. He might conclude, "Well, I've got control and I don't really think that there's any danger here and I would like to have a drink and this person seems friendly so we'll sit down and we'll chat." Someone else might say, "No, I've been away for two weeks and I'm kind of desperate and I don't know whether I could handle this or not." Now the Church cannot tell us what to do in each and every situation. It cannot make a rule: "Don't have drinks with attractive women at bars." That's where conscience does its job. The conscience judges at this instance whether one ought to do this or that.[1]

Notice in this excellent example that the application of general principles is not as cut-and-dried as it may seem at first. It requires knowledge of the norm, but also knowledge of yourself and how you will react in different situations. This self-knowledge takes into account your past behavior and habits, your personal strengths and weaknesses. In this example, the same person may honestly reach a different conclusion on two different days, depending on his present state.

For this reason, formation of conscience at the level of specific moral judgments especially entails growing in the virtue of *prudence*. Prudence means more than cautiousness and circumspection, or knowing when to hold back. As one of the four cardinal virtues, prudence refers to wisdom and right judgment in practical affairs. It is the ability to apply principles well and to sort through the relevant values, norms, consequences, and human goods to be able to come to a good moral judgment. As we have seen, conscience does not merely mechanically apply a universal norm to a specific instance. The process involved is dynamic and, along with knowledge of moral principles, requires knowledge of options and self-knowledge as well. Prudence helps us both to judge well and then to act according to the right judgment of conscience.

FOUR PRACTICAL WAYS TO FORM YOUR CONSCIENCE

We have already looked at some means for forming our consciences. Here we can sum them up in four practical tips. These are not the only means to form a good conscience, but they provide a good starting point for the person who sincerely wants to judge well and to do the right thing.

1. PRAYER

Since one of the major obstacles to good conscience is self-deception and rationalization, frequent conversation with God helps us to see our own behavior more clearly. We may be able to deceive ourselves, but we cannot deceive God. Prayer throws a special light on conscience—the light of God's truth. If you want to really clean a room, you throw open the drapes and let the sunlight bathe all the corners and surfaces. Suddenly you see dust and dirt where you hadn't seen them before. Prayer is like that. It reveals the deeper truths of our actions and helps us to be honest with ourselves.

Again, when we start avoiding prayer, it often means that we are ashamed of our behavior and afraid of what God may tell us. It may seem to go without saying, but living in the presence of God is indispensable for judging rightly. One of the principal fruits of prayer is the interior clarity that God gives to the one who prays. When we pray, we learn to see things as God sees them, and this includes our own moral choices.

2. FREQUENT EXAMINATION OF CONSCIENCE

We will devote the next chapter to this topic, so a simple word will suffice here. We have seen how good moral judgments require both knowledge of moral principles and self-knowledge. Examining our consciences—our moral choices, our victories and failures, our motivations and intentions— helps us to judge better and to make better decisions in the future.

Conscience is a tool, and tools work only when we use them. If we leave an appliance in the closet, it will never help us in our household tasks. Similarly, conscience helps us live well only when we exercise it. This exercise includes examining our moral choices. It requires time and attention away from the hubbub of daily activities. Conscience doesn't provide the service it should unless we give it the time and atmosphere it needs.

3. DOING THE RIGHT THING

This may seem more like the *result* of a good conscience than a *means* of forming it, but in reality it is both. Conscience not only influences our actions; our actions also have an effect on conscience. The more we obey conscience, the stronger it gets. When we habitually disobey it, it grows weaker and even changes its judgments. When we do not live according to what we believe, we eventually end up believing according to the way we live. Good conscience and good behavior support one another.

The philosopher Plato discovered that good people see things more clearly than bad people do. When we do bad things, our will is corrupted, but so is our *reason*. We no longer understand things the way a good person does. Yet the contrary is also true. When we start obeying conscience, we actually judge better and determine the right thing to do more easily.

4. SPIRITUAL DIRECTION

An objective third party can help us know ourselves better and sift through our own subjective way of seeing ourselves and our actions. When we honestly open ourselves to another person, he or she can assist us in forming better judgments and making better decisions. A good spiritual director will not just listen approvingly to everything we have to say but will challenge us to grow in our generosity with God and to purify our intentions.

An athlete can reach only a certain level of proficiency by himself. If he really wants to improve, he takes on a coach or personal trainer to help him get the best out of his efforts. A coach will analyze the athlete's strengths and weaknesses and correct the fine points of his style. He sees things from the outside that the athlete could never see. In the same way, a good spiritual guide helps us understand ourselves better and to see our behavior as God sees it.

Of these four means, examination of conscience is particularly important and merits deeper attention. In the next chapter we will explore this practice more deeply. We will discard mistaken notions about conscience examination and offer a number of practical hints to help make better use of this exercise.

Questions for Study and Discussion

1. For a Christian, what does it mean to grow up or be mature? What are the signs of a truly mature Christian man or woman?
2. Is virtue natural or does it have to be learned? How does this come about? What are the characteristics of a virtuous person?

3. What is conscience formation? How does it come about?
4. How do we grow in our purity of conscience and love of God? Give some practical suggestions.
5. How can we know the moral principles that should regulate our lives? What are some of these?
6. How do we learn to apply moral principles to our real-life situations? What are some practical means to forge an upright conscience?

Questions for Personal Reflection
1. Is love for God and his Son the greatest driving force in your moral choices? If not, why? What can you do to change this?
2. What are the moral principles that come up most often in your own life? Are you sufficiently well instructed in the moral duties proper to your specific state in life?
3. What are some of the practical means you employ to form your conscience?

13

MIDTERM EXAMS

The Hows and Whys of Examining Your Conscience

Few students actually *like* taking tests. Most fear them. Final exams, especially, mean the hour of truth, when we have to demonstrate how much we have retained from a given course and our ability to articulate our newfound knowledge. Despite our general dislike of exams, if we are honest, we also recognize their importance. They motivate us to study, allow our teachers to evaluate our performance, and also let us see how much we have or haven't learned.

To relieve some of the pressure of final exams, some teachers offer midterms—a partial exam in the midst of the course to help students gauge their performance. Instead of waiting until the end of the term to receive the unpleasant surprise that they are unprepared, students get a sense of how they are doing before that moment arrives. Midterms also furnish hints as to what the teacher will be looking for at the end of the course. They are like a trial run, or a dress rehearsal of the final. A bad midterm signals the need to study more and indicates where to put more emphasis while there still is time.

Christians believe they will be judged after death on their behavior. This "last judgment" is like a final exam on our lives. We will be judged on our deeds and on our response to God's love in our lives. We believe that this judgment will determine our eternal destiny—whether we are to spend it with God and the saints in heaven, or in eternal punishment.

No sane person would like to face this final judgment unprepared. We would like to be found in the best possible conditions, especially given the consequences. How can we guarantee a good outcome in this all-important exam? How can we know whether we are ready or not?

One extremely helpful means is the examination of conscience. Like a midterm exam, it reveals how we are doing and offers a measure of our progress without compromising our final grade. While we are on earth, there is always time to change our ways, to learn to love God more, and to follow him more closely. Rather than assume that everything is in order, making a good examination of conscience offers us the chance to adjust our behavior while there is still time.

As we move forward in life, we easily lose the innocence and simplicity of youth. This process has a positive side. We realize that not every moral question is as black and white as we once saw it. Many moral questions involve varying shades of grey. We also can become more compassionate toward others and more understanding of their difficulties.

On the negative side, however, we also learn how to rationalize immoral behavior and to justify our bad choices. As life progresses, many people lose moral clarity and grow wishy-washy in their ethical judgments. Sometimes, too, we simply stop looking at our behavior and suppose that everything is fine. It was the American comedian Steven Wright who said, "A clear conscience is usually the sign of bad memory." Examination of conscience jogs our moral memory and helps us regain moral clarity.

Do you remember the marvelous Dickens tale on conversion entitled *A Christmas Carol*? The miserly Ebenezer Scrooge is visited by spirits during the night before Christmas and realizes that he has his priorities all mixed up. When he awakens the next morning, he is overjoyed to discover that there is still time to change his ways. It is Christmas Day and he can still become the person that he knows he should be! A good examination of conscience can have the same effect in our lives as the visit of those spirits. It unveils our underlying attitudes and intentions and allows us to come to grips with the truth of our lives while there is time to change.

Examination of conscience isn't only useful as a preparation for Judgment Day, however. For those who sincerely desire to love God, it is an invaluable means of finding out how we can love him better and please him in all things. In this sense, it resembles an automobile tune-up. A smart car owner doesn't wait for a breakdown or flat tire to call in the mechanic. Every seven thousand miles or so, he or she takes the car in for a check-up and general retuning. The mechanic looks at the spark plugs, adjusts the timing, changes the oil, checks tire pressure, and adds fluid to the radiator and wiper system. This keeps the car running well and prevents unpleasant surprises. In the same way, we shouldn't wait for a moral meltdown in order to examine our conduct. A regular conscience exam works like a tune-up, exploring moral wear and tear and fine-tuning our behavior according to God's will for our lives.

Many people fall into a daily or weekly routine, aware of *what* they are doing but no longer conscious of *why* they do what they do. As Socrates wisely said, "The unexamined life is not worth living." Frequently reminding ourselves of what life *means*, and why we work so hard, motivates us to keep at it. It also allows us to break routines and work with a greater sense of purpose.

WHAT IS AN EXAMINATION OF CONSCIENCE?

In a technical sense, the term *examination of conscience* is a misnomer. We don't really *examine* our consciences, as if conscience were a storage shed full of our past actions of which we occasionally take inventory. More properly we *exercise* our consciences—the mind thinking morally—as a tool for evaluating our free choices and their conformity with goodness and moral truth. In other words, we *use* conscience to *examine* our actions. Still, since the expression *examination of conscience* has such a distinguished pedigree, we will continue to use it. Just bear in mind that conscience itself is not examined here; it does the examining.

An examination of conscience is a time of reflection and prayer in which we look over our moral choices and underlying attitudes, both good and bad. Examining our consciences involves an exercise in *memory*. We think back over our decisions, the way we acted toward others, the opportunities well used or wasted. *What is really important to me? Am I living in perfect agreement with what I profess to be? What obstacles are holding me back?* We consider the graces we have received, the occasions we have had to do good, what God is asking of us, and how we are responding.

Above all, an examination of conscience is a *prayer*, an encounter with God, in an atmosphere of dialogue with Christ. Before God, who knows us inside and out, we look over our lives and see whether or not they correspond to what he wants from us. The light of the Holy Spirit is essential to know ourselves well. Our question is not just a self-directed *Have I behaved well?* but addresses Christ himself: *Are you happy with me? What else would you like me to do? How can I please you better?*

Therefore, a conscience exam does not consist only in a simple listing of faults or a cold calculation of our personal triumphs and failures; it is an attentive exercise of a person who loves God and wants to love him more. Good companies that want to cut costs and maximize profits often conduct internal audits to discover how to better streamline their enterprise. These audits often reveal surprising ways to eliminate waste and increase productivity. Similarly, the person who ardently desires to love God better will often discover ways to do so when examining his or her conscience. It is not just a question of converting from bad to good but also of moving from good to better.

The fundamental motivating force behind the exam is love, the desire to uproot from our lives anything that could displease God or that could stain our friendship with him and to cultivate what pleases him most. Love seeks perfection. It doesn't distinguish between great and little, because everything is important when one loves.

Here we have touched on an essential element of a good conscience exam: it focuses on *loving God more*, and not merely on perfecting ourselves. One of the most subtle dangers facing anyone who seeks to advance in the Christian life is *spiritual narcissism*. Remember the story of Narcissus? According to the Greek myth, Narcissus was an extremely handsome young man who fell in love with his own image reflected in a pool of water. Leaning over to get a better look at himself, he fell in and drowned. Similarly, in our spiritual lives we can begin paying more attention to ourselves than to God. Instead of trying to please God more, for *his* sake, we become infatuated with our own spiritual beauty, like Narcissus staring at his image in a pool. We pick off our moral faults the way a man picks lint off his wool coat while standing in front of a mirror. If examining our conscience becomes a mere outlet for our self-love, it is useless or even harmful to our spiritual lives. We need to remind ourselves every day that the reason for our efforts doesn't lie in self-perfection, but as a means of growing in love for God.

Examination of conscience, then, is a means and not an end in itself. Among other things, it serves to grow in *self-knowledge*, which helps avoid unpleasant surprises and to better focus our spiritual work. The frieze of the temple to Apollo at Delphi bore the famous maxim *"Gnothi seauton"* ("Know thyself"). Self-knowledge means knowing not only *what* we do but *why* we do it. Conscience judges not only the moral quality of the actions we perform, to see whether they conform to the moral law, but also our attitudes, intentions, and deepest motives. This is not an easy enterprise.

We saw earlier that intelligence and goodness don't always go hand in hand. A good conscience, in fact, has little to do with native intelligence. If anything, intelligence can make self-deception easier through rationalization and subterfuge. The practical self-knowledge involved in the judgments of conscience is very different from abstract speculation. The main reason for this is that conscience affects our actions and choices, whereas speculative reasoning does not. In other words, we may have strong motivations to think in a certain way that rob our intellect of its objectivity.

Consequently, a person can be absolutely brilliant on the theoretical plane, and an absolute disaster when it comes to moral conscience. This is why King David could be perfectly clear on the punishment owed to a hypothetical scoundrel and equally blind to his own moral ruin. It is also why Jesus strongly recommends that we seek to extract the plank from our own eye before trying to remove the speck from our brother's.

Human beings are extraordinarily adept at deceiving themselves and believing what they want to believe. How is it that, time after time, criminals and even serial killers will declare that they consider themselves to be basically good people?

Self-deception isn't limited to ethics, of course. To take one egregious example, according to a 2006 survey, more than three-quarters of obese Americans said they have healthy eating habits and 40 percent said they do vigorous exercise at least three times a week. As one wag remarked on seeing the results, "These people must think that 'vigorous exercise' means walking from the car to the Dairy Queen." Or as Dr. David Schutt of Thomson Medstat, the Michigan-based health-care research firm that conducted the survey, commented somewhat more gently, "There is, perhaps, some denial going on. Or there is a lack of understanding of what does it mean to be eating healthy, and what is vigorous exercise."[1] Examination of conscience helps to overcome this tendency to self-deception by getting to know ourselves better, in God's presence.

Self-knowledge isn't the only fruit of the conscience exam. It also allows you to evaluate your *spiritual progress*, to see whether you have experienced improvement or setbacks and why. This keeps your spiritual work on track. It also is a moment to *refresh and renew your ideals and commitments* and recall what is most important in life. Finally, for Catholics, examination of conscience furnishes an invaluable tool to *prepare for the Sacrament of Reconciliation*, or confession. The better we understand what we have done and what it means for our relationship with Christ, the better we will express our sorrow and truly seek his forgiveness.

OBSTACLES TO EXAMINING OUR CONSCIENCES

We mentioned at the beginning of this chapter that most people don't like taking tests. Just as most people dislike scholastic exams, most dislike examining their consciences, too. This isn't because we are "graded" on our performance, but we do sometimes feel humbled. We are forced to confront our own mistakes and face the imperfect reality of our free choices. Yet this exercise, though sometimes painful, is ultimately liberating and joyful, since it allows us to live in the truth. It also provides the means of self-betterment.

Why is examining our conscience so difficult? If we can identify the main obstacles to examining our consciences, we should also be able to identify the necessary means to overcome them. Each vice has a corresponding virtue. There are three chief barriers to examining our consciences.

1. LAZINESS

A good conscience exam entails hard work. We have to think back over our conduct, which requires effort. It is hard to examine our actions. Beyond exploring *what* we have or haven't done, we also must dig deeper, to understand *why* we acted the way we did. This is harder still. Therefore, to examine our consciences well, we must have the courage and self-discipline to clear this first hurdle. We must decide to expend the effort necessary to get to know ourselves better.

The corresponding virtue to the vice of laziness is *diligence* or *willpower*. A willingness to take on difficult tasks provides the means to move beyond our natural sluggishness. If we forge in ourselves a spirit of hard work, we will have the willpower necessary to engage in this beneficial exercise. Our contemporary society encourages us to take things easy, to avoid whatever requires sacrifice or personal strain. Yet we also know that only those who overcome their laziness achieve the goals they set for themselves, be it in business, sports, or relationships. The same holds true for the spiritual life.

2. Pride and Vanity

All of us are susceptible to these two closely related passions of the human heart. We like to think of ourselves as better than we actually are. We paint a rosy picture of our state of affairs, sometimes deceiving even ourselves. Rather than acknowledge our faults and failings, we often justify them, rationalizing them away or at least lessening their importance. If a closer look at some area of our lives would be humiliating, we prefer to ignore it.

Examining our consciences requires deep *humility*. We must be committed to the truth and willing to see ourselves as we really are. This, too, is liberating. God knows us as we are, and as we get to know ourselves better, we see ourselves more and more as God sees us. Since humility is truth, those who possess this virtue recognize their qualities as well as their defects. They try not to make things darker or brighter than they really are.

When we take our spiritual lives seriously, we often seem to get *worse* before we get better. This is not because we are really getting worse, but because we are seeing our reality more clearly than before. C. S. Lewis expressed this beautifully in *Mere Christianity* when he wrote: "When a man is getting better he understands more and more clearly the evil that is still left in him. When a man is getting worse, he understands his own badness less and less. A moderately bad man knows he is not very good: a thoroughly bad man thinks he is all right."

3. Discouragement

It's no fun to fall down over and over again. It's especially annoying to fall back into faults we thought we had left behind. As a result, it can be frustrating to examine our consciences when we see no progress. If we don't look, maybe our faults will go away. We are not alone in the temptation to discouragement. Over and over again in the Gospels, Jesus has to tell his disciples to take heart, to have courage, to not be afraid. Discouragement leads nowhere, since it saps our moral energy and makes us wallow in our own failures.

The corresponding virtue is twofold: *courage* and *hope*. Courage gives us the strength to forge ahead despite the difficulties. We continue on without allowing our setbacks to keep us down. Hope, on the other hand, teaches us to trust in God who will give us the grace we need to improve. He never abandons us in our hour of need. He stays by our side, forgives our failings, and consoles us in our difficulties. United to him, we can truly do all things, even though progress seems painfully slow.

How to Examine Your Conscience

There is no standard method for examining your conscience. Still, I am often asked for suggestions on how to make better use of this exercise, so in the following paragraphs I will offer a possible dynamic to follow. Most of what follows takes the form of practical *tips*—elements to include or pitfalls to watch out for. You can adapt these to your personal use, incorporating what is helpful and leaving aside anything that just gets in the way.

The method of the exercise will also depend on the *frequency* with which we examine our consciences. Since examination of conscience involves an application of our memory, it should be fairly frequent; otherwise we simply can't remember our own behavior and intentions with any accuracy. If we examine our consciences often—say, every day—five or ten minutes is enough, since we are only looking over a day. We can go into greater detail and examine particular points. If we examine our consciences only once in a long while, we must necessarily concentrate on more general issues. The longer we wait between conscience exams, the more time we need to reflect on our conduct. The following suggested method may work for either case, but is better adapted to a more frequent exam.

Recall That You Are in God's Presence

Since a good conscience exam is a prayer, the best way to start is by recalling that we are in God's presence and asking the Holy Spirit to enlighten us. We ask for the grace to know ourselves better and to know his will. Just as we don't walk into someone's house without greeting our host, we don't begin this important prayer without acknowledging God and imploring his help to do it well. The great fourth-century bishop, Saint Augustine, often prayed with the simple Latin words *"Noverim me, noverim te!"* ("May I know myself and may I know you!") This is a perfect prayer with which to begin a conscience exam. If we truly wish to know ourselves better, we need God's help. Since the Holy Spirit knows us better than we know ourselves, he can reveal our deepest intentions and motivations and help us to come to grips with the truth about ourselves. He can also help us understand how we can improve and encourage us to do so.

Thank God for His Gifts and Blessings

A second important step in examining our consciences is to briefly recall God's gifts and blessings. Before turning to our own conduct, it helps to think of how good God is to us. This exercise helps us to consider our own behavior in relation to God, as a worthy or unworthy response to his love for us. Our actions don't happen in a vacuum. They happen *in relation* to God and his goodness. They are our worthy or unworthy response to his love. One of the best motivations we have for behaving well and reforming our conduct is the awareness that *God deserves better*. We recognize that sin reflects ingratitude toward the One who loves us up to the point of dying for us. The more we consider his blessings, the more clearly we see our own conduct in its true light.

Review Your Correspondence to God's Love

A third step involves *evaluating our correspondence to God's love and grace*. In the light of his immense blessings, how have we responded? Have our actions, thoughts, and words given glory to this good God? Again, in the form of dialogue, we can ask our Lord: *Was my conduct at work pleasing to you? Did I react well when my sister lost her patience with me? Have I taken advantage of the opportunities you gave me to love others and witness to your love?*

In this more concrete stage of our examination, we may make use of questionnaires that help us focus our attention on specific topics, such as the Ten Commandments. Another outline for self-examination looks first at our relationship with God (our prayer, our dependence on him, our desire to know and obey his will), then examines our relationship with other people (respect, kindness, attention, service, truthfulness, etc.) and finally looks at our relationship with self (our humility, responsibility, use of time, attention to duty, purity, etc.).

In this step, we analyze both the positive and the negative aspects of our fidelity to God and his will. It is not just a balance sheet of faults, but also a revision of our commitment to Christ. *How am I responding to Christ's love, to his grace? Am I trying to imitate him in my choices and in my pursuit of virtue? Does my Christian faith influence my decisions?*

Along with a more general self-examination, it is useful to direct our attention to some specific areas. The first is our *identification with God's will.* Like Jesus, we are called to seek his will in all things, not our own. *To what degree is God's will the standard of my behavior? Do I seek it in all things? Do I allow other factors to get in the way—like my own comfort, preferences, or what others think of me?*

A second central matter for our examination is our *practice of Christian charity.* Charity is the heart of the moral message of Christianity. Jesus came to save us from sin but also to show us how to love God and love our neighbor. He offers his own love both as an *example* to follow, and a *standard* for our own conduct. He calls it his new commandment: "Love one another *as I have loved you*" (John 13:34 NKJV, emphasis added). In this vein we can ask ourselves: *Do I build up others with my words and example? Do I actively serve my brothers and sisters? Do I make time for them and listen to them with my full attention? Do I avoid criticizing others or gossiping behind their backs?* We are called not only to avoid harming our neighbor but to build and edify in all things. After all, Jesus said that his followers would be recognizable by their love for one another (see John 13:35).

A good conscience exam considers not only our actions, but also our *intentions* and deeper *attitudes.* We need to dig beneath the surface to discover why we do what we do. Maybe even some of our good actions are done in order to be seen or thought well of. *Do we really act motivated by love of God, or is self-interest the principal reason for our choices? Did I do that in order to be seen, praised, thought well of? Did I choose that just because it pleased me, not because it was the right thing to do?* We might also discover patterns of behavior that reveal underlying habits or ingrained tendencies that need correcting. *Why do I get so angry when people disagree with me? Is it because I am proud and always have to be right? How can I become more like Jesus, who was "gentle and humble in heart"?* (Matt. 11:29 NJB).

One of the best ways to examine our intentions is to see how we act when no one is around to see us. It is relatively easy to do good when we are recognized and praised for it. It is much harder when no one sees us but God. This is called *purity of intention*, since it means acting for God alone and not to gain the appreciation of others. *How do I act when I know that no one can find out? Does my conduct change depending on who is around to see me?* In the gospel, Jesus teaches us to prefer to pray and do good works in secret and not to "let your left hand know what your right hand is doing," and promises that "your Father who sees in secret will reward you" (See Matt. 6:1–6).

Another key element to examine is our *omissions*. Rather than look solely at what we *have done*, we ought to also consider what we *haven't done*—the opportunities wasted, time squandered in front of the television, help we *didn't give* those in need. Since our Christian mission is to go out and transform the world with the message of the gospel and the practice of Christian love, we would be remiss if our days were to pass by without actively engaging in this mission. Maybe I haven't done anything wrong—*seriously* wrong, anyway—but *how much have I contributed to the mission of Christ and his Church? How have I witnessed to my faith? How much time have I devoted to others' needs rather than my own?*

INVOKE GOD'S MERCY

After considering the negative and positive points of our response to God's grace, we should *sincerely ask pardon for our faults* and thank God for the gift of his patience and forgiveness. We tell Christ we are sorry, confident in his mercy and love for us. The experience of his forgiveness helps us to be more lenient with other people, and to forgive them in turn. The person who is truly aware of how much he has been forgiven can never be hard-hearted or severe with others.

PURPOSE OF AMENDMENT

The fifth step in the conscience exam is traditionally called the *firm purpose of amendment*. This means that, after humbly recognizing where we have departed from God's will, we resolve never to do so again. This doesn't mean that we will never sin again. God is aware of our weakness and knows that we will fall. But a purpose of amendment reflects a serious intention to avoid sin, and whatever leads us to sin. It would be silly to tell God we are sorry, all the while intending to do the same thing all over again. We try to rectify our intentions, and to sincerely endeavor to do the right thing in the future, with God's help.

CONCRETE RESOLUTION

A final step in our examination of conscience entails the formulation of a *concrete resolution* as fruit of the exam. If we are examining our consciences in the evening, we can make a specific resolution for the next day. Maybe we need to be especially kind to a coworker who is getting on our nerves. Maybe we need to devote more time to prayer. Maybe we should better avoid occasions of sin, like wasting time surfing on the Internet. Whatever our area of work, we should formulate a practical resolution that will help us grow in our faithfulness to God, invoking his grace to continue working with constancy and determination.

QUALITIES OF A GOOD EXAMINATION

Along with a specific methodology or dynamic, there are certain essential qualities that mark a good examination. It isn't enough to run through the paces. Since the conscience exam is a prayer, it must be done with the right attitude and intentions in order to bear the spiritual fruit we are looking for. The following eight points describe some of the characteristics of a good exam.

1. TOTAL SINCERITY WITH YOURSELF AND WITH GOD

One of the big advantages of taking time to recall that we are in God's presence is that we begin with an attitude of *honesty*. We stand in the presence of the One who knows us perfectly and whom we cannot deceive. We can *often* deceive other people, *sometimes* deceive ourselves, but we *never* deceive God. Even though it sometimes hurts to look at ourselves as we really are, this is the only way to get to the truth. As long as we believe in God's power to transform us and trust in his merciful love, we won't be afraid to dig deep, to acknowledge the whole truth about ourselves. This is what Jesus meant by "com[ing] into the light" (see John 3:20–21).

Radical sincerity requires radical humility. We have to be willing to admit we have failed, that we are imperfect and in need of forgiveness. The conscience exam is not an exercise in self-justification or rationalizing our mistakes. We need to recognize our faults as they are, without excusing ourselves or minimizing personal responsibility. (*I was crabby and uncharitable, but only because my sister is unbearable and provoked me, and besides I didn't sleep well last night. . . .*) The conscience exam is not for examining others' faults, but our own freely chosen behavior. Sincerity is essential.

In practice, how can we do this? One good rule of thumb is to keep nothing hidden. We need to look at our failings and, with God's help, try to understand what moves us to act the way we do. It is often what we don't want to examine that we have the greatest need of examining. A second good rule is to call a spade a spade. For example, if we have been telling lies, we should not call that "stretching the truth" or "exaggerating." A lie is a lie. The same holds true for other faults. Again, the purpose of this is not to beat ourselves up or paint a picture darker than it really is. We simply want to live in the truth so we can please God more each day.

2. Concrete and Specific

A good examination gets down to brass tacks and pays *attention to the little things*. Often failures in conscience stem from looking only at the big picture. *Have I killed anyone today? Have I stolen anything?* Yet this is only a small part of the moral life. Just as a biologist uses a microscope to see what is really going on in an organism, so, too, we need to get down to details. In our moral lives we often become better or worse little by little, and not all at once through big decisions. Remember Jesus' important teaching: "Whoever is faithful in a very little is faithful also in much; and whoever is dishonest in a very little is dishonest also in much" (Luke 16:10). Our little faults—cutting moral corners—lead to a breakdown of conscience and open the door to bigger sins.

Therefore, rather than hanging at the level of generalities (*I guess I'm doing okay. My prayer life is all right. I should be more thoughtful.*), a good exam deals with *details* of thoughts, words, works, and omissions. If I realize that I am not considerate of other people, I should ask myself *when* and *with whom* this is expressed. Maybe our faults occur especially with one or two other people. Maybe there are specific situations we should be avoiding.

The more concrete and specific the exam, the more we get to know ourselves, and the more effective our work will be to uproot these faults.

Moreover, a concrete exam moves beyond what we *intended* and focuses on what we actually *did* or *didn't do*. In other words, if I often offend other people, it isn't enough to say that I didn't want to hurt anyone; I need to recognize that my actions *do* offend others, and figure out how best to combat this fault. A poem by Nixon Waterman beautifully expresses this attitude of getting down to specifics:

What Have We Done Today?

We shall do much in the years to come,
But what have we done today?
We shall give our gold in a pricely sum,
But what did we give today?
We shall lift the heart and dry the tear,
We shall plant a hope in the place of fear,
We shall speak the words of love and cheer,
But what did we speak today?

We shall be so kind in the after while,
But have we been today?
We shall bring to each lonely life a smile,
But what have we brought today?
We shall give to truth a grander birth,
And to steadfast faith a deeper worth,
We shall feed the hungering souls of earth,
But whom have we fed today?

We shall reap such joys in the by and by,
But what have we sown today?
We shall build us mansions in the sky,
But what have we built today?
'Tis sweet in the idle dreams to bask;
But here and now, do we our task?
Yet, this is the thing our souls must ask,
What have we done today?

3. DEEP

A good examination of conscience is not only specific; it is also *deep*. It plunges into the attitudes and dispositions that underlie our specific actions. Along with seeing what we are doing, we can further examine why we act that way (*Is it vanity? Self-centeredness? Envy because the other person has something I don't? Is it laziness, since I just can't be bothered?*). This exercise may seem unimportant, but in reality it has a huge influence on our spiritual work. A single fault could have different root causes. If we are inconsiderate of others, it could be because we are proud, but it also could be because we are lazy. Depending on the root cause, our plan of attack will be different. In one case, we need to become more humble and less self-centered; in the other case, we need to form our willpower and grow in determination to do the right thing, even when we don't feel like it.

If we examine ourselves in this way, we will often find that seemingly unrelated actions share a common root. A lazy person, for example, may also be irresponsible, inconsiderate, habitually late, neglectful of prayer, and unhelpful. In this case, these particular faults will all be rooted in a deeper tendency: laziness. We don't do many things we should do, because it takes too much effort. This search for root causes allows us to fine-tune our spiritual work. When we grow in the opposing virtue (diligence and a spirit of hard work), we find that we start overcoming many of our related faults at the same time.

4. OBJECTIVE

Like a pendulum, we human beings tend to swing toward opposite extremes. When we are feeling good, everything seems bright and cheery, and we see even our faults in a positive light. When we are down, everything takes on a darker hue, and we feel we are good for nothing, incapable of anything but failure. In reality, we are somewhere in the middle. A good conscience exam aims at *objective* self-knowledge. We seek to know ourselves and our conduct as they really are. Not everything is negative, nor is everything positive. We need to see both the good points and the bad. In other words, we recognize the progress we have made, but also our need for further growth.

The better we know ourselves, the more we will acknowledge our real deficiencies and our need to improve. The funny thing is, the *less* we examine our consciences, the *better* we think we are. That is why the saints often see themselves as big sinners. The closer we draw to the Light, the better we see how far we are from our ideal.

On the other hand, this self-knowledge—when united to confidence in God—doesn't lead to defeatism, but to a healthy distrust of self and greater dependence on his grace. The exam looks not only at our own behavior, but also the action of God in our lives. Seeing how interested he is in us, we realize that we are not alone in our spiritual work. He is pulling for us!

5. CONSTRUCTIVE

A good conscience exam doesn't consist solely in discovering what we have done wrong. It is not a session of nit-picking, faultfinding, or self-bashing. Rather, we examine our consciences in order to *grow in our love for God*. This is the first and most important fruit we seek through this exercise. Even our recognition of our faults has this end in mind. A runner sizes up hurdles in order to leap over them, not to get depressed by them. We examine our conduct in order to *improve* it and to please God better.

If our self-examination gets stuck at the level of our faults, we easily fall into discouragement. Our examination should be part of a larger, pro-active process of spiritual work. Discouragement is a terrible enemy of Christians, since it makes us wallow in our misery and self-pity. It drains spiritual energy and keeps us from doing the good we are called to do. This is why the purpose of amendment and practical resolution are so important. When we fall, we immediately get back up, ask for God's pardon, and set to work. Failure and occasional defeat are a part of every life, and we cannot let them keep us down. God doesn't want it. With renewed hope in him, we are called to keep building.

6. TRUE COMPUNCTION

Love brings with it *sorrow* for our sins and faults. Since self-examination is a prayer, and an exercise of love for God, we realize that our sins are not simply infractions against the law. They are a failure to love our Lord as he so richly deserves. God is not just the lawgiver; he is our best friend, our Father, our number-one benefactor, our dear brother who gave his life for us. There is a difference between offending a person on the street and offending your father or mother. In the same way, our offenses against God reflect ingratitude toward the One who loves us most.

Remember the poignant words of the psalmist, which represent Jesus' cry to each one of us:

> It is not enemies who taunt me—
>   I could bear that;
> it is not adversaries who deal insolently with me—
>   I could hide from them.
> But it is you, my equal,
>   my companion, my familiar friend,
> with whom I kept pleasant company;
>   we walked in the house of God with the throng.
> (Psalm 55:12–14)

Sometimes sorrow for sin comes spontaneously. We truly regret offending God and feel terrible about hurting him. Remember that when Saint Peter denied Jesus three times, he went out into the night and "wept bitterly" (Matt. 26:75). He loved Jesus so much that his sin weighed heavily on his soul. Other times, however, though we *recognize* we have done wrong, we *feel* nothing. Here we must beg God for the gift of compunction—a deep sorrow for our sins. It is a blessing when our feelings correspond to the truth of what we have done.

Not all compunction is *true* compunction, however. Sometimes we confuse *wounded self-love* for godly sorrow. We feel bad for our mistakes, not because we have been unfaithful to God, but because we haven't lived up to our own expectations. We thought we were better than that, and our failure humiliates us. Our pride chastises us for our weakness. There is a self-centered sorrow, just as there is a God-centered sorrow. Even in our sorrow, then, we need purity of intention. We need to be sorry for the right reasons: because God deserves better and we have let him down.

Sorrow for wrongdoing leads to a sincere rejection of sin and a firm resolve to work harder. Like other emotions, sorrow can serve as a positive motivating force to encourage us to act as we should. Though conscience operates at the level of knowledge, rather than emotion, the feelings that often accompany it can be very helpful in our spiritual work. The more we feel remorse for offending our Lord, the harder we will try to love him better and to avoid whatever displeases him.

7. TRUSTING IN GOD

Knowledge of our sinfulness and spiritual poverty could easily lead to despair, unless accompanied by a deep confidence in God. We need to remind ourselves that God's greatness is infinitely greater than our misery. Hope is an important Christian virtue that leads us to see that with God *all things* are possible. What was the main difference between Judas and Peter? Both betrayed our Lord. Both were sorry for what they had done. Yet Peter, after weeping for his sins, returned to Jesus, trusting in his mercy and love. Judas, on the other hand, thought that his sin was too great to be forgiven and went and hanged himself. We all sin, and Christ offers us his forgiveness without limits or conditions.

This confidence in God's mercy and the power of his grace helps us persevere in our good proposals despite little visible progress. We do not become saints overnight. The Christian life entails many falls and the willingness to get up and start all over again. Love keeps pushing. It doesn't give up after one or two setbacks. And again, this is possible only when we have great confidence in God's merciful love for us.

This confidence stems from the *experience of God's mercy.* When we have tasted the forgiveness he offers us, we learn to trust in him more and more. We even become ambassadors of his mercy, teaching others to trust in him as well. To trust in God means realizing that it's not all about us. We need him, and he is worthy of our confidence. Even though we do not merit his grace, he gives it to us in abundance and refuses nothing to the person who places his whole trust in God.

8. CHRIST-CENTERED

A good conscience exam, finally, takes as its point of reference our transformation into Christ. We do not evaluate our conduct according to some abstract ethical system, but according to our resemblance to Christ. Our moral work aims at becoming more and more like Jesus, and our self-examination adopts the same touchstone. Therefore we do not simply reflect on whether we are doing right or wrong, but on whether or not we are "putting on Christ" and growing in our likeness to him.

A Christian doesn't adopt Jesus as a model, for instance, with the aim of growing more charitable; rather, he aims at growing more charitable in order to resemble Christ more. Our real goal is to become like Jesus, not to become abstractly good. In *Mere Christianity*, C. S. Lewis expressed this concept with his characteristic eloquence:

> There are lots of things which your conscience might not call definitely wrong (specially things in your mind) but which you will see at once you cannot go on doing if you are seriously trying to be like Christ. For you are no longer thinking simply about right or wrong; you are trying to catch the good infection from a Person. It is more like painting a portrait than like obeying a set of rules. And the odd thing is that while in one way it is much harder than keeping rules, in another way it is far easier.

Like a precision tool, our consciences need to be whetted and exercised. Using our consciences keeps them supple and in good working order. For centuries Christians have recognized the benefits of examining their consciences as a way to follow Christ more closely. Saint Paul wrote to the Corinthians:

> Examine yourselves to see whether you are living in the faith. Test yourselves. Do you not realize that Jesus Christ is in you?—unless, indeed, you fail to meet the test! I hope you will find out that we have not failed. But we pray to God that you may not do anything wrong—not that we may appear to have met the test, but that you may do what is right, though we may seem to have failed. (2 Corinthians 13:5–7)

We show our appreciation for the great gift of conscience when we use it well. Forming it, examining it, applying it in our daily lives, and heeding it are the ways we become the Christians that God calls us to be.

Part of being Christlike is knowing where our allegiance lies and taking responsibility for our own actions. Jesus was true to his Father at all times, regardless of the sometimes painful consequences. To be true followers of his, we need the same moral clarity. Sometimes our responsibilities to God and moral truth conflict with our obedience to state laws or reigning social norms. In these cases, conscience is put to the test. Let's look more closely at the much debated topic of conscientious objection.

Questions for Study and Discussion

1. What is an examination of conscience, and what role does it play in a Christian's moral and spiritual life? Why is it important?
2. Why do people have such a tough time examining their consciences? How can this natural resistance be overcome?
3. What are some of the fruits of examining one's conscience?
4. What are the basic dynamics and content of a conscience exam? How important are structure and method here?
5. What are some qualities of a good conscience exam? What are some of the pitfalls to watch out for?
6. What is the difference between wounded self-love and godly sorrow?

Questions for Personal Reflection

1. How often do you examine your conscience? Does this exercise help you to love God more and to be a better Christian?
2. How well do you know yourself, including your deeper motivations and intentions? Does conscience examination help here?
3. What areas of your moral and spiritual life merit closer examination and attention?

14

YOUR RIGHT TO SAY NO

Conscientious Objection and Personal Responsibility

Morality is all about accountability. Since we are free, we are ultimately responsible for our own choices. Personal accountability doesn't disappear when other people are around. When others invite or encourage us to do wrong, it is still we who say yes or no. Even in the case when legitimate authority *commands* us to do evil, the final accountability for our choices rests firmly in our hands.

Nowhere was the question of personal accountability brought out more forcefully than in the Nuremberg War Trials. There Wilhelm Keitel and other members of the S.S. offered the celebrated excuse "I was only following orders" for war crimes, including arranging the transportation of Jews and others to the concentration camps like Auschwitz and Dachau. The Nuremberg Trials helped discredit this rationale as a justification for evil action, and it is now commonly accepted that we are responsible for our own actions even when we are obeying our superiors.

In the U.S. military, soldiers are strictly bound to obey a *lawful* order, but not any order whatsoever. The Vietnam War presented the United States military courts with more cases of the "I was only following orders" defense than any previous conflict. The verdicts for these cases reaffirmed that obeying manifestly illegal orders is not a viable defense from criminal prosecution. In *United States v. Keenan*, for example, Keenan was declared guilty of murder after he followed an order to shoot and kill an elderly

Vietnamese citizen. The Court of Military Appeals held that "the justification for acts done pursuant to orders does not exist if the order was of
such a nature that a man of ordinary sense and understanding would know
it to be illegal."

This principle was upheld once again more recently in the case of
the Abu Ghraib prison abuse. In his trial defense, Charles Graner Jr., the
suspected ringleader of the abuse, said that in mistreating and sexually
humiliating detainees, he had only been following orders. This defense
carried no water. A military panel, consisting of four officers and six enlisted soldiers, convicted Graner on January 15, 2005, of five charges:
conspiracy, dereliction of duty, maltreatment of detainees, assault, and
committing indecent acts. In addition to a ten-year prison sentence,
Graner was reduced to private and dishonorably discharged.

One of the twentieth century's most famous and controversial pieces
of psychological research involved the willingness of persons to inflict
pain on others, simply on the orders of an academic authority figure. In
the early 1960s, Yale social psychologist Stanley Milgram, PhD, conducted
an experiment to analyze the conflict between obedience to authority
and personal conscience ("Behavioral study of obedience," 1963).

Dressed in a white coat, the experimenter told the subject that the exercise had been set up to study the effects of punishment on learning. The
subject's job was to teach a volunteer learner in an adjacent room to
memorize a list of word-pairs. Every time the learner made an error, the
teacher-subject was to punish the learner by administering to him increasingly severe electric shocks by pressing levers on a shock machine.
There were thirty levers whose shock values ranged from a low of fifteen
volts to the maximum of 450 volts. In actuality, no electric shock was involved. The "learner" was an actor who only pretended to receive them,
but the subject did not know this. Despite the learner's increasingly ago-
nized screams and pleas to stop, a majority of subjects (more than 60 percent) obeyed the experimenter's commands to continue and ended up
giving the maximum "shock" of 450 volts. Not one subject stopped before reaching 300 volts. At times, the worried "teachers" questioned the
experimenter, asking who was responsible for any harmful effects resulting from shocking the learner at such a high level. The experimenter as-
sured them that he assumed full responsibility, and the teachers continued

shocking, even though some were obviously extremely uncomfortable in doing so.

I first learned of this experiment in a college psychology class in 1981. It turns out that it is one of the staples of psychology courses everywhere, as well as providing scientific fodder to the movement to "question authority" popularized in the 1960s and 1970s. In his conclusions, Milgram argued that once people have accepted the right of an authority to direct their actions, they relinquish responsibility to him or her and allow that person to define for them what is right or wrong.

Though these examples do not exempt us from our obligation to obey legitimate authority, they do underscore the personal nature of morality. In the end, each of us must answer to God for his or her own actions. The fact that we were told to do so, or that everyone else was doing it, simply won't matter.

What Is Conscientious Objection?

Since we are obliged to obey God's law and moral truth before any human authority, we occasionally find ourselves in the uncomfortable situation of having to say no to authority. Whenever pressure is exerted on a person to behave in a certain way, and the person refuses to comply on the grounds that to do so would be morally wrong, we call this *conscientious objection*. Conscientious objection was made popular during the Vietnam War, when a number of draftees refused to serve, saying that they considered it morally wrong to do so.

Though conscientious objection immediately makes us think of the military, there are many other areas where the same principle comes into play. When an employee is told to offer a bribe to shore up a business deal, or an accountant asked to cook the books, or a government official ordered to spy on a rival, or a prison guard told to beat a prisoner's confession out of him—all of these give grounds for conscientious objection, when a person must simply say, "I cannot do that."

Conscientious objection doesn't occur only when we are told to do something illegal. Whenever there is a conflict between what is legal and what is moral, the possibility of conscientious objection also arises. For example, medical students today may be obliged to learn about and sometimes even participate in abortion procedures. Students who believe that killing an unborn baby, though legal, is always immoral will find themselves in the position of having to disobey the norms and requirements of their school, often to great personal disadvantage, in order to be true to their consciences.

Conscientious objection always refers to *moral* obligation. Let's go back to the classic example of military obligation. Reasons for avoiding military service vary. Some soldiers are married and don't want to leave their wives and children. Others are simply afraid and would prefer not to risk their own skin. There can be as many reasons for not going to war (especially to the front!) as there are soldiers. Yet none of these reasons constitutes *conscientious objection*. Only those who honestly believe that participation in the war would be a *morally evil* thing for them to do can rightly appeal to conscientious objection. Conscientious objection is not the same as disagreeing with one's superior, nor simply a question of ducking out for fear or inconvenience. It must be truly a moral objection, i.e., that one would be committing moral evil if he were to obey this command.

Sometimes conscientious objection takes subtler forms. The pressures exerted on our moral character by the reigning social and cultural trends can be even stronger than officially constituted authorities. How many times are we told to "get with it," that "everybody's doing it," and to "get over our moral hang-ups"? We can even be made to feel guilty for adhering to traditional Christian morality, when it disagrees with a more permissive mentality. Yet if we are obliged in conscience to disobey even legitimate authority when it commands something evil, how much more are we obliged to disregard the authority of political correctness when it contradicts the objective moral law!

BIBLICAL BASIS

The idea that morality comes before legality is a matter of moral common sense, but it is firmly grounded in sacred Scripture as well. You may recall the case recounted in the book of Exodus of the Hebrew midwives who were ordered by Pharaoh to kill every male child born. Because the Egyptians feared a growing Hebrew population, they sought to limit their numbers. The king of Egypt said to the Hebrew midwives, "When you act as midwives to the Hebrew women, and see them on the birthstool, if it is a boy, kill him; but if it is a girl, she shall live" (Exod. 1:16).

The biblical account goes on to say that "the midwives feared God" and for this reason they did not do as the king of Egypt commanded them, but they let the boys live. Since they preferred doing what was right before God, rather than what human authority commanded, God was pleased with them. Thus we read that "God dealt well with the midwives; and the people multiplied and became very strong" (Ex. 1:20).

Jesus taught very simply that we are to render unto Caesar what is Caesar's, and to God what is God's (see Matt 22:21). In other words, the civil authorities have legitimate claims on our loyalties and our obedience. We are to pay taxes, respect laws, and work for the common good. But God also has his rights over us. He, too, has legitimate claims on our obedience to his moral law, and his claims are superior to those of any human authority.

From a Christian perspective, in fact, the key criterion for obedience concerns not the *legality* of the act enjoined, but its *morality*. No one should ever do what he knows to be immoral, even if it is legal. An emblematic case involved Saint Peter and his run-in with the Jewish authorities for continuing to witness to Jesus' death and resurrection. Peter had been ordered not to preach about Jesus, but he continued to do so. Therefore the high priest had the temple guard bring Peter before him and said: "We gave you strict orders not to teach in this name, yet here you have filled Jerusalem with your teaching and you are determined to bring this man's blood on us." To this Peter and the apostles replied, "We must obey God rather than any human authority" (Acts 5:28–29).

In the end, our first allegiance must be to God himself as our Creator and Lord. We obey civil law because it is the moral thing to do and is pleasing to God. When civil law no longer upholds morality but enters into conflict with God's will, it loses its authority. We must obey God rather than men.

EXAMPLE OF THE MARTYRS

This conviction has been a mainstay of Christianity from the very beginning. In the early centuries, the Roman Empire sought an absolute loyalty from its subjects that sometimes created a conflict of conscience for Christians. Under certain regimes, divine worship was demanded for the reigning emperor, which for Christians meant idolatry. Christians were perfectly willing to "render unto Caesar what is Caesar's" but unwilling to give to Caesar what belonged to God alone. Sometimes emperors or local governors went even further, requiring an explicit renunciation of the Christian faith. This tension sometimes went so far as to require the supreme sacrifice of martyrdom itself.

A sterling example of this is the martyrdom of Polycarp, the eighty-six-year-old bishop of Smyrna (today known as Izmir). Polycarp had been a disciple of Saint John the Apostle and was martyred in AD 155 during the reign of the Roman emperor Antoninus Pius. At the time Christianity was illegal, and hatred of Christians, especially in the Roman provinces, was widespread. Fortunately we possess a good eyewitness record of Polycarp's martyrdom, since the story was circulated for the edification of the faithful.

Having been found out as a Christian, Polycarp was conveyed to the stadium for execution. On the way, the head of police sought to persuade him, saying, "What harm is there in saying 'Lord Caesar' and in offering sacrifice?" To this Polycarp was silent, but when they continued to urge him, he simply said, "I shall not do as you advise me."

Polycarp was brought to the stadium before the proconsul of Asia, who tried to convince him to deny Christ, saying, "Respect your age," and "Swear by the genius of Caesar, repent, say: 'Away with the Atheists'" (meaning the Christians). Finally the proconsul said to him: "Take the oath and I let you go, revile Christ." In response, Polycarp offered his now-famous testimony, "For eighty and six years have I been his servant, and he has done me no wrong, and how can I blaspheme my King who saved me?"

Soon after, Polycarp continued, "*I am a Christian*. And if you wish to learn the doctrine of Christianity fix a day and listen." On seeing that neither persuasion nor threats had any effect on Polycarp's resolve, the proconsul handed him over to be burned alive on a pyre.[1]

Another such martyr was Sir Thomas More. More, chancellor of England from 1529 to 1532, was beheaded by his "good friend" King Henry VIII for refusing to take an oath recognizing Henry as head of the church in England. It was a question of conscience. Though he was afraid of dying, Thomas More couldn't bring himself to swear to something he knew not to be true. In 1960 the British playwright Robert Bolt wrote the brilliant drama *A Man for All Seasons*, subsequently made into a film that won the Oscar for Best Picture in 1966. Bolt—himself a non-Christian—was so captivated by Thomas More's strength of character that he made him the object of his study and his art. "What first attracted me," Bolt wrote, "was a person who could not be accused of any incapacity for life, who indeed seized life in great variety and greedy quantities, who nevertheless found something in himself without which life was valueless and, when that was denied him, was able to grasp his death." [2]

Thomas More is rightly considered the patron saint of lawyers and statesmen. He provides a moving example of fidelity to truth and allegiance to God's law over human pressures, even at the cost of one's own life. How much better the world would be today if we had more politicians of this integrity and moral caliber, truer to their moral convictions than to volatile popular opinion!

CONSCIENTIOUS OBJECTION

Having looked at the nature of conscientious objection, its grounding in Scripture, and its exemplification in the lives of Christian heroes, we are prepared to dissect it into its component parts. A series of principles, or theses, combine to set the groundwork for conscientious objection. The following ten theses can help us better understand why conscientious objection is a moral imperative for people of goodwill.

TEN THESES

1. One must always obey the certain judgment of conscience, regardless of the consequences. This thesis seems obvious, especially in the light of the preceding chapters, but here we must insist on the absoluteness of this principle, even when the personal consequences are painful. It is never morally acceptable to do wrong in order to avoid unpleasant fallout. As we have seen, this has led many in the past even to the shedding of blood, in order to be true to their moral and religious convictions.

In the gospel Jesus asks: "What will it profit a man to gain the whole world, and lose his own soul?" (Mark 8:36 NKJV). In the end, popularity fades, riches wear out, and even our lives on earth come to an end. God alone will judge us. He will judge us on our adherence to the truth and our steadfastness in following his Son Jesus, with all that that entails. Conscience testifies to God's truth and obliges us to act uprightly, no matter what the consequences.

Standing up for moral truth may seem rosy at a distance, but it often entails heart-wrenching decisions. Sometimes it means the loss of good friends, a prestigious position, the possibility of career advancement, or even one's livelihood. In these cases, with so much at stake, one is obliged to refuse to collaborate only when doing so would clearly mean infidelity to Christ and the moral law. Unfortunately these cases do present themselves, and much courage is needed to be faithful to conscience!

2. You are always responsible for your own actions, even when ordered by another. Freedom, as we have seen, implies responsibility for one's actions. Unless we are drugged or brainwashed, our personal choices are imputed to us and we are accountable for our actions. This includes the *choice* to obey an order. We may not abandon our critical moral reasoning just because we have been told to do something. Before God, all representatives of authority will have to render an account for the orders they have given, but we will also have to render an account for our free choice to obey or disobey.

Remember the Genesis story of the first sin of mankind, when Adam and Eve tried to pass the buck and shirk their own moral responsibility (Gen. 3:11–19). When God asks Adam why he ate of the forbidden fruit, Adam replies that it was the woman's fault—she gave it to him. When God turns to the woman to question her, she blames the serpent who tricked her into eating it. God does indeed punish the serpent, but he doesn't let Adam and Eve off the hook, either. He holds them responsible for their own actions.

True, we do not always know beforehand all the consequences of our actions, and we are responsible only for those that can reasonably be foreseen. What remains clear is that we, and no one else, will be held accountable for our choices. We are responsible for what we know, and for what we do.

3. One must always obey legitimate authority, unless one is commanded to do moral evil. We are called to obey civil laws and those in positions of authority, not only because of what will happen to us if we don't, but because it is the right thing to do. Here Saint Paul's words are exceptionally clear: "Let every person be subject to the governing authorities; for there is no authority except from God, and those authorities that exist have been instituted by God. Therefore whoever resists authority resists what God has appointed, and those who resist will incur judgment" (Rom. 13:1–2). He later adds that we should do so, not out of fear of punishment, "but also because of conscience" (Rom. 13:5).

The obedience asked of a Christian extends to all legitimate authority, not just civil magistrates. Therefore Saint Peter could write, "For the Lord's sake accept the authority of every human institution, whether of the emperor as supreme, or of governors, as sent by him to punish those who do wrong and to praise those who do right" (1 Pet. 2:13–14). Children should obey their parents, employees should obey their supervisors, and soldiers their superiors. Yet this obedience extends only to morally good actions. Whenever we are ordered to do something evil, we have a moral obligation to resist.

Legitimate authority deserves the benefit of the doubt. We should not systematically question every disposition of our superiors or ask for a point-by-point justification for everything asked of us. Sometimes authority will benefit our personal interests; other times it will make heavy demands on us—presumably for the sake of the common good. It is when we know or suspect that what is being asked of us is unethical that we have the moral obligation to question it or, in certain cases, to refuse to obey.

4. Legality is not morality. Western society increasingly tends to conflate the moral and legal realms, as if morality and legality were the same thing. From this perspective, the only moral virtue is being "law-abiding." As long as you break no laws, you are okay. How many times have you heard the excuse for a given behavior, "It's not against the law!"

Yet while both the civil law and the moral law are important, they are not the same thing. Civil laws require only an external conformity to a legal code, while morality encompasses the whole sphere of free human action, and extends to deeds, words, omissions, and even thoughts. Many moral obligations lie outside the purview of the law but oblige in conscience nonetheless. As theologian John Courtney Murray wrote in his celebrated work *We Hold These Truths*:

> It is not the function of the legislator to forbid everything the moral law forbids, or to enjoin everything the moral law enjoins. The moral law governs the entire order of human conduct, personal and social; it extends even to motivations and interior acts. Law, on the other hand, looks only to the public order of human society; it touches only external acts, and regards only values that are formally social.

Since civil law exists to promote the common good and secure a just social order, it will naturally draw on basic moral norms or principles and codify some of them into civil laws. It is therefore ridiculous to assert, as some do, that "you can't legislate morality." We legislate morality all the time. Laws prohibiting murder, rape, theft, and extortion all translate fundamental moral principles into a civil code, producing a substantial overlap between legality and morality. Nevertheless, many moral norms will never, and should never, be formulated as civil laws.

5. Civil laws can be just or unjust. Therefore, some behavior permitted by civil law may be immoral. Just as "only following orders" provides no justification for illegal actions, so, too, "Hey, this is legal" provides no justification for committing immoral acts. Legality does not automatically confer morality on our actions. Abortion and euthanasia, for example, are moral crimes that no human law can ever legitimize. They will always be morally evil, no matter what civil laws may exist.

Some legal prescriptions could even oblige in law what is forbidden in conscience. The precedence of morality over legality was brought out forcefully in a comment made by Orthodox rabbi David Kaye, a U.S. Air Force chaplain, in an address delivered at the annual Canterbury Medal Award dinner in 1997. Kaye remarked that during the Holocaust, "no Jew was killed illegally, only immorally."

Civil law is as fallible as the human beings who make it and must be judged on some other basis than its own internal authority. The moral law, in fact, preexists civil society and serves as a yardstick for evaluating the justice of a given rule of law. Universal moral norms allow us to distinguish between "good laws" and "bad laws."

6. Unjust laws do not bind in conscience. Human laws, to be legitimate, may *go beyond* the moral law, but they cannot *contradict* it. For instance, human laws legitimately order society by laying down regulations and restrictions that are not moral in nature. Traffic laws, fiscal legislation, and laws regulating commerce, for example, are not immediately derived from the moral law, but nor do they oppose it. On the other hand, a law that commanded citizens to do evil (such as turning over the names of all Jews to the public authorities) would be no law at all, and citizens would be obliged to disobey it.

Laws and decrees enacted in contravention of the moral order, and hence of the divine will, can have no binding force in conscience. In fact, we may even be morally bound to disobey them. Therefore Saint Thomas Aquinas could write that "human law is law inasmuch as it is in conformity with right reason and thus derives from the eternal law. But when a law is contrary to reason, it is called an unjust law; but in this case it ceases to be a law and becomes instead an act of violence" (*Summa Theologiae*).

7. The fact that a law is democratically passed doesn't mean it is morally right. Democratically determined legislation bears no guarantee of moral infallibility any more than other edicts or decrees. It must be judged according to its conformity to the objective moral law. Nor does the acceptance of a given behavior by the majority of persons confer moral goodness. Consensus has never been a good measure of morality. As Yahweh commanded the Israelites: "You shall not follow a majority in wrongdoing" (Exod. 23:2).

We know from historical experience, after all, that the majority can be mistaken as easily as an individual. Remember, for instance, that Adolf Hitler himself was elected democratically. Slavery, too, was embraced by a majority for many years, and abolitionists—whom we now look upon as heroes—were seen as fanatics at the time. Future generations will no doubt look back upon our own and regard certain "legal" practices like abortion and euthanasia as vestiges of a darker age and wonder incredulously how a supposedly "enlightened" society could have permitted such unspeakable barbarities. The majority has no monopoly on truth, nor guarantee of infallibility.

As Pope John Paul once wrote: "Everyone's conscience rightly rejects those crimes against humanity of which our century has had such sad experience. But would these crimes cease to be crimes if, instead of being committed by unscrupulous tyrants, they were legitimated by popular consensus?" (*Evangelium Vitae* 70).

8. Everyone has the obligation to be informed about morality, especially in his or her particular field of work. That means that parents have a special obligation to form their consciences in the area of education, doctors in the area of medical ethics, and politicians in the area of political morality. Since we are personally responsible for our moral choices, we are bound to know the demands of moral truth as they apply to our situation.

In a democratic state, the temptation to abdicate one's personal conscience can be even greater than in a dictatorship. In the case of a dictatorship, citizens naturally distrust and despise the orders of the ruling regime, and cultivate a critical attitude. In the case of a democracy, however, we naturally assume that laws and mores embraced by the majority bear some degree of reasonableness. This well-founded trust can, unfortunately, lead us to surrender our personal responsibility to act always in a moral way.

The gentle pressure of a democratically instated rule of law can even make us doubt our own moral convictions when they conflict with those of the majority. This leads many to hold, at least in practice, that in carrying out one's duties, the only moral criterion should be what is laid down by the law itself. Individual responsibility is thus turned over to the civil law, with a renouncing of personal conscience, at least in the public sphere. Thus we easily fall back on public consensus as an excuse for our lack of critical moral judgment: *If everyone does it, it must be okay.* Unfortunately— as we have seen—this isn't the case.

9. It is morally reprehensible to force a person to act against moral conscience. A corollary to the duty to act in conscience is the immorality of forcing another to act *against* his conscience. It is paramount to obliging him to sin. Conscience is the most intimate core of a person, where he is alone with God, and merits the most profound respect. Saint Paul taught that we should respect the dignity of others' consciences, even when we believe them to be mistaken. He uses the example of those who still believe that food sacrificed to idols is somehow morally unclean and should not be eaten. He tells the Christians of Corinth that they should avoid eating this food (even though it isn't really morally unclean), because it could scandalize those whose consciences are weak (see 1 Cor. 8:7–13).

This respect for conscience has limits, of course. First, we can and must help others to reach the truth. If a friend has a poorly formed conscience, we cannot stand idly by and allow him to damage himself and others but must charitably try to persuade him of the truth. We cannot force him, but must appeal to reason and faith. Second, if a person's actions are harmful for the community, he must be stopped, even though he appeals to conscience. Wrongdoing cannot be justified in the name of personal conscience, and the public authority has the responsibility of insuring that the actions of individuals do not disturb the social order. Society has the right and the duty to protect itself against the abuses that can occur in the name of conscience and under the pretext of freedom.

10. Public authorities should make allowance for conscientious objection. Since conscience is sacred, and people should not be made to act against it, public authorities should accommodate people's religious and moral convictions. Whenever possible, exemptions should be written into the law to permit citizens to act in accord with their moral and religious beliefs. Nor should people be penalized for being faithful to their convictions. A good government will not try to impose religious truth, but nor should it stifle religious practice or make it difficult for people to fulfill their religious and moral obligations.

Going back to our example of pacifism, if a citizen is convinced that to serve in the military as a soldier would be morally wrong, he should be given the opportunity to serve his country in some other way, for a corresponding length of time. Doctors and nurses should not be obliged to perform abortions or euthanasia and should not be made to suffer for this moral choice. Pharmacists should not be obliged to distribute death-dealing drugs, even if these drugs are legal. A good legal system will try to promote an ethical citizenry and will support and encourage fidelity to conscience.

These reflections are not just hypothetical. On June 20, 2005, the American Medical Association approved a measure that would force pharmacists to fill prescriptions for all legal drugs, even if filling those prescriptions violated their consciences. This was in response to lawsuits by three Illinois pharmacists to stop Governor Rod Blagojevich's executive order mandating pharmacists to dispense all legal drugs. The lawsuit claims the governor's order violated state law, which allowed health professionals to opt out of acts they consider morally offensive.[3] These issues were brought to the fore by the abortifacient Plan B (the "morning after" pill), also euphemistically known as "emergency contraception." A real war is going on, and men and women of goodwill need to continually step forward to insist that laws must accommodate people's right to freedom of conscience.

These ten theses encapsulate the moral principles involved in conscientious objection. In the end, we can summarize them still further: No matter what, do the right thing! No matter who tells you otherwise, no matter what the consequences may be, no matter how uphill the road may seem, do the right thing!

Still, doing the right thing isn't always so easy. In today's society, moral decision making seems to get harder and harder. We can do so many things that were impossible just a generation ago. From embryonic stem cell research to economic speculation in the futures market, many of today's moral questions are quite complex. How can we best face moral dilemmas? What guidelines do we have at our disposal for more complex moral problem solving? Let's look more closely at these important questions.

Questions for Study and Discussion
1. What is conscientious objection? What are some historical examples that exemplify this principle?
2. What does the Bible tell us about conscientious objection? Give some specific examples.
3. What is the difference between conscientious objection and mere cowardice or personal convenience?
4. How do the martyrs exemplify true conscientious objection? Give some concrete examples.
5. If a Christian should always obey legitimate authority, how can we justify disobedience? How can we know when we must disobey?
6. In today's society, where do Christians most often face situations where they may be called to exercise conscientious objection?

Questions for Personal Reflection

1. Are you ever asked to do things that you know are immoral? How do you respond?

2. How much influence does peer pressure exert on you? Do you ever compromise your principles out of fear of what others may think or say?

3. Are you proud to be a Christian or do you sometimes find it embarrassing? Are you willing to suffer for Christ and for his name?

15

DIFFICULT CHOICES

Moral Dilemmas and How to Resolve Them

What would you do if you were on a sinking ship with eleven people, and the only available lifeboat could hold just ten? Whom would you leave out—the elderly brain surgeon, the young mother, the ten-year-old boy? We have all heard these hypothetical ethical dilemmas put forward to stump students and supposedly teach them to reason ethically. Many modern methods of teaching ethics involve placing students in a moral bind and helping them work through it. The moral dilemma—an extreme situation that seems to have no good ethical solution—serves as a paradigm for making choices. Students are asked to consider the many conflicting values that come into play and to defend various ways of reaching a morally acceptable solution.

Unfortunately, this common method suffers from a fatal flaw from which many students of ethics never recover: the inclination to see dilemmas as the moral *norm*, rather than the *exception*. Just as in jurisprudence "hard cases make bad law," so, too, in ethics moral dilemmas make bad ethical models. The fundamental problem with dilemma-based morality is that it leads one to suppose that making moral decisions regularly entails a Herculean effort at moral calculation, involving countless variables, which rarely, if ever, yields an ethically certain outcome. Morality begins to look like such a complicated affair that, in the end, one is tempted to throw up one's hands and exclaim, "There is no right or wrong answer! It's anybody's call!"

Compare this, for a moment, with your own experience. How often each day do you find yourself in situations where you simply *don't know* what the best course of action is? How many times a day do you scratch your head wondering what in the world God wants you to do? Granted, these occasions *do* exist, and we have all experienced them, but they are far from the norm. Often, too, we may scratch our heads wondering what in the world *God* is doing in our lives, or *why* he does what he does, but we usually know *what* he wants from *us*, at least in the present moment.

Here we could distinguish two types of moral dilemmas. Each is resolved in a very different way. The most common moral dilemma occurs when the voice of conscience is clear. We know what we ought to do, but it demands sacrifice. We really don't want to do it. We waver not at the level of *conscience* (knowing what we *should* do), but at the level of *choice* (deciding what we *will* do). Will we take the easier way out, avoiding a mountain of problems by renouncing our consciences, or will we do the right thing, no matter what the consequences may be? Sometimes by telling a lie—to take one example—we can get out of many difficulties, but at the cost of moral compromise.

This first sort of moral dilemma is resolved through the formation of virtue and the humble petition of God's grace. In its original sense, *virtue* means *strength*. It means the ability to do the right thing even when it's difficult. This demands tremendous courage and moral mettle. The more we build up the habit of doing good, the easier it becomes, since we ourselves are morally stronger. But even the strongest Christian needs God's grace. Prayer and the sacraments give us access to God's omnipotence and reinforce us in our weakness. Some of the most extraordinary examples of moral heroism often come from the weakest among us, even mere children. God chooses the weak and gives them his own strength (see 1 Cor. 1:27–29; 2 Cor. 12:9–10).

A second type of moral dilemma occurs when conscience offers insufficient light to guide us. We sincerely want to do the right thing but cannot figure out what it is. Like a navy captain, we desperately want to guide our craft surely through the night, avoiding shoals and shipwreck, yet sometimes the fog becomes so thick that we simply cannot see where we are going. For all our caution and goodwill, we still waver in our decision because we do not *know* what to do. This is a doubt of conscience or moral dilemma in the true sense. Its resolution involves more than courage and virtue—it requires education and counsel.

It probably goes without saying, but this second type of moral dilemma concerns those who are sincerely committed to doing the right thing, no matter what. A person who is willing to compromise with conscience, cut ethical corners, and make moral "deals" will never have a true moral dilemma (except maybe of how far he is willing to bend!).

AGONIZING OVER ETHICS

One solution to moral dilemmas is the *anguish theory*. For some, to be an ethical person means that the most important thing is not to choose well but to agonize over one's decisions. We see this all the time in the newspapers. "It's the hardest thing I've ever done," Annette Faulkner said of her decision to "interrupt," in her own words, a pregnancy. "Twelve years on, there is not one day that I don't think about it." Stories of heart-wrenching and ultimately immoral choices, like this one described in the July 4, 2004, issue of Australia's *Sun-Herald*, increasingly find their way into leading newspapers. The more one reads these stories, the more a common thread emerges: whatever you do, no matter how terrible, it's okay as long as you had to anguish over the decision.

The May 13, 2007, issue of the *New York Times* delivers a similar line. "For many women and their partners, the decision to terminate a pregnancy after a prenatal diagnosis of a serious genetic defect can be harrowing, often coming after a painful assessment of their own emotional and financial resources." Another article in the *New York Times* (July 14, 2004) narrated the agonizing internal struggles of Mrs. Florence Tauber, leading up to her decision to procure a lethal dose of medicine so her husband, Al, could take his life, in accordance with Oregon law. Al had recently been diagnosed with chronic lymphatic leukemia, and doctors estimated that he had six months to live. "It was a very difficult decision for me," Mrs. Tauber relates. "But he made it easier by saying he was giving me the best of himself and not leaving me with ugly memories of him diminishing."

Or take this further example from the May 20, 2004, issue of the same newspaper. The story describes the deliberation of family members of eighty-two-year-old Macie Mull, an Alzheimer's patient, over whether or not to have a feeding tube inserted, since she could no longer eat on her own. The entire article is framed in terms of the intense emotional struggle of those who must make these ethical choices. Reference to numerous conflicting voices and opinions—all of apparently equal moral weight—accentuates the turbulent nature of the decision. Even the title of the piece—"Stolen Minds, Tough Choices"—underscores the vexation of those who must deal with these ethical issues. In this particular case, the family eventually chose to insert the feeding tube, but the article ends with the "crisis of conscience" of geriatrician Douglas Nelson, who filed a position paper with his state medical society affirming that tube feeding was not good medicine for end-stage dementia patients. "My advice is to let the patient die peacefully," Nelson announced.

Intended or not, this style of "unbiased" reporting serves a specific purpose—the shaping of public opinion on key moral issues ranging from prenatal testing and embryonic stem cell research to euthanasia and gay marriage. The message is not that one side is right and the other wrong, though a clear proclivity toward the liberalization of laws and moral codes clearly comes through. Rather, we learn that good arguments can be made for all sides of nearly any case and that, in the final analysis, right and wrong reside within the individual. Proof of "good intentions"— manifested by anguished internal debate—suffices to justify any final outcome.

On reading these accounts, one is gently but firmly pushed toward the conclusion that many moral choices are so hopelessly complex that no right or wrong moral answers exist. If even the experts disagree, who are we to naively propose black-and-white principles to follow? Such moral simplicity is a throwback to medieval obscurantism, one surmises. In the end, provided you have lost enough sleep over your dilemma—the reader concludes—you are morally entitled to elect any option.

I do not wish to casually dismiss these dilemmas as if such moral choices were easy. Nearly all people suffer terribly over the hard decisions they must make during life. A lack of clear alternatives and family support, or the prospect of seemingly unbearable future difficulties, can even make some feel that they have no choice. And, indeed, some situations really do present moral dilemmas that require expert guidance, prayer, and prudence.

Yet from the earliest appearance of ethical theories some twenty-five hundred years ago, praise and blame were given according to the correctness of people's moral choices, and not according to the difficulty they had reaching a decision. The purpose of moral deliberation was to reach a good moral choice. The formation of virtue aimed at making right choices easier and more "natural." The current focus on the interior struggles involved in choosing seems to be a subtle way of justifying what another, less-sophisticated generation might have called "bad choices." Politically incorrect Christians might be tempted to call it a *rationalization of sin*.

As we have seen, many times the difficulty we experience in making moral choices doesn't proceed from the complexity of the factors involved, but rather from the sacrifices entailed in doing the right thing. In other words, we would rather not. We scrape around for reasons to justify choices that, though immoral, make life easier. It comforts us to know that informed opinions vary all over the map, and that we have taken our choices seriously, even to the point of agonizing over them. But in the end, this anguish-based ethics serves only as a sedative to conscience and to relieve us of our real responsibility to do the right thing.

COOPERATION IN EVIL

All this being said, we must still recognize that authentic moral dilemmas do exist. There are times in our lives when we must make decisions— often big decisions—and the ethical road is anything but clear. In these cases, how do we illuminate conscience to make good ethical judgments? What aids do we have to clear up our doubts?

A particular problem of conscience arises when we are associated professionally or socially with those whose actions are immoral. We ourselves would not willingly choose to engage in their behavior, but the help we provide can make us wonder whether we have an obligation to speak out or to formally disassociate ourselves from their actions. Though this problem appears relatively simple in theory, in practice it can be tremendously difficult to discern.

Let's say, for example, you work at a publishing house that also produces pornography. Are you obliged to protest or even to quit? What about owning stock in a pharmaceutical company that manufactures contraceptives and abortion pills? Or what if the company you work for engages in unethical practices overseas, such as child labor that may even border on slavery? What if you work for a firm that is hiding an important defect in its product? Are you obliged to publicize the truth, or even to resign?

The hypothetical cases are far too many to enumerate. Traditional Christian morality offers guidance in forming one's conscience to be able to decide the moral path to take. Ethicists make a fundamental distinction between *formal cooperation* (where you directly participate in the immoral action or share the intention of those who are doing so) and *material cooperation* (where you play some indirect part in the process, without intending or willing the outcome). Since formal cooperation means making the evil act your own, it is always morally wrong. Material cooperation can sometimes be permitted, when we disassociate ourselves from the evil actions of others and do not directly participate in their wrongdoing. On the other hand, we must also try to avoid scandal and be willing to bear witness to the truth, even when to do so may be personally disadvantageous.

To refuse to take part in committing an injustice is not only a moral duty; it is also a basic human right. No one should be forced to perform an action that is incompatible with human dignity. What is at stake is an essential right, which should be acknowledged and protected by civil law. For example, the opportunity to refuse to take part in the phases of consultation, preparation, and execution of acts against human life should be guaranteed to physicians, health-care personnel, and directors of hospitals, clinics, and convalescent facilities. Those who have recourse to conscientious objection in these cases should be protected both from legal penalties and also from any negative effects on their careers or earning possibilities.

Resolving Moral Dilemmas

In chapter 12 we outlined some important sources of moral knowledge that will help us in evaluating tough moral cases. The first was knowledge of God's Word, including the Ten Commandments, but also encompassing a closer familiarity with Christ and his moral criteria. A second source was the natural law, the unwritten expression of God's eternal law on the human heart. The third guide we discussed—Church teaching—is especially important for the resolution of moral dilemmas. As we saw, the assistance that the teaching Church offers proves particularly precious in these difficult times where moral quandaries abound. Modern society presents many new ethical enigmas unheard of in past generations. Many issues not explicitly dealt with in the Bible—such as assisted suicide, tax fraud, and use of the "morning-after pill"—*have* been considered by the Church. Under the guidance of the Holy Spirit, she offers sound principles for assessing modern moral conundrums.

Along with these sources of moral truth, over the centuries ethicists have also developed a series of helpful insights that can assist us in facing tough moral choices. First, we ought to apply general moral guidelines to our specific case. Let's look at some of these.

REALIZE THE END DOESN'T JUSTIFY THE MEANS

In other words, we cannot do evil to achieve good. A good result doesn't legitimize bad means to get there and it's not enough that "everything worked out in the end." We are responsible not only for the final outcome of our choices, but also for the choices themselves—with all that they entail. The choice to commit murder in order to save other people can never be a good choice, since the act we are committing (murder!) is never justified by a good end. You've probably heard of the television series called *24*. Maybe you saw the episode of Season Three where the hero, Jack Bauer, is told by terrorists that unless he executes his boss, Ryan Chappelle, they will unleash a deadly virus on the world. Unfortunately, Jack makes the morally evil choice of carrying out the terrorists' wishes. Some commentators mistakenly wrote that Jack was "forced" to execute Chappelle, but one can never be forced to do evil. We would all like to avert evil in the world, but we cannot do so by committing evil ourselves. If one innocent person is expendable, then a million people are no less expendable.

PRACTICE THE GOLDEN RULE

A second principle is the *Golden Rule*: do unto others as you would have them do unto you. Many of our moral doubts are resolved when we put ourselves in the other person's place. We naturally seek our best interests, so by putting ourselves in another's shoes, we more readily discern the best way to act. Since we would like to be treated fairly, we should be fair toward others. Since we would like a second chance when we have made a mistake, we should give others the same opportunity. Since we would like to be forgiven when we have apologized for our errors, we should extend the same mercy to others. We spontaneously tend to be softer on ourselves than on others, excusing our own actions and judging others with severity. The Golden Rule helps us to be more objective and impartial in our moral judgments.

CONSIDER IT BETTER TO SUFFER EVIL THAN TO DO EVIL

Socrates makes this remark in the *Gorgias,* when he is arguing against Polus's conception of the good life. A person who cares about his true well-being should be concerned never to do injustice. Being an unjust person, *in itself,* is a bad state to be in. No matter what benefits might result from one's vicious actions, it is always better to choose the virtuous course of action. From Socrates' point of view, doing wrong harms the soul. Since in his view the soul is the most valuable thing there is, it is important to protect the soul from this harm. Suffering evil, in contrast, doesn't harm the soul. It might harm the body. It might be psychologically difficult. But it doesn't harm the most valuable thing. So doing evil is worse than suffering it.

This reminds us of Jesus' rhetorical question, "For what does it profit a man if he gains the whole world and loses or forfeits himself?" (Luke 9:25 RSV). He also counsels his followers to have no fear of those who can kill the body, but cannot kill the soul (Matt. 10:28). No bodily benefit can outweigh the good of our souls, and this is why the physical evil we suffer can never be as bad for us as the moral evil we commit. The martyrs bear a wonderful witness to the lengths to which some will go to live out this principle. Sometimes our faith is costly. Following Jesus means a willingness to follow him to the cross.

USE THE PERSONALIST PRINCIPLE

A fourth general norm is called the *personalist principle*, which states that a person should always be treated as an *end* and never as a mere *means*. This norm has profound consequences for our ethical choices. We cannot simply apply a utilitarian calculus to decide how to act, where persons are involved. According to the utilitarian spirit that pervades our society, the best human actions are those that are most useful to the majority. We judge the worth of our actions by their net results. This doesn't work in the case of persons. According to a Christian worldview, persons are not "useful"—they are good for their own sake. They cannot be evaluated simply by their productivity or the "quality" of their lives. They not only possess value for others, they possess *dignity* in themselves. Persons and nonpersons are fundamentally different, since persons exist for their own sake whereas things exist for the sake of persons. Persons have an intrinsic worth that must always be recognized and respected. *Things* are to be used; *people* are to be loved. In other words, we should never treat the people in our lives as mere instruments for achieving our own purposes.

These general principles should guide our moral judgments, but they may not always be sufficient for determining the correct choice in every case. Where no clear moral norm exists regarding a proposed sort of behavior, we need to turn to the best consensus of theologians and holy persons. We can receive helpful guidance for applying moral norms from people who sincerely love the Lord, are docile to the Church's teaching, and devote themselves to the study of ethics and morality. When the teaching Church offers no clear guidance, this is our best option. Fortunately these cases are few and far between, but they do exist. Here, too, consensus isn't always easy to come by.

Let's take, for instance, the case of the adoption of frozen embryos. Is this a good ethical choice or isn't it? Is it permissible to "adopt" or "rescue" a frozen embryo? Here the Church has yet to make an official pronouncement. Moral theologians—even good ones faithful to Christian tradition—are not in full accord. Some think that embryo adoption is an offense against marriage or even against the unborn child himself. Others are convinced that embryo adoption is a morally commendable act and offers unborn children the one thing they need to survive. In such cases where no consensus exists, Christians must choose the course that seems best to them after listening to the arguments and praying to the Holy Spirit for guidance to know God's will.

On examining specific cases, it becomes evident that there is no magic formula for determining the right thing to do in every possible situation. Again, the vast majority of our moral choices don't involve such intense deliberation. Most are rather simple. As we have seen, the more we strive in every moment to do God's will and to love him with all our hearts, the more spontaneously we reach good moral judgments. Nothing helps moral conscience like the pureheartedness of a soul in love with the Lord.

Conscience will continue to be a matter for debate for decades to come. Some will use conscience as an excuse for doing as they please—claiming that no one has the right to question the decisions they make in conscience. Others will insist that conscience is a vestige of an earlier stage of human evolution, no more useful or reliable than the appendix. For those who sincerely seek a morally good life—Christians and non-Christians alike—conscience will be a precious gift, and the best tool we have to reach sound moral judgments. Christians especially will thank God for this invaluable instrument for knowing God's will and living it out in their daily lives.

Questions for Study and Discussion
1. What is wrong with a dilemma-based morality?
2. Describe the two types of moral dilemmas. What is the difference between the two? Which is more common?
3. How important is anguish in our moral decision-making? Is it an accurate marker of the quality of our choices?
4. What is meant by "cooperation in evil"? How does this come about?
5. What is the difference between formal cooperation and material cooperation? How important is this difference?
6. What tools do we have at our disposal for the resolution of moral dilemmas?

Questions for Personal Reflection
1. What were the three hardest moral choices you ever had to make? What exactly made them so difficult?
2. Are you ever called upon to take part in other people's wrongdoing? How do you react in these cases?
3. Whom do you turn to when you have serious moral doubts? What are the most trustworthy means you have to know what God expects from you?

NOTES

CHAPTER 6

1. Nietzsche's vitriolic attacks on the Jews make one shudder in the light of their later incarnation in the actions of Hitler. One incendiary passage reads as follows: "All the world's efforts against the 'aristocrats,' the 'mighty,' the 'masters,' the 'holders of power,' are negligible by comparison with what has been accomplished against those classes by *the Jews*—the Jews, that priestly nation which eventually realised that the one method of effecting satisfaction on its enemies and tyrants was by means of a radical transvaluation of values, which was at the same time an act of the *cleverest revenge*" (*Genealogy of Morals*, 16–17).

CHAPTER 7

1. Executive Board of the American Anthropological Association, "Statement on Human Rights," *American Anthropologist* 49/4 (October–December 1947): 539.
2. Pope John Paul II, encyclical letter *Evangelium Vitae* (March 25, 1995), no. 4.
3. Ibid.

CHAPTER 8

1. Cf. *Protagoras* 345de, 355b–358a; *Gorgias* 488a; *The Sophist* 228cd; *The Laws* 731c; *Timaeus* 44b, 87ab.

CHAPTER 9

1. Richard Dawkins, "Let's All Stop Beating Basil's Car," *Edge: The World Question Center*, 2006: http://www.edge.org/q2006/q06_9.html.

CHAPTER 10

1. Billy Joel, "Only the Good Die Young," © 1977 Joelsongs (BMI). All rights reserved.

2. Pope Benedict XVI, *Homily on the Solemnity of the Immaculate Conception of the Blessed Virgin Mary,* December 8, 2005; http://www.vatican.va/holy_father/benedict_xvi/homilies/2005/documents/hf_ben-xvi_hom_20051208_anniv-vat-council_en.html.
3. Dr. Janet Smith, unpublished lecture *"Humanae Vitae* and Conscience."
4. Robert Hazard, "Girls Just Want to Have Fun," © 1979 Heroic Music (ASCAP). All rights reserved.

CHAPTER 12

1. Smith, *Humanae.*

CHAPTER 13

1. Mike Stobbe, "Survey: Most Obese Claim to Eat Healthy," Associated Press, August 2, 2006.

CHAPTER 14

1. "The Martyrdom of Polycarp" in *Apostolic Fathers*, trans. Kirsopp Lake (Loeb Classical Library, 1912); http://www.earlychristianwritings.com/text/martyrdompolycarp-lake.html.
2. Robert Bolt, *A Man for All Seasons* (New York: Random House, 1962).
3. Associated Press, "Illinois Pharmacists Told to Fill Birth-Control Prescriptions," April 4, 2005.